Marquis de Sade

Marquis de Sade:

His Life and Works

By
DR. IWAN BLOCH

**Fredonia Books
Amsterdam, The Netherlands**

Marquis de Sade:
His Life and Works

by
Dr. Iwan Bloch

ISBN: 1-58963-567-1

Copyright © 2002 by Fredonia Books

Fredonia Books
Amsterdam, The Netherlands
http://www.fredoniabooks.com

All rights reserved, including the right to reproduce this book, or portions thereof, in any form.

In order to make original editions of historical works available to scholars at an economical price, this facsimile of the original edition is reproduced from the best available copy and has been digitally enhanced to improve legibility, but the text remains unaltered to retain historical authenticity.

Contents

THE AGE OF MARQUIS DE SADE

General Character of the Eighteenth Century in France   3
Debauchery in France.

French Philosophy   7
Philosophy and Pleasure.

French Royalty in the Eighteenth Century   10
Orgies in the King's Bordello; Nobility and Eroticism.

Nobility and Clergy   15
The Abbé and the Knight; The Clergy and Ungodliness.

Paris Police Reports on the Immorality of the Clergy   18
The Clergy and Immorality; The Clergy and Lust; Priests and Prostitutes.

The Jesuits   26
Seduction by Jesuits.

The Black Mass   29
Orgies in Satan's Church; Sexual Black Mass; Secret Rites of the Clergy.

Convents   35
Prostitution in the Convents.

Women   38
Idealization of Prostitution; Sadism and Women; Women and Marriage.

The Erotic Literature   45
Erotic Literature; Philosophers and Pornography; Rétif de la Bretonne; Fetichism and Literature; Lascivious Poems.

CONTENTS

Art — 56
Erotic Pictures; The Erotic Drama.

Fashion — 61

Bordellos and Secret Pornologic Clubs — 63
Description of a Bordello; Bordello Keepers; Bordello of Madame Paris; Negro Bordellos; Pornographic Love-Clubs.

The Prostitutes — 76
Golden Age of Prostitution; Growth of Prostitution; Famous Prostitutes; Pimps and Pimpesses.

The Palais Royal and Other Public Places for Prostitution — 85
Prostitution in the Palais Royal; Prostitution and Sunamites; Soldiers and Prostitutes.

Onanism — 92

Tribadism — 94
Confessions of a Tribade; A Tribadic Cult; Rites of Tribadism; Initiation of a Tribade.

Pederasty — 103
Cults of Pederasty.

Flagellation and Phlebotomy — 107
Whips and Passion.

Aphrodisiacs, Cosmetics, Abortions and Quackeries — 110
Renewal of Virginities; Nostrums for Venereal Diseases; Syphilitic Panaceas; Aphrodisiacs and Dildos.

Gastronomy and Alcoholism — 119
Alcoholic Debaucheries.

Crime and Murder — 121
Crimes and Murders in Paris.

Poisoning — 123
Wholesale Poisonings.

Public Executions — 125
Execution of Damiens; Mass Pleasure in Executions; Revolution and Murder.

Ethnological and Historical Examples — 132
Vice and Cruelty of Savages; Curious Erotic Crimes.

Conditions in Italy — 137
Debauchery in Italy; Sexual Orgies in Naples.

CONTENTS

THE LIFE OF MARQUIS DE SADE

His Ancestors 147
Hereditary Influence.

The Childhood of Marquis de Sade 150
Description of Marquis de Sade.

Youth 152
The Marriage of Marquis de Sade; Imprisonment of Marquis de Sade.

His Prison Life 156
The Kellar Affair; Different Versions of the Crime; The Marseilles Scandal.

Imprisonment in Vincennes and in the Bastille 162
Mirabeau and de Sade.

Participation in the Revolution and Literary Activity .. 165
Literary Activity of the Marquis; De Sade and the Revolution; His Life in the Asylum.

His Death 171
Will of Marquis de Sade.

THE WORKS OF MARQUIS DE SADE

"Justine" and "Juliette" 175

The Preface 176

Analysis of "Justine" 177
Perils of Virtue; Orgies in An Abbey; Crimes in a Castle.

Analysis of "Juliette" 185
Torture and Prostitution; Crimes of a Politician; The Perfect Criminal; Society for the Friends of Crime; Heights of Vice; An Anthropophagic Monster; Orgies of the Priests; Orgies of Royalty; Arrangement of Bordellos; Fortunes of Vice.

Philosophy in the Boudoir 206
Philosophy of Libertinism.

Other Works of Marquis de Sade 209
Napoleon and Virtue.

Character of the Works of Marquis de Sade 212
Napoleon on de Sade.

The Philosophy of Marquis de Sade 213
Philosophy and the Universe; Philosophy and God; Philosophy and Christianity; Degradation of Virginity; Crime and Perversions; Perversity as a Virtue; Murder and Libertinism.

THEORY AND HISTORY OF SADISM

Introduction	231
Anthropophagy and Hypochorematophily	232
Other Sexuo-Pathologic Types of De Sade *Curious Sexual Passions.*	234
Arrangement of Erotic Individualities *Erotic Positions.*	237
Lying and Sexual Perversions *Virtue and Society.*	239
De Sade's View of the Nature of Sexual Perversion *Nature of Sexual Perversion.*	240
Definition of Sadism	242
Judgment of the Man, de Sade, According to His Life and Works *The Professor of Crime.*	244
The Spread and Effect of the Works of Marquis de Sade *Rétif and Villers.*	248
Sadism in Literature *Some Sadistic Works; Memoirs of a Singer.*	251
Some Sadistic Moral Crimes *Case of Michel Bloch.*	255
Bibliography	261

Introduction

The Marquis de Sade, whose life, works and personality we treat of, was preëminently a man of the eighteenth century. He was at the same time a Frenchman. But we believe that true light can be shed on this strange man only if we try to explain him through his age, the France of the eighteenth century. Medicine has apparently voiced its opinion on Marquis de Sade. But this judgment from the mouths of the most important alienists and specialists must remain one-sided until we investigate and consider the external conditions, the milieu in which this remarkable life grew, fashioned itself, and produced its effects.

For it is always of the utmost importance to understand from which decade and century, from which land and people, the data is borrowed. In a word, it is not the individual but the social conception that can lead to a true knowledge of de Sade's personality. A truly scientific judgment of a personality is possible only in this way. We must accept as a basis for our study of Marquis de Sade the views of an important sociologist, Theodore Achelis: "The personal ego forms, in general, only the pinnacle and bottom of psychic motives. Psychiatric investigations on the mutilation and degeneration of our ego have brought us to this conclusion: our personality is not the beginning, but the end of an infinitely long psychic activity, reaching far into the abysses of the unconscious, and which we cannot always bring back to the prime cause. By the observation of the social life and, in particular, the constant intercourse of the individual with the surrounding society an hypothesis is raised to a scientific datum. Here, in most cases, premeditated deliberation and completely voluntary self-determination are not decisive; it is rather customary adaptations, the work of dark unconscious instincts and impulses. Custom and usage, lawful, æsthetic and religious forms are, for the most part, organic developments without a decided, purposeful desire on the part of the individual. Our feelings and sensations spring in spite of their own individual character from those depths of the unconscious which precede the social fixation of the ego."

So we seek in this section the threads which connected the subjective spirit of Marquis de Sade to the objective spirit of his age. He was both a representative of the *ancien régime* and of the Revolution. His two most notorious masterpieces were unmistakable results of the great French Revolution.

Thus we must investigate what de Sade received from his age in order to discover what he gave to it. We will not repeat familiar facts in the history of French culture, but rather explain the works of Marquis de Sade by all the internal and external relations of the social life in the eighteenth century.

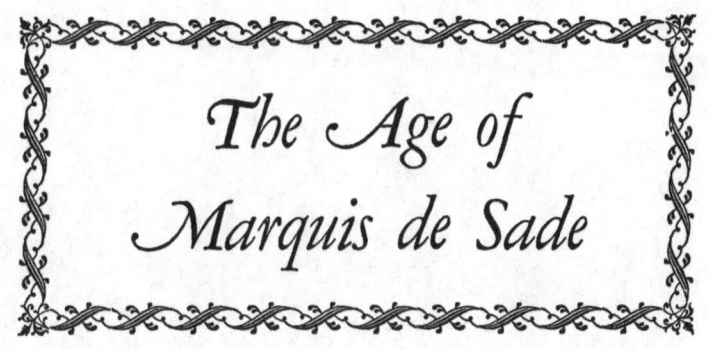

The Age of
Marquis de Sade

General Character of the Eighteenth Century in France

*D*e Sade called the eighteenth century "the age of complete corruption" (Justine I, 2) and in another place had Noirceuil say: "It is dangerous to desire to be virtuous in a corrupt century" (Juliette I, 261). The consciousness of the general evil of the century was sufficiently impressed upon him as on others. Hegel in his *Philosophy of History* has the most pertinent expression for this epoch: "The whole state of France at that time was a dissolute aggregation of privileges against ideas and reason; in general, a mad state with which, at the same time, was bound the highest depravity of morals and spirit—an empire of injustice with the growing consciousness of that state."

The eighteenth century belongs to that frivolous era, whose essence was masterfully described by a student of Hegel, Kuno Fischer, in his *Diotima:* "Frivolous times are those which always conclude a moribund era and completely destroy the life of mankind so that it can start afresh." Fichte once called it "completed sinfulness." In all great turning-points of history the traits of the different ages resemble one another. They are weakened and appear so flabby and impotent, that one despairs of new ones. And in fact, when an era has completely lived itself out, there remains from its customary life but the external shell, and this needs artistic charm to excite it again, for the inward power is lacking which alone can bring it forth in its youthful freshness.

"It is unrestrained and yet a feeble life; it is unfettered, and yet dull powers which complete the drama of life. There is no character, no formation in such times; everywhere the prose of selfishness without its power; the impotency of pleasure without its poetry." The world of the Cæsars, the age of expiring popery, the French monarchy before the Revolution were all such periods. The second was the complete sinfulness of Catholicism; the last, the complete sinfulness of the monarchy.

Pleasure, *à tout prix*, was the watchword in the eighteenth century. But the man who wants enjoyment at any cost is the egoist. Never was egoism so prolific in France as in the *ancien régime* and during the Revolution. The minister Saint Fond, a true copy of a minister under Louis XV, said (Juliette II, 37): "A statesman would be a fool if he did not let his country pay for his pleasures. What matters to us the misery of the people if only our passions are satisfied? If I thought that gold might flow from the veins of people, I would have them blood-let one after the other, that I might cover myself in their gore."

De Sade found this expression characteristic of the *ancien régime*. Before the Revolution this egoism was encountered only in the ruling classes, monarch, nobility and clergy. In the Revolution it seized all ranks of the populace. Adolf Schmidt, who drew his description of the Revolutionary days from authentic contemporary documents, said: "It was the sharp expressed egoism, the selfishness and avarice, which not only pierced the higher ranks of society, but all classes of people and, foremost of all, the overwhelming number of peasants; indeed it was so powerful, that all other feelings, even those of country and of humanity, were deeply submerged and forgotten. It is astonishing and dreadful when one perceives how, amid all the gleaming declamations on liberty, equality and fraternity, on the rights of love and man, on sacrifice for the well-being of society, greatness and fame of the country, there was in almost all classes a race for wealth and property, a cold-blooded reckoning on taking advantage of the circumstances, an avaricious speculation on the misfortunes of the state and the misery of their fellow creatures. Each wanted to outwit and impose on the other." We will have to study this egoism, this chief trait of the eighteenth century, in its various forms.

For it brought to a head the search for pleasure which reached its summit in sexual abandonments. *The eighteenth century was the century of the systematizing of sexual pleasures and pursuits.* Paul Moreau distinguished three epochs in the history of sexual debauchery and aberration. The first is the epoch of the Roman Empire; the second embraces those great epidemics *de névropathie de toutes sortes* in the middle ages, especially the belief in the existence of the incubus and succubus, the cult of the so-called "Devil's Church" with its horrible sexual monstrosities. The third period falls in the eighteenth century, luminous in its peculiar French individuality by the saturnalias of the regency and Louis XV.

Debauchery! That is the word for the eighteenth

century, declare the best *savants* of that time, Edmond and Jules de Goncourt. "That is its secret, its charm and its soul. Debauchery is the air on which it breathes and lives. It is its atmosphere, its element, its inspiration, its life and its genius. It circulates in its heart, nerves and brain. It gives its own peculiar charm and savor to its customs, morals and works. Debauchery proceeds from the innermost being of the age and speaks from its mouth. From there it flies over this world, takes possession, is its fairy, its muse, the dictator of custom, style and art. And nothing has remained from this time, nothing from this century of woman, which was not created, moved and protected by debauchery."

What the French eighteenth century delineated, above all, in a manner never before nor after seen, was the systematizing of sexual love. It remained for this century to draw up a codex of machlosophy.

"The entire life strives for the sexual act: science, art, fashion, literature, gastronomy. Everything permeates the languishing breeze of purely physical love and leaves behind that heavy languor which enervates all spiritual energy. And as this arose in the great, glorious and unforgettable Revolution, which the new age had given birth to, that heavy perfume still hung on, carried the people again down, enslaved them and turned the heavily yoked forces into wild ferocity and pitiless bloodthirstiness."

The main characteristics of this century of injustice, egoism and sexual immorality, are to be observed at their highest in the life and works of Marquis de Sade; we must henceforth always seek, in relation to the personality of de Sade, the origin of that frivolity, and to investigate the factors which combined to form the general character of the century.

French Philosophy

The spirit of an age is most clearly and decidedly shown in its philosophy. French philosophy was the scientific expression of the egoism, the search for pleasure and sexual desire of that time. It was thoroughly sensualistic and materialistic. De Sade had Dubois say very definitely (Justine I, 122): "The principle of philosophy is the search for pleasure." Philosophy plays an important role in de Sade's works. Very often is this expression met: "The fire of passion is always ignited on the torch of philosophy." (e.g. Juliette I, 92, 158, 319, etc.). A good part of de Sade's works embraced long-winded philosophic excursions, which we will evaluate in a later section. Therein de Sade acted very eclectically and uncritically. He named, e.g., in one breath Spinoza, Vanini and Holbach, the author of *The System of Nature* (Juliette I, 31); then Buffon (Philosophy in the Boudoir I, 77), who made an attempt to soften the stark materialism. The names of Voltaire (Juliette I, 88), and Montesquieu (Juliette IV, 8) were, of course, present. But Montesquieu was a mere *"demi-philosophe."* Reminiscent of Rousseau sounds the expression: "Men are pure only in the natural state; as soon as they depart therefrom, they lower themselves." (Juliette IV, 242). La Mettrie appeared to have had the greatest influence on de Sade. At least it seems to us that the philosophic system of Marquis de Sade, if one may so name his eclectic potpourri, showed a preference for the thoughts of La Mettrie. Both sought to legitimize and exalt sexual pleasure in a philosophic analysis. In this connection La Mettrie was expressly mentioned (Juliette III, 211).

Montesquieu and Voltaire had acquainted France with the sensualistic philosophy of Locke; already the skepticism of Pierre Bayle had opposed the Christian belief as the higher and truer philosophy. As with English philosophers, so with Voltaire and Montesquieu: the sensualistic views were only developed theoretically; the sensualism remained essentially a theory of knowledge. But influences were being felt which tried to carry sensualism and its natural consequence, materialism, over to the practical field. Knowledge is a function of mind. The foundation of morals is personal well-being, egoism. The only eternal thing is movement which brings forth all other things and requires no creator. Free will and immortality of the soul, as well as the conception of God, are hence utopian. Matter alone is certain. There is no soul. Atheism is the only religion and finds its gratification in the adoration of nature, in a happy life and physical pleasure. From these representative formulae and propositions of La Mettrie and Holbach, the natural result was the special characteristic of French philosophy in the eighteenth century: the opposition to church and religion, the espousal of freedom for individuals.

Never had philosophy turned its attention with such vigor to all the life-relations and with such conscious desire to reform them. The French Revolution was pre-eminently the work of the philosophers; this was recognized very early. Barruel, a fanatic supporter of the *ancien régime*, said in 1793: "The Revolution was brewing for a long time and was planted by men who under the guise of philosophers had assumed the task of destroying throne and altar." There were hence political and religious philosophers. The chief representative of political philosophy was Mirabeau, the passionate attorney of the Third Estate. He wrote, however, that famous dictum: "If you want a revolution, you must first decatholicize France." How deeply imbedded in the people was the atheism of a La Mettrie and a Holbach is shown by an actual case reported by Dutard. Three priests were returning from a pious performance of their official duties. The foremost shoved out of his way with his silver cross a heavily laden porter who was walking by with a friend. "Say," called out the porter, "you there, clear out with that cross!" "Sh," cried his friend, "it is the good God!" "Aw, the good God!" answered the other, "there's no good God any more!"

There was consistent progress to the practical execution of the abolition of the hated religion. In the meeting of the Convention, November 17, 1793, Cloots declared that religion was the greatest hindrance to happiness; there was no other God than nature; no other master than the human race; the God of the people, Reason, must unite all men. Feirlich, on November 7, 1793, with a small body of clergy, in the pale of the convent of Bishop Gobel, abjured catholicism and christianity. The clergymen of the convent immediately followed his example. On November 10th in the Notre Dame church the strange cult "Reason" was initiated. Reason became flesh in the form of a pretty young girl whom the president of the convent embraced with a fraternal kiss. Abstract Reason became Concrete Sensualism. It is thus seen that the atheism which took such frightful forms with de Sade, was not peculiar to him but customary of the time. It is further seen how conclusively this whole atheistic conduct terminated in sexual pleasure, which took on enormous dimensions at the time of the Revolution.

De Sade mentioned La Mettrie's work *On Lust* with which *The Art of Enjoyment* was apparently joined (Juliette IV, 198). Here La Mettrie developed the rules for the enjoyment of physical love, which he prized as the most beautiful and valuable conduct in the world, for thereby was derived the satisfaction of all the "*caprices de l'imagination.*"

Philosophy, in which the spiritual movement of that time found the universal and most intense expression, fought for political, religious and moral freedom. It aligned itself against state, church and traditional custom. Marquis de Sade also made all these factors subjects of his weightiest attacks. We therefore essay an investigation of individual relations in state, church, literature and public life, insofar as they may shed light on the personality of Marquis de Sade.

French Royalty in the Eighteenth Century

Louis XV ruled in the youth of Marquis de Sade; Louis XVI at his maturity. In 1774 when de Sade was thirty-four years old the most corrupt monarch that ever ruled France, Louis XV, died. We pass over the following facts as too well known: the political misgovernment of the

French rulers in the eighteenth century, the great scandal involving John Law, and the loss of the most important colonies under Louis XV, the revolution under Louis XVI and the marked patronage of the nobility and clergy. The search for pleasure and the sexual debauchery of the monarchy were especially stigmatized by de Sade. Here, too, he had his prototypes in reality. "When a prince of the blood walks the way of vice he is accompanied by the entire society." The example given by the French rulers must have had the most corrupt effects on the out-and-out materialistically minded society of the *ancien régime*. The time of the Regency created the name and type of *roué*, which became a characteristic phenomenon of the whole century. The *roué par excellence* was King Louis XV, famous for the number of his mistresses and for his Deer Park. His life, as Moreau says, was a "steadfast prostitution." Hence, his mistresses, in spite of their great number and frequent exchange, could not keep him satisfied. In his famous Deer Park he had built the original of private bordellos, which played an important rôle in the works of Marquis de Sade. Imagine! A king maintaining a whole bordello for his private use! The Deer Park was built in 1750 in the hermitage at Versailles in the quarter called Parc-aux-Cerfs, by the Marquise de Pompadour who, in order to retain the reins of government, created this new sort of enjoyment for the king. The administrator of the bordello was a certain Bertrand; the purveyor of the young girls was called Lebel. In the beginning there were only two or three inmates in the house. After the death of Pompadour it became very crowded (*très peuplée*). According to another version (Mouffle D'Angerville), "the Marquise de Pompadour, since she was superintendent of his (the king's) pleasures, had incessantly to levy new and fresh beauties, in order to stock the seraglio, wherein she was sovereign; therefrom developed the so-called Deer Park (Parc-aux-Cerfs), that grave of innocence and virtue, swallower of masses of victims, who, when returned to human society, brought with them depravity, debauchery and all those vices, which they must have been infested with by the infamous keepers of that pleasure resort.

"Apart from the evil which this dreadful place did to the morals of society, it is horrible when one reckons the immense amount of money that it cost the state. And who can reckon the costs of this legion of master and minor pimps and pimpesses who were constantly on the go even to the farthest bounds of the empire to track out the objects of their investigations; the costs of conveying the girls to their destination; the necessary polish, dress, perfume and all the other means in the world for making them alluring? To this must be added the gratuities presented to those who were not successful in arousing the complete passions of the sultan, but had nevertheless to be paid for their submission, for their discretion, and still more for their being eventually despised. There were also the rewards for those nymphs who were more fortunate and received the monarch for a time in their arms and caused the fire of passion to burn in his veins. Finally there were the sacred undertakings to those girls who bore in their womb the precious fruit of their fecundity."

It was deduced that each girl cost the public treasury a million Livres. "If only two a week came (little enough), this mounts up in ten years to a thousand and the result is thus ten thousand million Livres. And even then the great number of children born in the Deer Park is not figured, a matter of no little account." It is accordingly viewed by many historians that the initial cost and upkeep of the Deer Park was the main cause of the financial ruin of Louis XV. Many rumors flitted about concerning the organized orgies in the Deer Park, which in any case have not been unduly exaggerated.

"The Saturnalia of the Romans at the time of the Cæsars, the horrible Lupercalia of Tiberius, Caligula, Nero or of Agrippina, Messalina, Locusta and other human monsters were but pale copies of the scenes that took place in the Deer Park. Intoxication was here multiple; induced by play, spices, wine and other beverages, perfumes, scenes from magic-lanterns, music and every conceivable kind of animal pleasure." Moreau, from authentic sources on the connection between religion and debauchery, wrote: "Every time Louis XV wanted to spend a night in the Deer Park he not only fulfilled his religious duties with fervor, but also could not bear the young priestesses of another cult to fail in the application of their Christian belief. As soon as he was closeted with one of his odalisks he commanded her to undress behind a curtain, while he did the same.

"Then clad in Adam's costume they genuflected on the carpet and said the daily prayer, while they wet their forehead with holy water, which was contained in a crystal flask at the head of the bed. After they had prayed and crossed themselves, the king stroked the naked bosom of his co-worshipper with his pious finger. Then they arose, stepped in bed, drew the drapes together, and the names of the Father, Son, Holy Ghost and the Virgin Mary were whispered again and again until the rites of love brought forth another vocabulary."

Louis XV also had his own official for the arrangement of his orgies in the person of La Ferte, *Intendant de Menus-Plaisirs* (the Minister of Dainty Pleasures). This cabinet-member was abolished by Louis XVI. On Thursday, May 19, 1774, when Louis XVI, nine days after the death of his predecessor, was strolling with his queen and child in the Bois de Boulogne, La Ferte presented himself. The king looked at him from top to bottom and asked: "Who are you?" "Sire, I am La Ferte." "What do you want of me?" "Sire, I am here to take the orders of your Majesty." "But why?" "Since—since I am the Intendant—of the *Menus*—" "What is that?" "Sire, it is the *Menus-Plaisirs* of your Majesty." "My *Menus-Plaisirs* consist in walking in the park. I do not need you." Thereupon the king turned his back on him and left.

Louis XVI and his consort, Marie Antoinette, are personally absolved from the reproaches of immorality. Still, under their rule the same sensual life at court continued and his brother, Prince d'Artois was indeed a noted libertine. It was impossible for the private life of the king and especially of the queen, who as an Austrian princess enjoyed small sympathy, to be free from suspicion. The well known necklace story was strongly taken advantage of, much to the queen's dismay. Indeed five years after Louis XVI's coronation there appeared an obscene poem, *The Loves of Charlot and Toinette*, later reprinted in numberless editions. The poem treated of the alleged love between Marie Antoinette and her cousin D'Artois (later King Charles X). The queen was here described in the most obscene verses as a true Messalina, whom the impotent king could not satisfy!

"Charlot," the Prince d'Artois, was indeed a chief participant in the orgies of the court nobility in the Residence, as was the Duke of Orleans, Philippe Egalité. At the famous nightly promenades in the Palais Royal the appearance of Prince d'Artois was a daily occurrence. In the *Nights of Paris* Restif de la Bretonne tells of a bordello in Saint Antoine, which the Duke of Orleans, the Prince d'Artois and others, frequently visited. "There took place all the infamies and bestialities which were later described by de Sade in his horrible novel *Justine or the Misfortunes of Virtue*."

De Sade called (Juliette IV, 16) Marie Antoinette *"la première putain de France"* (the first public prostitute of France) and allowed no opportunity to go by without insulting her (Juliette V, 235, 252, etc.). In general he cherished an overwhelming hatred against the House of Austria. He indeed wanted to wipe out all the kings of the earth and found a *"république universelle"* (Juliette V, 119).

Nobility and Clergy

The nobility and clergy play the main rôles in the novels of Marquis de Sade. Princes, Dukes, counts, marquis, and chevaliers accompany popes, cardinals, archbishops, bishops, monks of all orders, abbesses and nuns as erotic and atheistic monsters. All the corruption of the *ancien régime* passes before our eyes in his works. The nobility and clergy formed indeed only one class in France for the clergy were mostly recruited from the nobility. The oldest son of the nobleman became an officer, the second son a priest or monk, the daughters, who for lack of dowry could not be married, nuns. The patronage of the nobility by the state reached unheard of dimensions in the eighteenth century. All state officers, judgeships and military positions were usually given to the nobility. At eighteen to twenty the young noblemen, without having the slightest idea of military tactics, were given regiments. They passed their youth in luxury and debauchery with women.

A noted intermediary between clergy and nobility was the institution of *abbés*, that degenerate mixed breed which one found everywhere without any fixed official duties. Mercier declared that Paris was full of *abbés*, priests with tonsure, serving neither the church nor the state, passing their time in utmost sloth but playing no unimportant role as "friends of the house," pedagogues, writers, etc. They were at home in all bordellos, although at an early period every courtesan who could prove the visit of an *abbé* received 50 francs. But that ceased under Louis XVI. An excellent description of the *abbé* of the eighteenth century was given by that celebrated gastronomist, Brillat Savarin: "If a family of the nobility had many sons, one of them was set aside for the church. He first received simple prebends which sufficed for the costs of his education; he later became a canon, abbot or bishop according to his talent for the spiritual calling. That was the true type of *abbé*. But there were also many false ones, and many well-to-do youngsters appeared in Paris as *abbés*. Nothing was simpler and so convenient: by a slight change of attire the appearance of a benefice was simulated. One had friends, lovers and hosts, for every house had its *abbé*. They were small, fat, round, well-dressed, bland, obliging, curious connoisseurs, lively and insinuating." De Sade has drawn this type in Abbé Chabert, the friend of Juliette and teacher of her daughter (Juliette III, 280). The *abbés* also figure in the police reports of Manuel on the vice of the clergy in Paris which we shall quote in a later section.

A second characteristic phenomenon of the eighteenth century was the "knight," the chevalier. He also has found a loving commentator in Brillat Savarin: "Many knights had found it advantageous to present the fraternal kiss to each other. They were mostly pretty men. They carried their swords vertically, their heads high, their noses up, their bodies stiff; they were gamblers, seducers, squabblers and really belonged to the train of a lady of fashion. At the beginning of the Revolution most of the knights entered the army, others left the country and the rest lost themselves in the crowd. The few survivors can be recognized by their features. For now they are skinny and walk laboriously. They have the gout."

The champions of the cloth were, in de Sade's novels, the perpetrators of the most abominable outrages. With a special preference de Sade described the vices, hypocrisy, and the ungodliness of the clergy of every rank. He overwhelmed the cloth with the most vulgar insults. And he had excellent justification.

In the discussion of the wickedness of the French clergy we will present authentic historic documents. The discoveries of the police speak of and justify de Sade, whose works were placed on the *Index Expurgatorius* as much for their anti-clerical contents as for their obscenity. Thus Juliette called the pope an "old ape" (Juliette IV, 285); and the other prelates, monks, etc., did not fare much better. The tribade Clairwil cried (Juliette II, 336): "Who are the only true destroyers of society? The priests! Who daily seduce and rape our women and children? The priests! Who are the greatest enemy of every reign? The priests! Who continually deceive us with lies and frauds? Steal our last penny? Work most for the destruction of the human race? Defame themselves most with crimes and infamies? Who are the most dangerous and horrible persons? ... And yet we hesitate to put an end to these pestilent worms of the earth? Then we really deserve all these evils."

All the troubles of France were the work of the Jesuits (Juliette III, 169). Numberless were the orgies and debaucheries which the priests arranged in de Sade's novels. Therein appeared all the pathologic sexual types. The pederast, the pathicus, the *lécheur*, the *sanguinaire*, etc., etc. We here call attention only to the dreadful orgies of the Carmelites (Juliette III, 143), the Archbishop of Lyons (Juliette I, 234); the orgies in the catacombs of the Panthémont monastery between monks and nuns (Juliette I, 96); of Pope Pius VI and the Cardinals Albani and Bernis in Rome (Juliette IV, 100 ff.). All these clergymen were atheists and blasphemers. De Sade repeated—unique in his works—two obscene and blasphemous poems of Cardinal Bernis in *Juliette*.

We shall next present contemporary reports as proofs that de Sade was not unjust when he exposed the clergy in such an abusive manner in his works.

Paris Police Reports on the Immorality of the Clergy

*P*ierre Manuel has left us in his famous work *The Parisian Police Exposed* (Paris, 1794), a photographically true picture of the moral conditions of Paris before the outbreak of the great Revolution. Adolf Schmidt, one of the best *savants* of the history of France in the eighteenth century and who, like Manuel, collected similar reports in his *Tableaux of the French Revolution*, called Manuel's book one of the most reliable sources for the Eighteenth Century.

Manuel, in his famous work, had a chapter "Police, Priests and Prostitutes." He repeated in bitterly satiric words the vow of chastity of the priests and said: "I will reveal the lascivious actions of these missionaries of heaven, who themselves damn to Hades the passions of noble and sensitive persons. Naming these failings is not doing away with them. For the pure man is he who sleeps with his wife."

The following laconic records refer to the reports of the police-inspectors and commissioners, to the confessions of the culprits and their accomplices. We give verbatim some of the striking reports.

Franciscans:

February 12, 1760. Brother François Lortal, House of Toulouse. He reversed the maxim of Virgil in practice: *nudus ara, sere nudus!* Commissioner Thierion, Inspector Marais.

July 2, 1766. George le Payen, vicar in Cerny, lover on lover in the garden. Commissioner Grimperil, Inspector Marais.

Bernardines:

March 30, 1764. J. Ignace Xavier Dreux, licenciate, Professor of Theology, at Agathe, under the bed. Commissioner Mutel. etc.

Carmelites:

February 8, 1763. Jacques Brebi, from Maubert Place. He was under the name Jacques Mazure with the guards; he thought it was a church. Report of Prior Martin, etc.

Dominicans:

Pierre Simon, 46 years in the cloth. He described his pleasures with trembling hands. Commissioner Mutel, etc.

Capucines:

December 14, 1762. Laurent Dilly, mendicant friar from Rue St. Honoré, at the Boyerie, where he sang: *tirez-moi par mon cordon!* Report of the Father Guardian Grégoire, etc.

November 9, 1765. Joseph Biache, called Brother Constant, and Joseph Etienne, called Brother Constantine, from the monastery at Crépy; both in the inn, *The Mounting Deer,* where they asked for a bed for three, although they only had the image of the Virgin Mary with them. Commissioner Mutel, etc.

Recollects (strictest branch of *Franciscans*):

June 30, 1763. Noel-Clément Berthe, called Brother Paul, whipped at Leblanc. Com. Fontaine, etc.

March 1, 1765. Gabriel Anheisser, called Father Gabriel, in his nightshirt under the bed of Agnes Viard. He lived together with this former sutler for seven or eight years. Com. de Ruisseau, etc.

February 19, 1767. Father Constance between Victoire and Emilie, like the ass of Buridan. Com. de Ruisseau, etc.

Minimes (Paulines):

January 17, 1760. André Carron, while writing on the wall of the room of Zaire: "I am always ready for whipping." Com. Sirebeau, etc.

Feuillantines:

December 30, 1762. Dom Claude Jousse, 63 years old, at Marie la Neuve, where he was not abashed with the maidens. Report of Prior Jean Baptiste of St. Marie-Magdalene. Com. de Ruisseau.

Augustines:

November 5, 1763. Bernard-Nicolas, from Palais-Royal House, in the Avenue de Vincennes, with three Franciscans and Rosalie, who was a match for a dozen of them. Com. Mutel, etc.

October 26, 1765: "I, the undersigned, Honoré Regnard, 53 years old, canon of the holy Augustine order, procurator, House of St. Catherine, confirm that Inspector Marais found me at the St. Louis, rue du Figuier, to which I went yesterday of my own desire, in order to satisfy myself with Félix. I had her undress and caressed her with my hand concealed under the cloak. And today I played with Félix and her friend Julie, who took off my vestment and dressed and painted me as a woman. The inspector surprised me in this condition. I declare that I have had this desire for many years but which I have never been able to satisfy until today. As proof of authenticity I sign the following declaration, which contains the whole truth and nothing but the truth, with my name Honoré Regnard." Com. Mutel, etc.

July 18, 1768. Simon Boucel, with the Prévilles, Louise and Sophy.

Praemonstratenes:

March 17, 1760. François de Maugre, from rue Haute-Feuille, between Desirée and Zaire, all three happy. Com. Sirebeau, etc.

Penitents of Nazareth:

May 2, 1766. Brother Nicephorus, with Laville, who showed him every part of the body, including some internal ones. Com. Mutel, etc.

Celestines:

December 3, 1760. J. D. Tordoir, Prior of Nantes, at Mausy, in the garb of the prophet who awaked the son of the Sunamites.

Brothers of Mercy:

October 19, 1762. Jacques François Boulard, former overseer of novices and priors, at Lagarde, with Victoire and Julie, trying to take in as much as possible. Com. de Ruisseau, etc.

Order of St. Genevieve:

May 8, 1761. Jean Pierre Bedosse with Zephire, *per ipsam, cum ipsa et in ipsa*. Com. Sirebeau, etc.

August 2, 1752. Father Bernard, famous preacher. He chose two or three prostitutes at Lasolle. This cost him the wealth of a duchess. He gave six and a half Louisdors. And the surgeon, as a result, charged him forty Thalers and three Livres for the visit.

Eremites:

August 5, 1773. Brother Camille, from the monastery at Hayet, at Therese's where he described himself as "The Porter of Chartreux." Com. Mutel, etc.

Christian School:

September 14, 1763. Brother Firmin at Royer's, who compared him with those bad readers who begin a book and don't finish it. Com. Mutel, etc.

Order of St. Antoine:

September 27, 1765. François Vanova, at Lamourette's, *in flagrante delicto* by Commissioner Mutel and Inspector Marais.

Jesuits:

November 5, 1764. François Terrasse-Desbillon, 52 years old, at Mouton's, where he was enjoying himself in reversed rôles. Com. Mutel, etc.

Deans, Dignitaries and Canons:

April 3, 1764. Blaise Messier, Canon of Beauvais, at Blampié's. He appeared to have the same views as Rubens, liking his beauties around the 200 pound class. Com. Rochebrune, etc.

August 14, 1761. Marc-Antoine Montel, of the holy church, at Provençale's, working away. Com. de Ruisseau, etc.

July 8, 1760. Marie Mocet, Bishop of Tours, 60 years old. Gasping away. His hands doing the work of four men.

June 20, 1765. Jean Pierre Pellettier, curé, at Lambert's, devouring the work of God. Com. Mutel, etc.

August 22, 1760. Pierre Louis Thorin. Zaire in a three-quarter turn. Com. Sirebeau, etc.

Abbés:

October 27, 1763. Charles Marie Thibault was sent to St. Lazare, having been found at Aurora's for the third time. A poem was found in his pocket praising what Hebe showed the goddesses.

Doctors of the Sorbonne:

May 9, 1765. J. Baptiste R. . . . who lay inert with his useless fire-piece at Guerin's.

May 23, 1763. Fel. Auguste Tomalle turning over the pages at Desnoyer's. His third thesis.

Teachers:

February 24, 1761. P. . . . Teacher of the children of Marquis de P. . . . at Pearl's. Looking for gems at the altar of Venus. Com. Sirebeau, etc.

These are some out of a long, long list. A commentary would be superfluous. *Facta loquuntur*. These facts from authentic documents afford a satisfying proof and justification for the description in de Sade's novels of the orgies of the clergy; and also for the hatred which the priests were looked on not alone by de Sade. Manuel remarked at the end of his tale that no Bishop was named therein. He explained it from the fact that one may not even speak of the illnesses of a Bishop, let alone his sexual adventures.

Besides these reports of Manuel there exists a very great work on the immorality of the French clergy. After the storming of the Bastille in 1789 there was found in that prison two volumes on *The Chastity of the Clergy Exposed*. Louis XV had the reports of the visits of the clergy in bordellos sent to him every morning. These bulletins were called the *Paris Nights*. The two volumes contained 189 reports from April 10, 1755 to June 7, 1766. They appeared more to have served "the revival of the dead libido of the king" than the interests of morals and the honor of the king.

In the same category was the affair of the Vicar of Bagnolet with Mademoiselle Mimi. In the autograph-collection of Lucas Montigny there is a letter from the Archbishop of Paris to Police Superintendent Le Noir:

"I have been informed that the Vicar of Bagnolet when

in Paris visits a prostitute, Mimi, who lives in the rue Pierre Poissons. If you can verify this, I would be extremely grateful, for I am very interested in discovering the truth."

The letter had the following notation by Le Noir: "Get Quidor to verify the fact immediately and send me his report."

Further interesting details on the conduct of the Parisian clergy are found in the *Confessions of a Young Girl*. We are introduced to the bordello of Madame Richard. Sapho, (for so the young girl is called), looks through the peephole at the *tête-à-tête* of the madame with a priest. The madame takes out a cuirass of doubled horse-hair, bordered by a mass of blunted iron nails, enfolds the breast and back of the priest with it, ties him tightly on all sides with heavy cord, fastens an iron chain around his belly, which supports some kind of suspensory around his groin. This suspensory is also braided with strong coarse hair, in a way not preventing the use of the hands on the sources of pleasure. Similar "bracelets" are placed on the wrists. Tumescence then follows. Now the madame begins the flagellation and the other incitations of love.

Sapho tells further how she becomes the mistress of a bishop, whose vicarage follows him in his mode of life and presents a lively picture of the immoral conduct of the clergy in this diocese. She has an adventure with four priests, one of whom is a pederast, having a motto: *tout est cunnus dans une femme*.

The sexual dissoluteness of the clergy is also found in poems and pictures. The following verse is to the point:

> *One has chosen five bishops,*
> *All marked by syphilis,*
> *To reform the gay monks.*
> *Can one whiten ebony with black ink?*

This poem refers to a Board of Morals composed of the Archbishops of Rheims, Arles, Narbonne, Bourges and Toulouse. This Board of Censorship was indeed a mark of the age! But how they were judged by public opinion these verses best show.

The Jesuits

In *Persian Letters* Montesquieu had Rica visit a monastery library where a monk described the contents of the works. Under the theologians were named especially the *casuists*, who bring the secrets of night into the daylight; who create in their fantasies all the monsters that the demon of love can produce, collect, compare and form as eternal objects of their thoughts. Yet fortunate if the heart is not enmeshed and does not become the plaything of the many delusions which are so naively described and so nakedly painted!

In this field of "sexual casuistry" we find the jesuits masters in the eighteenth century. No order understood so well how to legitimize pleasure by religion and how to clothe their own immoral actions with a cover of mysticism and piousness. It was not necessary for the jesuits to find their pleasures in bordellos (Manuel found only one jesuit in these resorts, explained also by the fact that they were too clever to be caught in such traps). In his dual rôle as father confessor and teacher it was easy for him to satisfy his, by no means weak, sexual feelings which were protected from police inspection as "divine inspiration." Early in the seventeenth century Cornelius Jansen inveighed against the jesuit father confessors, "who regulated the gallant sins of the household and permitted the nuns to be fingered lewdly on their bosoms and thighs by their comforters." For the jesuit Benzi taught expressly: to pinch cheeks, bosoms, and to shamelessly handle the genitals. As a result of these precepts, de la Chaise, father confessor of Louis XIV, violated the ladies of the court and had mistresses sent to the King of England. Young ladies in Holland let themselves be whipped by the jesuits for their pleasure. Similarly the ladies in the court in Lisbon under Nuñez. The jesuit Herreau in 1642 taught that it was permissible to use abortive medicines. In the sixteenth century in Lyons the jesuits influenced the ladies to wear open *chemises;* this practice was copied in 1789.

The notorious "Theology of Murder" of the jesuits, in no way inferior to the apology of murder by de Sade, may be originally blamed to the treatise of their founder, J. de Mariana (1599), as well as the famous work of Blaise Pascal, *Provincial Letters* (1657), describing the entire immorality of the jesuits. In the eighteenth century the commanders of the order allowed the father confessors obscene tracts, insofar as it was favorable to the order. Thus the last commander of the order before the Revolution, Lorenzo Ricci, wrote on how the young jesuits ought to act to the young—and rich—widows. They took every possible care to keep them from a second marriage, pointing out indefatigably the inconveniences of such a state, the danger to the soul, etc., etc. "But when in spite of all this the young widows have a great yearning for a second marriage, when they find themselves in the state: it is better to marry than to burn, then a clever and discreet father may offer his services against the seductions of the flesh."

World famous was the scandal of the relation between the jesuit, Jean Baptiste Girard, and his penitent, Catherine Cadière, which started at Toulon in May, 1782. The affair occasioned an immense literature and served as a model for many pornographic novels. The case was fully documented in *The Girard Case* (1791). A folio volume of etchings portrayed the most piquant situations; its collection has been variously ascribed to Marquis d'Argens, Count Caylus and Mirabeau. It has also been asserted that Marquis de Sade was moved to write *Justine* by the above work.

The jesuit Girard, as rector of the seminary and as naval chaplain at Toulon, had started a private penitential school for women, in which Catherine Cadière, the pretty and pious daughter of a merchant, entered. Girard, by the application of the most cunning sexual mysticism, succeeded in seducing the innocent maiden and utilized fully her visions and dreams for his lustful desires. Carnal flogging, indecent embraces, and the horrible mental prostitution soon lead to acute hysterics and in the course of time she became pregnant, but by reason of jesuit precepts abortive drugs stopped the process. Finally action was brought against him, but, to the wrath of the public, he was freed.

Voltaire, under a picture of Girard and Cadière, wrote the following verse:

> *The beauty saw God, Girard saw the beauty:*
> *Ah! but Girard is happier than she.*

The Black Mass

The height of religious sexual mysticism was reached in the cult of the so-called "Satan's Church." Satan here became the "Personification of the Physical Mysterium of Copulation" as a protest against the exclusive mastery of the "Metaphysical Mysticism of Idolization." The history of this remarkable sect has been written for all time by Stanislaw Przybyszewski in his *The Cult of Satan's Church*. Satan-Satyr, Satan-Pan, and Satan-Phallus was the ancient "God of instincts and corporeal passions, equally honored by the highest and lowest in spirit, the inexhaustible source of joy in life, enthusiasm and intoxication.

"He taught women the art of seduction, men to satisfy their feelings in their double sexual desires, he ran riot in color, discovered the flute and set the muscles in rythmical movement, until the divine mania embraced the heart and the divine Phallus with its opulence sowed the fruitful womb."

That was the age of the pagan mysteries of motherhood. Then came the Judeo-Grecan Christianity and preached the supernatural, ascetic mysticism of fatherhood. The church tore man forcefully from nature. "She destroyed the unconscious selection of nature, which expressed itself externally in beauty, power and splendor; she protected everything that nature would uproot: dirt, ugliness, sickness, cripples and eunuchs." But nature did not allow itself to be rejected. And so the church had to give in and amalgamate the pagan creed with its own. "The bacchanalias at the feasts of Ceres Libera were celebrated with greater freedom than ever before on Lady-day, and until the thirteenth century the people celebrated, in common with the priests, lascivious and orgiastic festivals, the feast of the Ass, the feast of the Idiots. The remainder of the Phallus cult stole away to the church; the columns and pillars swarmed with obscene figures, a favorite theme for the reliefs in the church was Noah sleeping with his daughters." But the real cult of "Satan's Church" was founded by the Manichees in southern France. "From here began the monstrous triumphal procession of Satan through all Europe." The secret societies of "Perfect Beings" formed everywhere, serving exclusively the most obscene sexual vices. "They insulted and stoned the priests, violated the holy objects with their obscene purposes and parodied the Catholic services in their rites." In spite of the persecution of the church the sect and its motto persevered: *Nemo potest peccare ab umbilico et inferius;* it found continual support from "unsatisfied" priests. Sins slay sins! That was the great principle of their sexual orgies. The priest sanctifies all women who sin with him. The nuns are "consecrated," i.e. they become the mistresses of the priests. The black death in the fourteenth century, flagellation, dance-mania, famine, all heightened immeasurably the sexual hysteria. Now the sect of devil worshippers enjoyed their triumphs. Since then, in spite of persecution, they remained in the self-same position and further celebrate their public masses. Even in modern times they have appeared in various forms. The "Adamites" or "Nicolites," "Picards," who congregate nude and enjoy wives in common, were founded by John Ziska on an island in the Luschnitz River. They appeared again in 1848 in five villages as "Moroccanes." The name was chosen due to their expectation of the extirpation of all Catholics by an enemy coming from Morocco. Similarly the name "Oneida" or the older name of "Perfecti," later "Perfectionists" in New York State (since 1831). Even today the Satan cult is carried on in Paris, as is described by J. K. Huysmans in *Là Bas:*

> The sacrifice ceased. The priest descended the steps backward, knelt on the last one, and in a sharp, tripidant voice cried:
>
> "Master of Slanders, Dispenser of the benefits of crime, Administrator of sumptuous sins and great vices, Satan, thee we adore, reasonable God, just God!
>
> "Superadmirable legate of false trances, thou receivest our beseeching tears; thou savest the honour of families by aborting wombs impregnated in the forgetfulness of the good orgasm; thou dost suggest to the mother the hastening of untimely birth, and thine obstetrics spares the still-born children the anguish of maturity, the contamination of original sin.
>
> "Mainstay of the despairing Poor, Cordial of the Vanquished, it is thou who endowst them with hypocrisy, ingratitude, and stiff-neckedness, that they may defend themselves against the children of God, the Rich.
>
> "Suzerain of Resentment, Accountant of Humiliations, Treasurer of old Hatreds, thou alone dost fertilize the brain of man whom injustice has crushed; thou breathest into him the idea of meditated vengeance, sure misdeeds; thou incitest him to murder; thou givest him the abundant joy of accomplished reprisals and permittest him to taste the intoxicating draught of the tears of which he is the cause.
>
> "Hope of Virility, Anguish of the Empty Womb, thou dost not demand the bootless offering of chaste lions, thou dost not sing the praises of Lenten follies; thou alone receivest the carnal supplications and petitions of poor and avaricious families. Thou determinest the mother to sell her daughter, to give her son; thou aidest sterile and reprobate loves; Guardian of strident Neuroses, Leaden Tower of Hysteria, bloody Vase of Rape!
>
> "Master, thy faithful servants, on their knees, implore thee and supplicate thee to satisfy them when they wish the torture of all

those who love them and aid them; they supplicate thee to assure them the joy of delectable misdeeds unknown to justice, spells whose unknown origin baffles the reason of man; they ask, finally, glory, riches, power, of thee, King of the Disinherited, Son who art to overthrow the inexorable Father!"

Then Docre rose, and erect, with arms outstretched, vociferated in a ringing voice of hate:

"And thou, thou whom, in my quality of priest, I force, whether thou wilt or no, to descend into this host, to incarnate thyself in this bread, Jesus, Artisan of Hoaxes, Bandit of Homage, Robber of Affection, hear! Since the day when thou didst issue from the complaisant bowels of a Virgin, thou hast failed all thine engagements, belied all thy promises. Centuries have wept, awaiting thee, fugitive God, mute God! Thou wast to redeem man and thou hast not, thou wast to appear in thy glory, and thou sleepest. Go, lie, say to the wretch who appeals to thee, 'Hope, be patient, suffer; the hospital of souls will receive thee; the angels will assist thee; Heaven opens to thee.' Impostor! thou knowest well that the angels, disgusted at thine inertness, abandon thee! Thou wast to be the Interpreter of our plaints, the Chamberlain of our tears; thou wast to convey them to the Father and thou hast not done so, for this intercession would disturb thine eternal sleep of happy satiety.

"Thou hast forgotten the poverty thou didst preach, enamoured vassal of Banks! Thou hast seen the weak crushed beneath the press of profit; thou hast heard the death rattle of the timid, paralyzed by famine, of women disembowelled for a bit of bread, and thou hast caused the Chancery of thy Simoniacs, thy commercial representatives, thy Popes, to answer by dilatory excuses and evasive promises, sacristy Shyster, huckster God!

"Master, whose inconceivable ferocity engenders life and inflicts it on the innocent whom thou darest damn—in the name of *what* original sin?—whom thou darest punish—by the virtue of *what* covenants?—we would have thee confess thine impudent cheats, thine inexpiable crimes! We would drive deeper the nails into thy hands, press down the crown of thorns upon thy brow, bring blood and water from the dry wounds of thy sides.

"And that we can and will do by violating the quietude of thy body, Profaner of ample vices, Abstractor of stupid purities, cursed Nazarene, do-nothing King, coward God!"

"Amen!" trilled the soprano voices of the choir boys.

Durtal listened in amazement to this torrent of blasphemies and insults. The foulness of the priest stupefied him. A silence succeeded the litany. The chapel was foggy with the smoke of the censers. The women, hitherto taciturn, flustered now, as, remounting the altar, the canon turned toward them and blessed them with his left hand in a sweeping gesture. And suddenly the choir boys tinkled the prayer bells.

It was a signal. The women fell to the carpet and writhed. One of them seemed to be worked by a spring. She threw herself prone and waved her legs in the air. Another, suddenly struck by a hideous strabism, clucked, then becoming tongue-tied stood with her mouth open, the tongue turned back, the tip cleaving to the palate. Another, inflated, livid, her pupils dilated, lolled her head back over her shoulders, then jerked it brusquely erect and belaboured herself, tearing her breast with her nails. Another, sprawling on her back, undid her skirts, drew forth a rag, enormous, meteorized; then her face twisted into a horrible grimace, and her tongue, which she could not control, stuck out, bitten at the edges, harrowed by red teeth, from a bloody mouth.

Suddenly Durtal rose, and now he heard and saw Docre distinctly.

Docre contemplated the Christ surmounting the tabernacle, and with arms spread wide apart he spewed forth frightful insults, and, at the end of his forces, muttered the billingsgate of a drunken cabman. One of the choir boys knelt before him with his back toward the altar. A shudder ran around the priest's spine. In a solemn but jerky voice he said, *"Hoc est enim corpus meum,"* then, instead of kneeling, after the consecration, before the precious Body, he faced the congregation, and appeared tumefied, haggard, dripping with sweat. He staggered between the two choir boys, who, raising the chasuble, displayed his naked belly. Docre made a few passes and the host sailed, tainted and soiled, over the steps.

Durtal felt himself shudder. A whirlwind of hysteria shook the room. While the choir boys sprinkled holy water on the pontiff's nakedness, women rushed upon the Eucharist and, grovelling in front of the altar, clawed from the bread humid particles and drank and ate divine ordure.

Another woman, curled up over a crucifix, emitted a rending

laugh, then cried to Docre, "Father, father!" A crone tore her hair, leapt, whirled around and around as on a pivot and fell over beside a young girl who, huddled to the wall, was writhing in convulsions, frothing at the mouth, weeping, and spitting out frightful blasphemies. And Durtal, terrified, saw through the fog the red horns of Docre, who seated now, frothing with rage, was chewing up sacramental wafers, taking them out of his mouth, wiping himself with them, and distributing them to the women, who ground them underfoot, howling, or fell over each other struggling to get hold of them and violate them.

The place was simply a madhouse, a monstrous pandemonium of prostitutes and maniacs. Now, while the choir boys gave themselves to the men, and while the woman who owned the chapel, mounted the altar, caught hold of the phallus of the Christ with one hand and with the other held a chalice between "His" naked legs, a little girl, who hitherto had not budged, suddenly bent over forward and howled, howled like a dog. Overcome with disgust, nearly asphyxiated, Durtal wanted to flee. He looked for Hyacinthe. She was no longer at his side. He finally caught sight of her close to the canon, and, stepping over the writhing bodies on the floor, he went to her. With quivering nostrils she was inhaling the effluvia of the perfumes and of the couples.

"The sabbatic odour!" she said to him between clenched teeth, in a strangled voice.

The Marquis de Sade gave evidence in his novels of being a fanatic Satanist. Many black masses appeared in *Justine* and *Juliette*. A mass in a monastery was fully described in *Justine* (II, 239). A maiden, as the Holy Virgin, with arms raised to heaven, was bound in a niche in the church. Later she was laid naked on a great table, candles were lit, a crucifix decorated her buttocks, and "they celebrated on her buttocks the most absurd mysteries of Christianity." Then a mass was read on the same place. As soon as there was a Host of God, she seized the monk Ambrose and held fast to his member, whereby the believers in the Host were derided with the maddest expressions.

Two black masses were read in the privates of two tribades (Juliette III, 147), then the Host was placed in the dung, after which the main altar became the place of the wildest orgies.

Pope Pius VI, himself, read a black mass in St. Peter's church, the Host being placed in the anus of a young girl.

Convents

So many comments have already been made on the life of nuns in the eighteenth century that we can be content with a short description. The Panthémont Convent in Paris described by de Sade (Juliette I, 1 ff.) actually existed! "The great convent of the eighteenth century, after the convent at Fontevrault, is Panthémont, the royal convent where the princesses were educated and where the greatest nobles sent their daughters." Panthémont was the most expensive of all convents.

In the eighteenth century the convents were becoming more and more secularized. "The motto of the convent of the Nouvelles Catholiques, *vincit mundum fides nostra*, had for a long time been a dead letter. The world had stepped into the convent." Of course, the secular students lived separately from the nuns. But nevertheless intercourse between them easily sprung up and the nuns were informed as to the events of the outside world by the lay-sisters. Gossip and scandal were never far from the convent; then, too, the intercourse with the father confessors and the intimate companionship of so many young and old women did not allow the sexual aberrations of the previous centuries to cease in the convents. The brothers de Goncourt wonder how a book like Mademoiselle d'Albert's *Escapades of a Jolly Girl* could have ever been written at the Panthémont convent. We rather wonder how the de Goncourts in their expressed preference for the eighteenth century, for "the good old times," failed to recognize the immorality in the spiritual convents. It is true we haven't many reliable reports on the French convents. We can find, for example, only a few scandalous stories about the Panthémont convent. But what does that show? The entire spiritual corruption was open as day. From the beginning of the century till the French Revolution clear-seeing minds condemned it with grave reproaches. One reads, for example, the account of this situation, derived from reliable reports, in Buckle's *History of Civilization in England*. Or the other citations, the dissolution of the jesuit order, the historically confirmed intercourse of the *confesseurs* with the nuns. Tocqueville says: "The clergy preach of morals but they are compromising by their actions." Buckle calls special attention to this state of affairs in his authoritative work.

What the de Goncourts have further overlooked is the decisive proof: the affairs in the convents became objects of public ridicule in contemporary drama, represented in Lanjon's *Nunnery, Popess Johanna, The Dragoon, The Convent Girls,* etc. That is shown further by the enormous spread of tribadism in France in the eighteenth century, which we shall later investigate, and which found its favorite centre in convents. It is proven finally by the famous novel of Diderot, *The Nun,* and the many pictures of the corruption in the convents, as well as the erotic writings of the eighteenth century.

So we can well believe de Sade when he said (Juliette, I, 1): "The prettiest and most immoral girls in Paris are those that come from the Panthémont convent" and also when he had the tribade, Zanetti, say (Juliette VI, 156): "The churches serve as bordellos," and when he described an instrument of pleasure, much used by women, as the "jewel of the 'sisters' ".

At any rate, immorality in the convents of neighboring Italy had reached a very high degree. Gorani, whose reliability is well known, reported wild orgies in the Neapolitan convents. The discovery of sexual debaucheries of the nuns at Prato (near Florence) brought to light one of the most noted spiritual scandals of the Eighteenth Century. Reumont related: In Prato as well as in Pistoia there were firmly entrenched in the Dominican convents disorders of the worst kind, a mixture of pietism and physical aberrations that bordered madness, and which had been no secret to the spiritual leaders for a long time. Some sort of order was established in Pistoia, but in Prato, where most of the compromised nuns were sent, there was an outbreak at Easter in 1781. The Grand Duke led an investigation by the police commissioner, the two principal culprits were locked up at Prato, then sent to Florence for trial. The Dominicans were forced to break all connections with the convent and were threatened with expulsion in case of disobedience. The entire affair made a grand sensation because of the vice and the fact that the nuns who were incriminated came of highly respected parents. A detailed description may be found in the biography of the Bishop of Prato, Scipione de' Ricci, by Potter.

Woman

The eighteenth century is, at least in France, the century of women. Georg Brandes rightly believes that the de Goncourts, those refined worshippers of women, felt drawn to the history of the eighteenth century, since "the influence of women was highest at that time." *Woman in the Eighteenth Century* by the de Goncourts is one of the most pleasant historical works, dealing with the highlights instead of the sidelights of its subject.

There is an unequalled description of the powerful influence of women in the chapter *The Mastery and Intelligence of Women* of the above work. "The soul of this age, the center of this world, the point from which everything radiates, the mount from which everything descends, the pattern that forms everything else, is the Woman." From the beginning to the end of the century woman ruled: Mesdames de Prie, de Mailly, de Châteauroux, de Pompadour, du Barry, de Polignac. Woman ruled in state, politics, and in society; her influence was felt in every field of life. War and peace were decided by the caprice of a woman, and not by the welfare of France. And in the famous salons of Du Deffand, Necker, Lespinasse, Geoffrin, Grandval, women set the fashion in the discussions of questions of the day and scientific affairs. Here was formed the modern "cultured society."

The age also showed that where the influence of women became predominant, the family broke up, love took on immoral forms, and was accompanied by a contempt for the feminine sex.

Love in this age was thoroughly sensual. It had become debauchery. Passion was recruited from the curious; the husband taught his wife all the tricks of love of a mistress. Philosophy aided in justifying debauchery and in apologizing for its shame. "At a supper in the house of a famous actress, at the table of a Quinault, among the obscene talk of a Duclos and Saint-Lambert, one heard women in all stages of sweet drunkenness speak of modesty: Pretty virtue! It should be fastened with pins." Convenient sophisms confused all moral conceptions of the woman. The purely physical love, which was proclaimed as the ideal by naturalism and materialism, finally appeared in women "in all its brutality."

The sexual relations followed wholly sensual purposes, and those which tried to beautify love were confined to making more pleasant and lasting the coarsest curiosities by light hindrances and by a mixture of such embellishments, which had more appeal to the mind than to the heart. The word "gallantry" received an entirely new meaning. It signified immoral manners and conduct which only differed from the wantonness of common whores by such forms as would increase the pleasure and serve as preservation of the appearance of esteem before the public. Bernhard's famous imitation of Ovid's *Art of Love* preached conventional behaviour in the greatest lewdness. Not much better were the "platonic loves," the "*liaisons* of society," the "private affairs" of that time. The Abbé Baliani says: "The women did not then love with the heart but with the head." Love was "complete freedom in the making." One realized in it the dirtiest dreams of a decadent artist, the temptations of spiritual corruption, the strangest fancies of an insatiable lechery. Love became an exciting play in which all the refinements of spiritual prostitution were essayed in order to increase the pleasure.

They prepared themselves for these pleasures by indulging in the most obscene conversations. Repeatedly de Sade mentioned in his novels how the pleasures of love were increased by conversations employing the dirtiest words and topics. This experience was taken directly from reality. Mercier tells that the great number of public whores had incited the youths to a very free speech which they used in addressing the most honorable women. The conversation with the most respected women was seldom delicate but reveled in dirty jokes, puns and scandals.

Therefrom resulted an unheard of immodesty in women. At thirty, woman lost the last particle of feeling of shame. There remained but "elegancy in vice," grace in debauchery. The woman took on all the counterparts of a male libertine; her greatest pleasure was "to enjoy fully the shame of her calling." So also the women in de Sade's novels rejoiced and exulted that they were prostitutes, that they belonged to the whole world and could bear the honored name of "whore." Even so pious a soul and so tender a heart as Madame Roland knew no feeling of modesty and reserve. She described herself and her body in all details in her *Autobiography;* she told of her breast, hips, legs, etc., so coldbloodedly that it would avail for a criticism of a statue. Shall we wonder then that de Sade had Juliette describe her own charms with a boundless cynicism (Juliette IV, 103)?

Genteel women carried their immodesty so far as to rent *petites maisons*, just like male roués. Indeed even women from the aristocracy went so far as to seek their pleasure in bordellos. Rétif de la Bretonne recognized Princess d'Egmont as a prostitute in a bordello. Conversely, it was no rarity for a prostitute to marry into polite society. In his *Contemporaries*, de la Bretonne says further: "I have indeed seen something far worse than this: a daughter of a hunchback, after she had passed through the hands of the madames, had a child, lived in the St. Honoré as a public prostitute, etc., etc.; she then married a rich man, had children by him and moved in polite society." Yet another example: Du Barry! Daughter of a low tax-collector, first a model in Paris, then a prostitute in the house of Madame Gourdan, of whom we shall speak more later. Here in the bordello she met Count Jean du Barry, to whose brother she was later married on her advancement to the position of the mistress of Louis XV. No wonder that the aristocracy eagerly copied such an example and inaugurated a true hunt of the *beautés populaires*. Thence arose a new fashion-word *s'encanailler*.

Thus the nearer one approaches the time of the Revolution the more moral corruption lay hold of the women of the country. It was prepared and nourished by the famous "convulsions," that remarkable, hysterical epidemic of convulsions lasting from 1727 to 1762 and attacking mainly the lower classes. Its center was the courtyard of the St. Medardus church. "From all quarters of the city the crowds turned to St. Medardus in order to participate in the trances, fits, cramps, convulsions and similar ecstasies. The entire courtyard and even the neighboring streets were packed tight with girls, women, invalids of all ages, etc., who strove to outdo one another in convulsions." Women, lying stretched out, begged the spectators to beat their bellies and were not satisfied until the weight of ten or twelve men were piled high on them with full force. Passionate dances, like the famous "*saut de carpe*" of Abbé Bécherand, soon gave an erotic color to these "convulsions."

Dulaure told what final rôle lust played in this notable form of hysteria and how these convulsions assisted in spreading sexual licentiousness. One can recognize the erotism in these convulsions in that the young maidens in their "fits" "never called to women for aid, but always to men, and to young, strong men at that." Hence they dressed very indecently, always showed an inclination for adamite nudeness, assumed lascivious postures, threw longing looks at the young men running to help them. Indeed, some cried out loudly: *Da liberos, alioquin moriar!* Thus vice and debauchery did not wait in abeyance; when the women in their orgasms invited the men "to use as a promenade their belly, bosom, thighs, etc., to fight with them," there was, of course, the natural result from the absolvement of morals by the convulsions.

Hysteria (*Vapeurs*) was prevalent with the French women throughout the century. Sauvages rightly holds that the origin of this hysteria was the crass egoism *(amour excessif de soi-même)*, the weak, vicious life of the women of that time. The *hysteria libidinosa* then also brought to a head notable eccentricities.

Woman in the Eighteenth Century created what a later age designated as "sadism," and which we shall later define in a significantly broader meaning. The *méchanceté*, the evil, and the *noirceurs*, the malicious tricks, became fashionable in love; the sinful sentiment *(scélératesse)* became a necessary ingredient of sexual pleasure. "Debauchery became an art of cruelty, perfidy, treachery and tyranny. Machiavelli was the master of love." Shortly before the Revolution, after the *petits maîtres* of love there appeared the *grands maîtres* of perversity, the heartless advocates of theoretical and practical immorality. With some women debauchery even reached satanism. They tormented respectable women, whose virtue was offensive to them; they also dastardly and with evil joy had the objects of their hate and also their love removed. They embodied the lustful pleasure in evil, the *"libertinage des passions méchantes."*

Real people gave the stamp to this society; their existence was confirmed by numerous personalities. The de Goncourts named the Duke of Choiseul, the Marquis de Louvois, Count de Frise, etc., as such lustful devils. And a respectable Dame of Grenoble, the Marquise L. T. D. P. M. was the feminine counterpart of these heroes, perhaps the pattern for de Sade's Juliette. The age of terror for love had broken out long before the reign of terror of the great Revolution, even before de Sade, intoxicated by the flowing blood from the guillotine, depicted in the most notable literary documents: *The Terror of Love!* And as in the age of terror under Chaumette's leadership the "theosophical orgies of lust" were celebrated, as the "goddesses of reason" were honored by a Maillard, a Moncore, an Aubry, in their bestial fashion, there suddenly appeared the *"tricoteuses de Robespierre,"* the *"flagelleuses"* and the horrible *"furies de guillotine."*

The four greatest thinkers of France in the eighteenth century: Montesquieu, Rousseau, Voltaire and Diderot all taught contempt for women. One has only to think of Voltaire's bitterly sarcastic expressions on his true friend Madame Du Chatelet. Woman, according to Rousseau, was created only for man's enjoyment. For Montesquieu man has power and reason, woman only gracefulness. Diderot saw in woman only an object of passion. "So a woman to Diderot is a courtesan, to Montesquieu a graceful child, to Rousseau an object of pleasure, to Voltaire—naught." In the Revolution Condorcet and Sieyès appeared for the family and political emancipation, but their protests were quickly stifled by the "mighty voices of the three great continuers *(continuateurs)* of the eighteenth century, through Mirabeau, Danton and Robespierre." The reason for this contempt is clear. Marriage, as Westermarck has shown in his classical work, is that institution to which humanity owes its moral perfecting; it is the absolute moral institution. In marriage the woman is of equal rank with the man, since she completes him. Outside of the marriage the woman cannot compensate him and consequently appears inferior.

We close with an almost unbelievable example of the contempt of women. The reference will be found in Buckle's *History of Civilization in England*, Part I, Chapter XII: "In the middle of the eighteenth century, there was an actress on the French stage by the name of Chantilly. She, though beloved by Maurice de Saxe, preferred a more honourable attachment, and married Favert, the well-known writer of songs and of comic operas. Maurice, amazed at her boldness, applied for aid to the French crown. That he should have made such an application is sufficiently strange; but the result of it is hardly to be paralleled except in some eastern despotism. The government of France, on hearing the circumstance, had the inconceivable baseness to issue an order directing Favert to abandon his wife, and intrust her to the charge of Maurice, to whose embraces she was compelled to submit (Grimm, Corresp. Lit., Vol. viii, pp. 231-233)."

The Erotic Literature

The French literature of the Eighteenth Century is brand-marked pornography! At no other time in the history of the world, even under the Cæsars, had literature been made a tool of vice in such a systematic fashion as in the *ancien régime*. Of course, the representation of sexual passion was an old story in French literature, and was even present in the numerous *fabliaux* of the middle ages; but it was not until the eighteenth century that the healthily coarse naturalism and naiveness of these older forms of erotic stories were replaced with pictures of sensuality, whose studied premeditation served as a malignant stimulus to an enervated society. The eighteenth century produced the greater part of the pornographic literature existing today; and in the number of individual erotic works more than all the other centuries combined. The lion's share in the production of pornography falls in the period from 1770 to 1800 when only eroticism could move the public. These books made the worship of flesh their main theme. They recognized nothing but lascivious experiences and all the forms of sexual pleasure. The bordello was a paradise, the prostitute far nobler than the most faithful wife. "What age has so dirtied itself with obscene books as this great century?" asked Janin, "that even men like Voltaire, Rousseau, Diderot, Montesquieu and Mirabeau fashioned their works according to the taste of the time." Shortly before and during the Revolution machlosophy appears to have suppressed all nobler motives. The book-stores were literally pornographic libraries. Mercier declared in 1796: "Only obscene books are displayed, especially those whose title-page and frontispiece mock and jeer at modesty and good taste. Everywhere these monstrosities are sold in baskets and pushcarts, near the bridges, the doors of the theatres and the open streets. The poison is not expensive: ten sous a book." The principal market was the notorious Palais Royal, of which we shall later speak. This center of all vice was also the principal market for the obscene writings that flooded Paris. One found these works even in the toilette rooms of Parisian ladies. Bernard has an interesting tale about this which also serves to show the enormous spread of the writings of Marquis de Sade: "A respectable lady both in age and position had written out a list of books she intended to take to the country for herself and children and asked me to procure them for her. On the list was *Justine or The Misfortunes of Virtue*, which she thought was a pedagogical work!" That such writings were plentiful in bordellos was not strange and, indeed, such is the case today. Napoleon I ordered all such books found in the possession of prostitutes to be seized and destroyed; only one example of each to be saved for the National Library where they are still preserved in a special corner of the building.

De Sade forever talked of obscene books. Juliette and Clairwil ransacked the dwelling of a Carmelite monk, Claude, and found a select library of pornography. Juliette said: "You have no idea what obscene books and pictures we found there!" First they note the *Porter of Chartreux*, "more a comic than a dirty book, which the author, nevertheless is supposed to have written on his death bed." Second, the *Academy of Ladies*, well conceived but poorly carried out. Third, the *Education of Laura*, a wretched work which had too little vice, murders and *goûts cruels* for Juliette. Finally, *The Philosopher Therese*, the enchanting book of Marquis d'Argens with pictures by Caylus, the only one of the four books that combined vice and atheism. And the monk had, of course, a number of the "wretched brochures that are found in all the cafés and bordellos."

The Marquis de Sade, indeed, intended his works to serve as models for all later obscene works.

We present as an orientation a short survey of the most important French erotica of the eighteenth century. For a complete list the student is referred to Gay's *Bibliography of Erotica* (six volumes).

The Ovid of the Eighteenth Century was Pierre Joseph Bernard (1708-1775). In 1761 appeared his *l'Art d'aimer*, a coarse imitation of Ovid's *Art of Love*. Nevertheless it caused great excitement and was present in the toilette table of every respectable lady. The verses were bound together with rose-bands and were appropriately about billing and cooing. But these latter were very passionate and the plainness of speech compared with Ovid. Bernard enfolded in his poem a whole course of refined sexual life, in which he recommended strongly the reading of piquant works.

The younger Crébillon (Claude Prosper Jolyot de Crébillon, 1707-1777) can be called the real creator of lascivious writings in the eighteenth century. His writings were characterized by an "elegant cynicism and graceful vice." The most famous was *The Sofa, a Moral Tale*, whose title indicates the content of the work. Of a similar kind were *The Loves of Zeo Kinizal, King of Cofirons* (1746), which described the love-adventures of Louis XV; *The Night and*

The Moment (1755), *Oh! What a Story!* (1751), *The Sins of the Heart and the Spirit* (1796), etc. In Crébillon's novels the tendency is apparent: to prettify and justify the commonest sensuality with a philosophic cover.

Jean François Marmontel (1723-1799) created the type of anti-clerical novel in *The Incas,* and had unmistakable influence on the representation of the clergy in later erotic novels.

Sidelights on the History of M. Dirrag and Mlle. Eràdicée, in addition to the case of Girard (Dirrag) and Cadière (Eràdicée), portrayed the sexual debaucheries of the jesuits. De Sade, as we have seen, ascribed this work to Marquis d'Argens and the pictures to Count Caylus.

André Robert Andréa de Nerciat (1739-1800) was for two years librarian in Cassel and was later confidant of Queen Charlotte at Naples. He wrote the notorious *Félicia* and a sequel *Monrose or a Libertine by Fate*.

That pornography at that time was fashionable and in good taste was shown most strikingly by the circumstance that the greatest figures of the age did not disdain the earning of this cheap fame. We have already mentioned that *savant* of the classical times, Caylus. But such men as Mirabeau and Diderot did not shrink from sullying their literary works by the production of obscene stories. Mirabeau especially was often quoted by de Sade and there is no doubt that Mirabeau's *Education of Laura* served as the model for *Philosophy in the Boudoir*. In *My Conversion* Mirabeau described the experiences of a male prostitute, who had respectable ladies, nuns, etc., pay for his services. A third obscene book of Mirabeau's was *Erotica Biblion* (1783).

In Denis Diderot's *Jacques the Fatalist* were presented obscene stories that put him below Crébillon's class. His famous *The Sister* which, "when first published, was thought to have been written by a nun, dealt with the torture to which a nun was put by the perverse lubricity of her abbess, for whom, it was said, Diderot found a model in the Abbess of Chelles, a daughter of the Regent, and thus a member of a family which for several generations showed a marked tendency to inversion." (Havelock Ellis in *Sexual Inversion*.) His *Indiscreet Joys* was also erotic and contained a number of paradoxical assertions and paranomasias in the sexual field; this feature probably gave occasion to de Sade's preference for Diderot.

Choderlos de Laclos was the Petronius of "a less literary and more degenerate epoch than that of the real Petronius." His much quoted *Dangerous Liaisons* described the corruption of the aristocracy, of which the author, the friend of the notorious Philippe Egalité, had first-hand knowledge.

Less cynical in his description of the debaucheries of the nobility was J. B. Louvet de Couvray who drew the type of the "chevalier" in his *Loves of Chevalier de Faublas*. In Faublas' rich love-adventures the hero (borrowed from the artificial effeminization of the real Chevalier d'Eon) played a rôle also found at the end of *Juliette* where Noirceuil, dressed as a woman, married a man.

Next to the Marquis de Sade the most famous erotic writer of the Revolutionary period was the productive Restif (Rétif) de la Bretonne. We shall later evaluate Rétif de la Bretonne as one of the first critics of de Sade. We are at present interested in him only as a contemporary of de Sade and in his influence upon him. It was plainly Rétif, whom de Sade referred to unfavorably in his novels: "R. . . . floods the public and needs a printing press next to his bed. By good fortune they groan alone under his frightful products; a dull decrepit style, nauseous adventures in the worst society; no other merit but a great verbosity for which only the store-keepers will be thankful." May not professional jealousy have played a part in his judgment? We will later see that Rétif did not think much better of de Sade. It may also be that the highborn Marquis thought himself far removed from the lowborn Rétif.

Indeed Rétif de la Bretonne (1734-1806) mainly occupied himself with the representation of the moral corruption in the lower classes, thus supplementing the work of Marquis de Sade, with whom he had otherwise much in common. Eulenburg declares: "An infinitely closer figure to de Sade than Rousseau is that *Rousseau du ruisseau*, Rétif de la Bretonne. He was lashed by a powerful sensuality and driven into a kind of exhibitionism by the idolatry of the ego. Therefore he was unequalled in understanding how to analyze the origin, essence and power of sexual life and to devote the ego to a greatly refined worship." There we have the germs of a literary de Sade but far weaker, more passive and less passionate. Were Rétif more active and impulsive, of a less contemplative nature, and were the means and milieu of the *célébré Marquis* given to the poor peasant's son from youth onward, then perhaps a second de Sade would have resulted, who would have been literally equal in power and in sensitiveness of description. Not aimlessly does Rétif praise above all this unusual sensitiveness, this "sensibility, sometimes delicate, sometimes horrible, cruel and wicked." We add to the characteristics of this remarkable writer that he was a passionate connoisseur of women and, unsatisfied with his very numerous mistresses, would run after every pretty girl he met on the street, and would not rest until he had made her acquaintance. He was personally of the greatest uncleanliness. He writes in the

Contemporaries: "Since 1773 till today, December 6, 1796, I have brought no new clothes. I have no underwear. An old blue coat is my daily garment." Rétif hence loved cleanliness—in women. He continually spoke thereof, gave detailed information in this connection in his *Pornography*, and approved the spread of this virtue among the Parisian prostitutes.

Despite his own patient observations he did not hesitate to avail himself of the adventures of others. Count Alexander of Tilly told in his *Memoirs* that Rétif de la Bretonne came to him with the request that he tell him his erotic adventures so that he could put them in a book. Very important was the relation of Rétif to Mathieu François Pidanzat de Mairobert (1727-1797), the famous author of *The English Spy* and the editor of *Secret Memoirs of Bachaumont*. The latter not only had his works printed at the secret press of Rétif but also collaborated with him in many works. One valuable treatise that appeared from there was Rétif's *Pornography* on the sixteen classes of prostitutes and panders. Also the *Contemporaries*, the *Owl* and the *Paternal Malediction* were enriched by Pidanzat de Mairobert.

The greatest work of Rétif was undoubtedly *Nights of Paris*, an inexhaustible thesaurus for the moral life in the Revolutionary period, the only representation of its kind of the moral physiognomy of Paris at the end of the eighteenth century, the true *Nocturnal Tableaux of Paris*, whose content rendered necessary a twenty years' work. "Every morning," said Rétif, "I wrote down what I had seen in the night." The result was eight voluminous volumes from which unfortunately space does not permit us to quote.

In *Monsieur Nicolas* (Paris, 1794-1797, 16 vols.) Rétif de la Bretonne told the story of his life more truthfully than the authors of such similar works as *Faublas, Clarissa* and *Heloise*. Of especial interest is the thirteenth volume, *My Calendar*, in which Rétif, day by day, wrote down all the women, whose acquaintance he had made and whom he had seduced and made pregnant.

His *Contemporaries* is a collection of tales that are founded on actual experiences. The heroes of these adventures were supposed to have authorized the author to use their real names. They are essentially tales of the moral life of the people.

The Farmer and the Perverted Farmer's Wife or the Dangers of the City are the *liaisons dangereuses* of the lower classes, which preach the sad truth that virtue through constant intercourse with vice necessarily is destroyed.

Fanchette's Feet is the story of a young modist from the Rue Saint-Denis, whose small foot enchanted Rétif, for he was an outspoken foot-fetichist. He had a fanatic *passion* for pretty women's feet and shoes. Fanchette's feet are indeed the heroes of the story.

"Her foot, her small foot, that turns so many heads was shod with a pink pump, so beautifully made and so worthy of enclosing such a beautiful foot that my eyes once fixed on that charming foot could not turn themselves away. Beautiful foot! I said very softly, you don't walk on Persian or Turkish carpets, a beautiful carriage does not guarantee you the fatigue of carrying that superb body, that masterpiece of the graces, but you have an eternal throne in my heart."

He really did see "Fanchette" one day in the Rue Saint-Denis, and her feet, "her wonderfully small feet," inspired him to write the story.

The work of Rétif that sounded most like those of the Marquis de Sade was *Innocent Saxancour or the Divorced*

Woman, supposedly the story of his unhappily married daughter, Agnes. Rétif in this work "crossed the boundaries of the boldest cynicism" and the author himself said that one will find in the work "all things that are called atrocities." The unfortunate wife after the marriage had to submit to all the moods of a degenerate *roué* from her husband; she suffered the most unbelievable infamies and horrors of her passionate tyrant.

We will refer to some other works of his in a later, more pertinent section. In conclusion to our short survey, which stresses only the characteristic works, we wish to remark on two very well known obscene poems of the eighteenth century. The first is *Fourtromania, a Lascivious Poem for Connoisseurs*. It contained six stanzas, each of 600 verses. The "foutromania" is the good luck of the gods, that drives away the boredom. But it also makes men happy. The author led the dance of these fortunates with Mlle. Dubois, an actress of the *Comédie Française*. Then follow the ladies Aroux and Clarion. At the end of the first stanza appear the duchesses and ladies of the court, who satisfy themselves with their lackeys. Finally the inexhaustible libido of old Polignac de Paulien is described.

The second stanza starts with the description of the charms of a young girl, who succumbs to the passions of a young *roué*. Inserted is a poem *Father Chrysostome* against sexual debaucheries in the convents. Later a man suffering from satyriasis breaks into the convent. Then follows an attack on tribadism and pederasty. The old Duc d'Elboeuf was one of the first who introduced the sect of pederasts to France. The conclusion is an excursion on syphilis.

The third stanza is almost entirely devoted to the rôle of syphilis in love. First the high perfection in the healing of this grave ailment is praised; then the "syphilitic heroes of love" are extolled. Archbishop of Lyons, Sire de Montazet, etc., are named together with the Duchesse de Mazarin. After highly indecent expressions on the Duke of Orleans and Madame de Montesson the liaison between the Duchess of Orleans and de l'Aigle as well as de Melfort is disclosed, the last two receiving syphilis from the duchess. Finally, high praise for Aretino, the discoverer of the "plastic positions."

The fourth stanza is devoted to the praise of the bordellos. The famous procuresses and madames are presented: Paris, Cardier, Rockingston, Montigny, d'Hericourt and Gourdan. Description of the orgies in these infamous resorts. "Bed and Board" must then follow, hence German women are more susceptible to "foutromania." The author curses Italy where he lost health and wealth.

In the fifth stanza the syphilophobias are encouraged. Not *all* women have syphilis. Montesquieu had been in the fire as had been Rousseau and Marmontel. Great praise for Dorat, the *poète foutromane*. The Hollanders who love only money. Description of the immoral cardinals. Spinola sleeps at Palestrina's, Albani at Altieri's, Bernis at Saint-Croix, Borghese is. . . . It's too bad that the "Dames de France," the aunts of Louis XVI, live in celibacy.

Agyroni, the author of a popular work on the therapy of syphilis, is the hero of the sixth stanza. This charlatan had indeed cured the author of his complaint. Numerous medical details as in Robé's poem on syphilis. For a conclusion, "foutromania" is again praised as the soul of the universe.

The second poem, *Parapilla*, is a translation of the Italian original *Il Cazzo* (Phallus), the favorite word of Pope Benedict XIV. When a courtier pointed to the obscenity of the word, he replied: "*Cazzo, cazzo!* I will repeat it until it no longer sounds dirty." The French poem consists of five stanzas whose content, in short, is: Rodric receives from Heaven a certain instrument that makes all women happy. Firstly in Florence, the famous Donna Capponi. Then it thrives in a nunnery in the hands of Lucrezia, the daughter of Alexander VI. The debaucheries of this pope in Rome are then described and the poem closes with an obscene conversation between him and his daughter.

We could only touch on the most important erotic works of the French literature of the eighteenth century. Their influence on morals was tremendous and the Marquis de Sade was sensible of this influence. In his *Ideas on the Novel* he showed that he had recognized the significance of pornography. He said: "The epicureanism of Ninon de Lenclos, Marion de Lorme, Marquise de Sévigné and de Lafare, Chaulieu, St. Evremond, this entire society, tired of mere cytheric love, turned to Buffon, held that only bodily passions were worthwhile in love, and soon changed the style in novels. The writers found it simpler to amuse and corrupt these women than to serve and glorify them. They created incidents, descriptions and conversations more in the spirit of the time and developed its cynicism and immorality in a pleasant, easy and at times philosophic style."

Art

The French art of the eighteenth century was also a true mirror of the time. Architecture, painting, theatre and dance all served in excitation of the senses. The famous "rococo" was nothing less than a picture of harmony. Rococoism followed the inspirations of the artistically excited senses in the preference for detailed ornamentation, in intricate interlaced lines, in the representation of passionate scenes and delicately conceived *"nudités."* A splendid description of the graphic arts and especially of architecture was given by Georg Brandes: "What was sought after in architecture under Louis XIV was the impressive. Heavily interlaced and cumbersome details were the general style. The *petites maisons* of the time were a prerequisite of the man of the world. Every part of the room was designed to excite the mind. Indeed all the rooms smelled of passionate perfume. . . ."

The eighteenth century was expressed even more clearly in its painting than in its architecture. The desire for something new "to delight the blasé appetites" gave the artists a cunning talent for inventiveness. Fragonard, Lancret, the painter of *fêtes galantes,* disdained the simple naive nudity of the goddesses of Lebrun and Nicholas Mignard. Their *baigneuses* and *bergères* are no longer mythological figures but Parisian prostitutes who are displayed in voluptuous positions in bath or bed. These pleasant naiads and coquettish shepherdesses with bare breasts and more or less revealing dress were women of the time, ladies, "very much in vogue at the little parties at Trianon and Lucrinnes."

If books worked so much for the glorification of sexual passions, then their graphic representation must have been a thousand times more effective. "The realism of the painter shows itself in actions and in words, in books and in songs; it is bound to exert a bold influence on the youth by overexciting the sexual senses." And the Marquis de Sade, who told in his novels all the possible means of increasing sexual pleasure, had Saint Fond cry out after a wild orgy: "Oh! A painter should be here now so that he might hand down to posterity this passionate and divine picture!"

Hence it could not fail but happen that after the piquant *Nudités* of Fragonard and Lancret all sorts of obscene pictures would spread enormously. It was not unusual for mistresses to have painted for their lovers pictures or casts of themselves in the nude. Well known is the story of O'Morphi, mistress of Louis XV, inmate of the Deer Park, and for whom Louis XV had to thank the famous adventurer Casanova in this wise. Cananova, in one of his many love-adventures in Paris, had made the acquaintance of a Flemish actress, O'Morphi, who had a young sister of surpassing beauty, whose charms Casanova enthusiastically described. He had a painting made of this splendid body in the "divine manner" for six louisdors. The posture in which she was painted was "entrancing." "She lay on her belly, resting her arm and bosom on a cushion and held her head turned about as if lying three-fourths on her back. The artist has painted her bottom part with such great talent and truth that it is impossible to imagine anything more beautiful." A friend of Casanova was very eager to procure a copy of this painting. The painter exhibited in Versailles this copy which Saint-Quentin found so beautiful that he rushed off with it to the king. "His most Christian majesty, a great connoisseur in this field, wanted to convince himself with his own eyes whether the painter had made a true copy, and whether the original was as beautiful as the copy." Thus Casanova lost his mistress to Louis XV, who, after a payment of one thousand louisdors to her sister, had her brought to his Deer Park, where after a year she came down with child. The infant was immediately spirited away lest the queen be disturbed.

Casanova later showed this famous picture to a French nun in Aix, with whom he had an affair. The nun, too, had herself painted for Casanova, in the same obscene posture.

Especially before the Revolution the most immoral pictures were distributed in and about the bordellos without hindrance from the police. From 1790 to 1793 the most shameful caricatures of Louis XVI, Marie Antoinette, etc., were distributed to the customers in the bordellos. One can truly say that these places contributed greatly to the political breakdown of France. In the Reign of Terror such pictures were to be found not alone in the bordellos but in public shops and galleries where the boldest pictures imaginable of the most strange and obscene pictures hung in open display.

That erotica were richly illustrated with obscene pictures is understood. The novels of Marquis de Sade were no exception to the rule. We shall return later to this subject.

La Chronique Scandaleuse reported a remarkable hiding place for obscene pictures, "a new kind of obscenity, an epoch-making discovery." This was the *vestes de petits-soupers*. According to the fashion of that time coats or jackets were buttoned to the neck; hence the vests or waistcoats could not be seen. But during the orgies the gay young bloods would unbutton their jackets and show their vests decorated with paintings and stickers, which showed with true fidelity the very orgies themselves!

There was still another kind of obscene pictures we must discuss. For de Sade defecation was also an object of pleasure and passion. The faeces were delicious and were swallowed by men and women as a great delicacy. One can hardly believe it! Even the act of defecation was presented before the eyes of the Parisians. Reichart tells that poems, essays and pictures, all describing, praising and extolling this act were offered on every corner to passersby. Even respectable persons bought these pamphlets and treated the whole matter as a rich joke.

Sculpture also tried to extol the purely sensual in its limited fashion. Virgin nudity was profaned by the expression of sensual love. The women were almost always represented as *petites filles*, lascivious courtesans, wanton shop-girls, etc.

André Grétry, the chief representative of French music of the eighteenth century, who loved "*filles et fillettes*" all the time, showed in his musical works no noble passion but only lust.

That Marquis de Sade was a true product of the age was shown by the fact that he also was bitten by the mania of the age: "thespian madness, mimomania." He not only wrote many plays but also directed some amateur productions. The passion for the theatre, the "mimomania," ruled in France during the entire century with a force scarcely comprehensible to us today. Throughout the entire country amateur societies sprung up. There was a theatre in every castle, in every noble house. "It is an unbelievable mania," said Bachaumont, "even every pimp wants to have a stage and troupe in his home!" Theatrical madness also ran in the circle of the clergy. Louis XV, of course, by Pompadour's influence, had the plays presented in the Court.

The drama, especially in the last decade before the Revolution, had taken on an ever freer character. We have already mentioned Lanyon's convent plays. Shortly before and during the Revolution there came a real flood of obscene comedies against the king and church. The number of these so-called *Pièces révolutionnaires* is very great. The most extreme are by Guigoud Pigale (The Triumph of Public Reason), Léonard Bourdon (The Grave of Imposters of the Temple of the Revolutionary Truth, dedicated to the Pope), Sylvain Maréchal (The Last Judgments of the King), Desbarreaux (The Potentates Crushed by the Mountain and the Reason or the Deportation of the Kings of Europe). In the last-named play the princes of Europe quarrel about a piece of land. The Empress Catherine says to the Pope: "Have you swallowed your piece, Holy Father?" He answers: "Don't worry, you'll have the first try." Thereupon he boxes the ears of the King of Prussia who retaliates by stepping on his corns, and so the merry conversation proceeds with familiarities and obscenities.

The Marquis de Sade had a further model in the notorious *Théâtre gaillard* for his obscene comedies which he had his fellow-prisoners play in Bicêtre and in Charenton. The obscenity went further than mere words. In April, 1791, there existed in the Palais Royal a public theatre where a so-called savage and his mate, both nude, before the eyes of a crowded audience of both sexes, went through the act of coition. Coitus as a play! That must have pleased the numerous *voyeurs* of the city, who appear in de Sade's novels. La Mettrie had already said: "The pleasure that other people's pleasure afford us" in his *Art of Joy*. The magistrate finally had both actors summoned before him. It was discovered that the savage was a rascal from the suburb St. Antoine and that the female was a common whore who earned her money in this wise from the curious spectators.

The actresses, opera singers, chorus and ballet girls formed a very desirable number of the prostitutes, whom we shall treat of later. The foyers of the theatres were the "favorite hunting grounds for paramour, pander and prostitute."

Fashion

Clothing! That can make women seem more desirable by showing just slight hints of charms and arousing the passions of both sexes. That is the rôle which Marquis de Sade had Minister Saint Fond impart to fashion. Saint Fond also recommended to Juliette that she should show herself half naked in the streets to the public if she wanted to remove her last vestige of modesty.

Here, too, de Sade let reality speak. The advice of Saint Fond was actually followed. "On a quiet day of the year V of the Revolution two women paraded up and down the Champs-Elysées, completely nude and covered only with a thin gauze. Many women also showed themselves with wholly bare bosoms. The sight was not unusual."

The blaséness was shown in remarkable conceits. Young men and women tried to better nature and borrowed the white hair of age. The de Goncourts excellently describe the incessant changes in fashion in their bizarre fancies, their delicate concealment and unveilment, the gigantic *friseurs* of the women, their "make-up," beauty spots and patches, etc. Fashion paid homage to the age.

The nearer one comes to the time of the Revolution the more does nudity appear in fashion. The style of gauze, the preference for gossamer becomes more apparent. The clothing of the "Goddesses of Reason" becomes ever more transparent. Clothing retreated to the center to show its opposite semicircles, bosom and legs. Ankle bracelets and golden rings on the toes were the fashion. Terpsichore, in the Greek fashion, reigned in the public gardens. A journalist who attended the opening of the Parisian Tivoli, declared that the goddesses appeared in such light and transparent dress that nothing was left to the imagination. "The women in the audience are dressed as outrageously as possible. The indecency of their behavior is impossible to describe. In the last great ball in the opera house Madame Tallien appeared garbed only with jewels in the necessary place." These costumes, whose wearers were called *merveilleuses*, had been introduced in Paris by Therese Cabarries, the mistress of Tallien, after she thus publicly showed herself in the Reign of Terror in Bordeaux. The male *merveilleuses* were called *incroyables* and clothed themselves according to the ideal of offensiveness. For during the Revolution the highest ideal was not beauty but power and strength of muscles. Don Juan was changed to Hercules.

The perverse sexual impulses also found expression in

fashion. The wide spread paedicatio, also practiced between man and woman, brought the notable fashion of the so-called "Cul de Paris." It spread to such an extent that even the prostitutes delighted in this form of passion, since it was the "style." Under Louis XVI the seat in women's dress was so extended that they resembled "Venus Hottentote."

On the other hand, tribadism was a cause of rather strange costumes. The tribades with male inclinations had remarkably increased during the Reign of Terror. The virago on the streets was a daily incident. Her costume differed little from the man's. Since her hair was cut close and her voice was strident, it took a good look to make sure of the sex.

Bordellos and Secret Pornologic Clubs

Marquis de Sade had made his studies for his two notorious novels, *Justine* and *Juliette* in Paris. Here he, himself, experienced and conceived the greater part of the contents. Parisian incidents and experiences had permanently fructified his phantasy. And the models for the descriptions of individuals in his works are easy to discover. This will be shown in surprising fashion in the discussions of prostitution and sexual life in Paris. Even today Paris justifies the remark of Montesquieu in his *Persian Letters:*

"It is the most sensual city in the world where the fanciest pleasures are invented." De Sade's description of the great bordello with its ingenious contrivances and settings refers almost entirely to Parisian bordellos. Most of his heroines are Parisian prostitutes. It is therefore fitting that we should next consider these conditions.

In *Juliette* (I, 87) the Marquis de Sade describes the bordello of Duvergier in a suburb of Paris. This madame had a bordello for both men and women. In a private house, surrounded by a pretty garden, Madame Duvergier had her own cook, delicious wine and charming maidens who received ten louisdors for a *tête-à-tête*. The house had the requisite back entrance for safeguarding of propriety. The furniture was of the best; the boudoirs most fitting for their purposes. Duvergier, protected by the police, could celebrate more atrocities than her fellow-madames. The bordello supplied princes, nobles, and rich citizens with its wares.

When Juliette organized a house in Paris, six pimpesses (*maquerelles*) were sufficient to provide for girls from Paris and the provinces. Clairwil introduced Juliette into the house of the "Society of the Friends of Crime," which lay in the heart of Paris but was discreetly concealed. It had splendid drawing-rooms, boudoirs, *cabinets d'aisance* and harems or, as de Sade called them, seraglios in which both sexes disported themselves in wild orgies. The girls were, for the most part, torn from their parents, under the protection of the police. Here the respectable world was assisted by hangmen, jailers, floggers and flagellants (Juliette III, 33 ff.).

Alcide Bonneau believes that the Deer Park served de Sade as a pattern for his descriptions of bordellos. Nonetheless de Sade had made a thorough study of Parisian bordellos and had found many incidents to his liking. He wrote (Juliette I, 333) that in many bordellos in Paris turkey-cocks were much esteemed for lustful purposes in zoophilia. At any rate it cannot be denied that de Sade took his descriptions of Parisian bordellos from actual experiences. Authentic reports will conclusively confirm this. The most notorious bordellos of Paris, the secret pornologic clubs and the affairs of the prostitutes will be described in later sections.

The most famous, most sought after, most mentioned Parisian bordello in the Eighteenth Century was the House of Madame Gourdan on Rue des Deux Portes; under the reign of Louis XV and Louis XVI it served the court and nobility. This bordello was distinguished by the genteel attempt to satisfy every desire of male and female visitors. A short description of the place is appended.

1. *The "Seraglio."* This was a great salon with "*plastrons de corps-de-garde,*" i.e., twelve prostitutes who had always to be in a position such as to satisfy any whim of the visitor. There the price and details of their pleasure were agreed upon. Even the minute details were stipulated. Pidanzat de Mairobert at this description in *The English Spy* cries out: "Just imagine the horrors and infamies that took place in such a house!"

There is no doubt that de Sade expressed such a great preference for the word "seraglio" from this salon of Madame Gourdan. De Sade also discussed the understandings on the price of love in his novels and was particularly concerned with the analysis of the details for preparing an orgy.

2. *The "Piscine."* This was the bathroom of the bordello, where the girls, fresh from the provinces, were sent to the madame. There they were bathed, powdered and perfumed. Among the many essences and toilet waters

was the famous *Eau de Pucelle*. This was a strong astringent with which Madame Gourdan renewed "lost beauties" and restored that "which can be lost only once." Marquis de Sade often mentioned this remarkable miracle which will be discussed later under the section: Cosmetics and Aphrodisiacs. Also in the *piscine* was the *Essence à l'usage des monstres*, which made impotent persons potent again by its strong odor and excited them to passionate cruelty. The specific of Doctor Guilbert de Préval (we shall later say more of this charlatan) was truly a magic charm. For it served at one blow as a prevention, diagnosis and cure of syphilis! Truly a sexual panacea!

3. *The "Cabinet de Toilette."* Here the students of the Venus-seminar received their second lessons.

4. *The "Salle de Bal."* From this class-room a secret passageway led into the home of a merchant on Rue Saint Sauveur. Through his house the prelates and preachers (*gens à simarre*) as well as respectable ladies could enter the bordello. In this secret room were clothing of all kinds as well as "objects of delicacy." Here the clergy could turn into laymen, officials into soldiers, ladies into cooks. Here the respectable ladies permitted unflinchingly the powerful embraces of a coarse peasant, whom her trusty madame had chosen to satisfy her indomitable temperament. On the other hand the peasant believed her to be one of his own kind and was little embarrassed in expression and action.

5. *The "Infirmerie."* This was the room for the impotent. The attendants tried to incite and arouse drooping spirits by all possible means. The light fell from above; on the walls were passionate pictures; in the corners stood similar statues; on the table lay obscene books. In the alcove was a bed of black silk; its top and sides consisted of plate-glass so that it mirrored and reflected all the

objects and actions of this pretty boudoir. Perfumed thorny switches served for flagellation. *Dragées-pastilles* in all colors were offered for food; "only one was needed to make one feel like a new man." They were called *Pastilles à la Richelieu* because he had often given them to women as aphrodisiacs. Women were also taken care of in this *Infirmerie*. There were present so-called *pommes d'amour*, little balls of stone, to satisfy them. Mairobert could not discover if "the chemists had analyzed this stone which had a decided chemical reaction and was often made use of by the Chinese." The *consolateur* was an ingenious instrument "found in convents" as a substitute for a man. Madame Gourdan did a wholesale business with this artificial phallus. In her possession were numberless letters from abbesses and simple nuns asking her to send them *a consoler*. Great, black rings, so-called *aides*, served the men as artificial irritations in women. Many of these rings were covered with hard studs for increasing the pleasure. Finally there was a whole arsenal of *redingotes d'Angleterre*, which are today called condoms, and which, as Mairobert has it, "protect from the virus of love but dull the pleasure." Madame de Sévigné called it "protector of pain and despoiler of pleasure" in one of her letters.

6. *The "Chambre de la Question."* This was a private room in which one could see through a secret peep-hole all that took place. A contrivance for *voyeurs*.

7. *The "Salon des Vulcan."* In it was a *fauteuil* of a strange form. The moment one sat in it, one was struck a heavy blow. The person sank backwards with outstretched legs, which were fastened to the sides. This chair was a discovery of Sire de Fronsac, son of the Duke of Richelieu, and served him as a faithful aid to seduction. The *Salon des Vulcan* was so situated that the crying and wailing could not be heard outside the room. This

mechanization of vice will also be found in de Sade's writings.

Gourdan was the leading *madame* for the respectable world. She could satisfy all desires and was extremely wealthy. In Villiers le Bel she had a private country house in the forest to which she seldom went but often sent her sick and pregnant girls. The villa also served as a useful hiding place for especially delicate debaucheries. It was ironically called by the peasants *the convent*.

There were two kinds of *madames* in Paris; first, the seducers of virgins, second, purveyors of already deflowered maidens. Only the first were punished by being forced to ride backwards on an ass. Gourdan belonged to the second class and took care that her novices were officially prostituted by one of her assistants. But the head-madames had also to make regular reports of the physical health of their girls. We shall later give such a report.

In the House of Gourdan the mistresses were educated for the respectable world. The later Countess Du Barry had to thank her resplendent career to her early stay at the bordello of Madame Gourdan. Many aristocrats also sought new pleasures here. A respectable lady, Madame d'Oppy, was discovered in 1776 by the police at Gourdan's where she was officiating as a prostitute.

On November 14, 1773, Madame Gourdan delivered a funeral oration on her deceased colleague, Justine Paris, which was printed in *The English Spy* and is so full of sadism that we append a short summary of it. The idea for this funeral oration was conceived by Prince Conti, one of the most notorious adventurers of the *ancien régime*. It was read at an orgy in Conti's home. The "Funeral Oration of the very proud and very powerful Lady, Madame Justine Paris, Grand Priestess of Cytherea, Paphos,

Amathonte, etc., given November 14, 1773, by Madame Gourdan, fellow Priestess, in presence of all the nymphs of Paris" has the characteristic motto:

> *Syphilis, O my God!*
> *Has put me under the sod!*

On their dying-bed Justine's parents preach to her that immorality is the only redemption for the future. "Don't count the days you haven't consecrated to pleasure!" Justine immediately transposed this advice into action, which one finds on almost every page in the novels of Marquis de Sade, and dedicated herself to the advice of her parents. She then entered a Parisian bordello, where she made great advances in the service of Venus and became famous through an affair with the Turkish ambassador. Trips to England, Spain and Germany taught her to be phlegmatic with the Englishmen, serious with the Spaniards, and ardent *(emportée)* with the Germans. She finally came to Italy and in Rome was the "Queen of the World and the centre of *Paillardise*." She traveled through all Italy, honored and coveted by nobles and clergy. Unfortunately she was attacked from time to time by her hereditary syphilis but that did not prevent her at her return to Paris from celebrating new orgies, winning success and great honor as the proprietor of a bordello. She ended in a hospital.

Could this funeral oration have been unknown to Marquis de Sade? It is hardly probable; it is almost certain that Madame Paris was the prototype for Juliette who was celebrated throughout all Italy, in Florence, Rome and Naples as the queen of the world and as the ideal prostitute.

Casanova, the famous confidant, whose historic trustworthiness is attested by Barthold, told in his *Confessions* of a visit in 1750 to the bordello of Paris, the so-called Hôtel du Roule, and presented a living picture of the life and action in a Parisian bordello of the eighteenth century, which may here serve as an addition to the more systematic description of the house of Gourdan.

"The Hôtel du Roule was famous in Paris, but was as yet unknown to me. The proprietress has furnished it elegantly and has from twelve to fourteen splendid girls. One finds there all the desirable comforts: good table, good beds, cleanliness; her cook was excellent, her wine splendid.

"She is called Madame Paris, undoubtedly a pseudonym that pleases all.

"Protected by the police, she was far enough from Paris to be certain that the visitors to her place were persons well above the middle-class.

"The inside was well policed by servants, and all pleasures had a fixed tariff.

"One paid six francs for breakfast with a nymph, twelve for a dinner and double that for a night."

Here we pause for a moment and declare that the above description of Casanova tallies almost word for word with the description of Duvergier's in de Sade's *Juliette*. The house of Duvergier was just like that of Justine Paris.

Casanova died in 1798; his memoirs reaching only to 1773 remained in manuscript form long after his death and were not made public until 1822. *Juliette* appeared early in 1797. The only conclusion to be drawn is that both men have described independently the same bordello. To return to the description of Casanova.

"We enter a fiacre and Zatu says to the driver: 'To Chaillot.'

"After half an hour journey he stops before a gate on which is a sign, *Hôtel du Roule*.

"The gate was closed. A Swiss with a great beard stepped out from a side-door and seriously sized us up with his eyes. He found us respectable, opened the gate and we walked in.

"A one-eyed woman of about fifty years, but still showing traces of former beauty, greeted us and asked if we would like to dine.

"Upon my assent she led us into a very pretty salon, in which we saw fourteen young maidens who were all pretty and dressed in muslin.

"At our entrance they arose and made a charming bow.

"All were about the same age, some blonde and some brunette.

"Every taste could be satisfied here.

"We spoke a word to all and made our choice.

"The two chosen let loose a joyous cry, embraced us with a passion that was virginal, and we went to the garden expecting that we would be called to dinner.

"This garden was extensive and so arranged that it could serve the joys of love.

"Madame Paris said: 'Go, sirs, and enjoy the fresh air and reassure yourselves; my house is a temple of peace and of health.'

"During the sweetest occupation we were called to eat.

"We were very well served; the meal had aroused new longing in us, but with the clock in her hand the one-eyed attendant entered to inform us that our party was ended.

"Pleasure was here measured by the hour."

Finally Casanova and his friend were induced to spend the night in the bordello.

This house was mainly visited by the clergy. Madame Richard had started her career with the systematic seduction of young father confessors. This specialty gave her the idea of opening a bordello exclusively for the clergy. It flourished. Madame Richard became the purveyor of young girls for a "missionary home, for prelates and other clergymen." We have previously described an erotic scene in this house.

A *roué* in Venice always brought with him two Negresses in the bordello of Juliette because the contrast between white and black girls afforded him special satisfaction (Juliette VI, 152). Negroes also played a rôle in the anthropophagic dinner in Venice (Juliette VI, 204). In the castle of Cardoville at Grenoble, where Justine was led as a sacrifice to the passions of this *roué*, two Negroes are active accomplices at this orgy (Justine IV, 331). In the third volume of *Aline and Valcourt* there is an obscene picture on page 200 showing three naked women and four Negroes swinging heavy clubs at one another.

The Negroes are no invention of de Sade. Long before 1790 there existed a Negro bordello in Paris. This was in the house of a Mlle. Isabeau, first on Rue Neuve de Montmorency, later on Rue Xaintonge. In this bordello Negresses, mestizos, and mulattos were at hand. There were no set prices; the inmates were sold "like slaves in a caravan."

Fraxi believes that the taste for black women belongs exclusively to the French. At any rate one finds today in many bordellos in Paris and the provinces permanent examples of these black beauties. Hagen in his *Sexual Osphresiology* makes many references to this preference for Negresses by the French; he ascribes it to the charm of their odor.

For descriptions of the other great bordellos of Paris we must refer to the famous work of Rétif de la Bretonne,

Pornography and to the *Bordellos of Paris*. Yet we would like to mention the house in Faubourg Saint-Antoine, where, according to Rétif, the Duke of Orleans, Prince d'Artois, enjoyed the wildest debaucheries and atrocities, where those *bestialities* were encountered which the Marquis de Sade described is his *exécrable romance, Justine*.

Manifestly even this great number of bordellos could not satisfy the desires of the *ancien régime*. Passion must be made private. Hence the respectable gentlemen and rich *roués* of that time had in the so-called *petites maisons*, their own private bordello in miniature. Every one had his *little house* with some mistresses. That was the high tone in young and old. Casanova became acquainted in Paris with the eighty year old Chevalier d'Arzigny, the oldest of the *petits maîtres*, who powdered and perfumed himself, scented his heavy wig, pencilled his eyebrows, etc. Even this old worldling was devoted to his mistress, who managed his little house, in which he always ate at evening in the society of her friends, who were all young and lovable and gave up every company for his.

The Marquis de Sade also had his *petite maison* in Saint-Roch in 1772.

What Marquis de Sade described in the "Society of the Friends of Crime," and what we shall later delineate as the *mysterium of vice* in the novels of this author, actually existed. There were in Paris secret clubs whose members united for the practical study of debauchery. They had their temple with a statue of Priapus, of Sappho and other symbols of sexual passion; they had also their own special speech and symbols.

The *Island of Happiness* or *The Order of Happiness* or *The Society of Hermaphrodites* was the notorious love-club. This secret society borrowed all descriptions, ceremonies and other forms of seafaring life, addressing their songs and prayers to holy Nicolaus. *Maître, Patron, Chef d'escadre, Viceadmiral* were the names for the individual grades of cavaliers and cavalieresses, who bore an anchor on their heart and had to swear eternal fidelity and silence if they wished to be borne to the island of fortune. In their more than gallant meetings the most obscene conversations were held. A very zealous member of this obscene club was Moët, the author of the *Code of Cytherea* and translator of the English work *Lucina sine Concubitu*. He wrote for his club the famous *Anthropophily or the Secrets and Mysteries of the Order Devoted to the Pleasure of Mankind*. It contained the rules and statutes of the organization, its vocabulary and poems. I chose a few expressions from the dictionary: "*chaloupe, petite fille; flute, grosse femme; frégate, femme; gabari, fille ou femme bien faite; goudron, fard; hisser une frégate, enlever une femme; mât, les corps; mer, amour; sondes, les doigts.*" The purpose of the club is given in the following verse:

> *Let us sail to the Island of Happiness*
> *In our good ship of hermaphrodites.*
> *We are sure to find complete success*
> *In our search for strange and new delights.*

Very mysterious was the *Society of Aphrodites* who by a holy oath, and by frequent change of their meeting-place sought to hide their secret. The men were given names from the animal kingdom; the women from the flower kingdom.

On the other hand in another club we have the manuscript of the statutes, signs of recognition, and index of members with the *noms de plaisir*. This was the *Société du Moment*. This manuscript affords a profound insight into the atmosphere in which this society of cynicism reveled.

A fourth secret pornologic society was the *Secte Anandryne,* the club for tribades, who celebrated their orgies in the *Temple of Vesta.* We will give later a detailed description of this club and its meetings.

The origin of this secret society is explained by Delbène (Juliette I, 25): "Vice need not be suppressed for that is the only fortune of our life. One must only surround it with such a mystery that will never be revealed." De Sade's description of the *Society of the Friends of Crime* was plainly designed from the above plans. This society had its own printing plant with twelve copyists and four readers. In the club building were many *cabinets d'aisance* which were served by young girls and boys who were forced to gratify all the desires of the visitors of this place. One found *seringues, bidets, lieux à l'anglaise, linges très-fins, odeurs.* But one could be cleaned by the tongues of boys and girls.

In both seraglios of the house were boys, girls, men, women and animals for the satisfaction of every kind of vice. Murder cost 100 Thaler. The novice entered nude into the assembly room with a crucifix at the end of which was a Bible. Before her admittance Juliette was asked if she wished to undergo the kinds of immorality and crime that are tolled off. After she assented she received *The Instructions for Women entering the Society of Joy.* The orgies taking place in this secret club will be described later in the analysis of *Juliette.*

The Prostitutes

It is apparent from the foregoing representation that the eighteenth century with its animal passion was the century of the prostitute. The prostitute was idolized and idealized. The more vice and pleasure she knew the higher she stood over the honorable woman. In the *Philosophy in the Boudoir* the novice Eugenie asked her teacher in love, Madame de St. Ange, what a *putain* was, a word she heard for the first time. The teacher replied: "So are called these public sacrifices to male debauchery who are always prepared to sacrifice their temperament and their interests. It is a fortunate and noble profession but is dishonored by the general meaning since it crowns joy. They are more useful to the state than all the prudes and virtue for they have the courage to serve it. They are indeed the women truly worthy of love, the only wise women in the world. Since I was 12 years old I have striven to be worthy of the name and feel most happy when in the middle of pleasure I hear myself called this, for then I fly into the heights of passion." This was what the de Goncourts called "enjoyment of the damage of a good calling" and stood as a universal monument of the women of the eighteenth century.

Rétif de la Bretonne rose to the following swansong of prostitution in his *Monsieur Nicolas:* "If you (the prostitutes) cannot marry do not therefore despair. You are still useful. By the pleasures which you can afford, by the joys of your profession you can bring the basest of men into the bounds of pure nature and prevent them from giving themselves to sick women and suffering loss of health. Never be defiant and irritable, always remember that maidens of your profession are the true joys of men, true priests of passion. Guard yourselves!"

This glorification of the prostitute often took on strange forms. The Chevalier de Forges often uttered the wish to die in the arms of a prostitute. In his lifetime he had sought his pleasure and fortune with prostitutes. He also wanted to find death there. This wish was granted him. He died in the middle of his pleasure in the arms of a prostitute.

This elevated opinion of prostitutes was mirrored most brilliantly in their relations with the police. We saw that de Sade had the bordello of Duvergier protected by the police. This was actually true at the time of the origin of *Juliette*, during the Reign of Terror and the Directory. Yet under the regency stray prostitutes were punished, individuals were even sent to New Orleans. *Manon Lescaut*, the famous tale of Abbé Prévost, need only be recalled to show the glorification of the prostitute in French literature. Sick prostitutes were sent to Bicêtre. Inspector Marais, as we have said, had to send regular reports on the prostitutes of Paris to King Louis XV. But a serious inspection was lacking. Parent Duchatelet has gone through the archives of the police prefect of Paris from 1724 to 1788 and made the following observations:

"That the toleration of the police in regards to prostitutes and bordellos was unlimited; that they entered only in very severe cases. That they never searched the houses unless upon repeated complaints by neighbors.

"That in many houses murder was committed, in some, maidens and men were thrown from the windows, the uproar was mainly from the soldiers; the neighbors ran the greatest danger in getting home and often were unable to pass.

"That in all arrests the greatest arbitrariness prevailed, everything depended on the mood of the police commissioner and his aides."

The Revolution was the golden age of prostitution. Those events which de Sade described in his works were actualities. According to Parent Duchatelet all rules and regulations were done away with in 1791. The profession of prostitution was no longer an especial object for legal statutes. It was recognized as a business which everyone was privileged to practice and held that any restrictions thereupon would be an affront to personal liberty.

So these maidens were to all intent free and were allowed to do as they pleased. They saw themselves emancipated, a state of affairs which they had at no other time and in no other land enjoyed.

An unbridled boldness, an unexampled scandal was the result. The Reign of Terror and Directory delineate the highest summit of freedom and undiscipline which prostitution had ever reached. We recall that Marquis de Sade spent the entire period of 1790 to 1801 in complete freedom in Paris.

The prostitute became the *Goddess of Reason* whom all must worship, and every woman became a prostitute. In July, 1793, a new play was presented at the Theatre of the Republic, entitled, *The Freedom of Women*. But in reality it described the boldness of vice. The chief character, a husband, dissolute by inclination, inconstant in character and enemy of propriety, declared: "The charms of my wife should be shared by more than one fortunate being!"

Public prostitutes multiplied on all the streets, especially in the Palais Royal, Maison Egalité and Champs Elysées; in the loges of the theatre, in the public houses and in the great restaurants one saw the most outrageous behavior. Paris became the cloaca of the whole Republic and drew to it all the dissolute characters of the provinces. Pleasure soon became brutality. In the summer of 1796 the Boulevard du Temple was the scene of unrestrained vice. In a great company of men and women, including girls of 12 and 13 years of age, there was carried on a truly animal relation. The animal passions took hold of them all and they gave way to the most shocking fornication. But in spite of all the indignation, even to attacking the police, there took place in the wide expanses of the Palais Royal and the Champs Elysées almost daily "scenes of the most horrible and most shameful immorality."

Here the ideal that Marquis de Sade had in his novels was actualized: mass-vice! The immoral conduct was accomplished by costumes *à la grecque* that led moral people into the maelstrom of vice. This infection of morals by the poison of vice has been excellently described by Rétif de la Bretonne in his account of the activity of a prostitute on the streets.

"The girls walk up and down the streets; some make themselves known by the elegancy of their clothing, but most by the unashamed revealment of their charms. Young men permit themselves the greatest of freedoms in public. Our children lap up the poison of their charms. The daughter of a worker sees a well-dressed woman walking down the street eagerly followed by some young men; they stop her, talk to her and embrace her. The innocent girl feels a longing to be like that well-dressed woman and to be the object of admiration of young men. Another easy convert to prostitution! Easy enough for the young boys and girls to find opportunity to sin. To step on the streets was to step into sin."

According to police reports in October, 1793, the galleries of the theatres were packed full of children from 7 to 15 years of age; both stage and gallery were scenes of unbridled lust. "Many of the children were stark naked and made lascivious gestures to the spectators." It is no accident that these monstrosities took place in the autumn of 1793 after that fateful September day when the blood flowed freely down the streets. It is no accident that the pinnacle of vice was reached in the days of terrorism. De Sade who in the December of this year had again been placed in prison had during this time viciously waded in blood and lust. It was the time when even the secret pornologic clubs became public and there were celebrated in the opera house "nude balls," the face alone being masked. The number of daily balls for prostitutes entered into the hundreds. "The Nudities of Greeks and Romans" was a daily sight in the theatres.

The number of prostitutes in Paris in 1770 is estimated by Parent Duchatelet to have been 20,000 in a population of 600,000. At the time of the Revolution it grew to 30,000.

If but a glance at the different kinds of prostitutes is vouchsafed it is apparent that the mistresses of the *ancien régime* were mainly recruited from the theatre-world. Actresses, singers and dancers were special favorites.

Mercier tells that the *filles d'Opéra* had decided favor with the men. La Mettrie emphatically declares: "Where can voluptuousness be shown off to its best limits than on the stage?" and praises the charms of the famous dancer Camargo. D'Alembert cynically believed that the good fortune and richness of the dancers and singers was "a necessary result of the law of movement."

Vivid light is cast upon these affairs by two anecdotes told by Casanova. His friend Patu introduced him to a famous opera singer, Mademoiselle Le Fel, favorite of Paris and member of the Imperial Academy of Music. "She had three loveable little children who ran all around the house. 'I adore them,' she said. 'They deserve it for their beauty,' I (Casanova) answered, 'although each has a different facial appearance.' 'I can well believe it! The oldest is the son of the Duke of Annecy, the second of Prince Egmont, and the youngest is due to Maisonrouge who has just married Romainville.' 'Oh, pardon me, I thought you were the mother of the three children.' 'But of course I am!' As she said this she looked at Patu and broke out into loud laughter with him. I was a novice and unaccustomed to seeing women usurp the privileges of men.

"But Le Fel was no bold creature and belonged to good society. Had I been better acquainted with the times I would have known that it was nothing unusual. The great gentlemen who strew about their posterity left their children in the arms of their mothers, paying them heavy pensions. As a result the more fecund these ladies were, the better they lived."

The second anecdote is yet more characteristic. One day Casanova saw at Lani's, the ballet master at the opera, five or six young girls from 13 to 14 years old, accompanied by their mothers. He began flattering them, while they listened with modestly closed eyes. One of them complained of headaches. While Casanova offered her his smelling-bottle, one of the girls said to her: "You must have slept very badly last night." "No, that's not it," answered the innocent Agnes, "I think I'm with child." At this so unexpected answer from the young girl whom from her age and appearance he had taken for a virgin, Casanova said: "I did not think that Madame was married." She looked at him for a moment surprised. Then she turned to her companion and they both laughed aloud.

The ballet dancers and chorus girls received no salary so that "many men had to make up for the deficiency of a honorarium." With few exceptions this caste took "pride in being disdainful." At that time there were many ballet dancers and singers who were more vicious than tolerable, had no talent and yet lived comfortably. For it was self-understood that such a girl must destroy every virtue in order to escape starvation.

A dialogue in *The English Spy* showed that the same was typical throughout the theatrical world.

The Duke of Bouillon spent 800,000 Livres in three months on the opera singer La Guerre. The prostitute La Prairie belonged to those women who ate in the nude at the *petite maison* of Marshal Soubise. "It's the custom of my friend, Abbé Terrai!" This moral priest had a precious bed in his house on Rue Notre Dame. When the dear visitor entered she found a covered painting which when uncovered revealed the pretty body of a nude woman. "Madame, it's the costume," the abbé cold-bloodedly remarked, showing her with these words that he would also like to have her in this costume.

The famous Mademoiselle Du Thé was originally "Rosalie" in chorus and as such initiated the young duke of Chartres into the practices of Venus. When she was discarded by this prince she went to London, ruined many lords there, returned to Paris, where she opened a gambling-hall that brought her much money and allowed only the rich to enter. This Messalina was thoroughly greedy and selfish. She later became the mistress of Prince d'Artois. But Du Thé did not always swim in gold. In a report of Police Inspector Marais of December 12, 1766 we find: "Yesterday Du Thé did not have a sou! She had to borrow a thaler and six livres in order to go to the Italian opera."

The actress Dubois made a catalog of her lovers reckoning on a twenty-year-activity 16,527, i.e. about three a day. "Her greed for gold was equal to her greed for pleasure." This well known history influenced Marquis de Sade. In the *Philosophy in the Boudoir* Madame St. Ange estimated that she had given herself to 12,000 men in 12 years.

La Chanterie, originally a chorus girl, was of a rare beauty. The artists often used her as a model. She was also painted as a madonna for the chief altar in a church. After an Englishman had seen her in the theatre, but not without a bitter after-taste, he came to the church, saw the head of the madonna and cried out in surprise: "Oh, it's the virgin who gave me a dose!"

Next to the theatrical profession the shop-girls were most in demand. The *jeunes ouvrières* appear in de Sade more than once. Rétif de la Bretonne described this class of prostitutes with especial preference in his works. He held for a long time a secret correspondence with the modists of a large establishment in rue le Grenelle Saint Honoré. The proprietor of this shop was a Madame Devilliers, who worked for Countess Du Barry. The later had also been a modist before she entered the bordello of Gourdan. The life and activity of these modists were described by Rétif in his *Le Quadragénaire*. According to Parent Duchatelet professional prostitutes gladly entered the shops during the Revolution. It almost seemed as if the shops had become adjuncts to the regular houses. Prostitutes were of course always present at the restaurants, cafés and bars. Casanova when in search for beauty would first visit a café. The Paris police-order fining the host 100 francs if caught having immoral girls was never enforced.

Pimping reached a high stage of development in the eighteenth century. Marquis de Sade described many types, for example, Dorval who through the work of his prostitutes owned thirty houses. Peuchet in 1789 spoke of pimps in his *Encyclopædia* and Rétif de la Bretonne discussed them in his *Pornography* (1770). The police lieutenant received an anonymous letter from a prostitute: "We girls cannot exist without protectors. Usually our choice falls on the wickedest scoundrel in the neighborhood so that he can protect us for better or worse. Once we have made our choice we must stick to it. We must tolerate his laziness, drunkenness, gamblings, beatings and vices. The only way to get rid of him is to find a worse scoundrel who can beat the old one up and is for that reason a worse tyrant and despot."

All kinds of pimps and pimpesses, that necessary correlative to prostitution, are found in de Sade's works. On the last page of the *Pornography* there is an index of these *mamans publiques*. Such women had many names. Those *companions* who could no longer practice their trade were called *pieds-levés*. The actual pimps and pimpesses were variously named *maquerelles, baillives, abbesses, supérieures, mamans*. The name *maîtresse* or *dame de maison* did not appear before 1796.

In *Justine* and *Juliette* all bordellos are richly provided with children, especially little girls, who served the purposes of vice and were given over to the brutal passions of the crowd. All this led to a great expansion in the traffic for boys and girls. We have already seen the extensiveness of the supply for the Deer Park. Similar places existed for the needs of private individuals. Rétif de la Bretonne gave detailed information on the *modus operandi* in Vol. 16 of his *Nights of Paris*. Under the arcades of the Palais Royal one saw children of both sexes being led by pimpesses. The death rate must have been fearfully high. "One pays the children," says Rétif, "as one pays for an animal. Parent and pimps come to an agreement on the price." Rétif remarks that this trade existed under the *ancien régime* and that it formed one of the chief sources of income to the Inspector of Prostitution, who no doubt had to share his profit with the police lieutenants. Needless to say the trade was never in danger of interruption from the police.

The Palais Royal and Other Public Places for Prostitution

The Palais Royal was a city within a city. It was the city of prostitutes of Paris and the centre of Parisian life in the eighteenth century. It formed a pretty little world all of its own with its gambling-dens, royal and jacobin conspirators, prostitutes and bandits, respectable yet degenerate customs, its luxury and poverty. The Palais Royal, not far from the Louvre, was built for Cardinal Richelieu in the years 1629 to 1634 by Lemercier in the spot of the former Hôtel de Mercoeur; it was inhabited for a time by Louis XIV who had it rebuilt and then presented it to his uncle, Duke of Chartres, and thus it was passed on to the Orleans family. The regent, Phillip of Orleans, inaugurated it as the chief city of pleasure and debauchery for respectable society. His great-grandchild, Duke Louis Philipp Joseph of Orleans, the notorious Philippe-Egalité, had the palace entirely reconstructed in the years 1781 to 1786 until it received its present form, consisting of a great number of palaces, gardens, arcades, market-halls, theatres, cafés, gambling-dens and other resorts for pleasure. The chief galleries of the Palais Royal were in the east, the Galerie de Valois, in the west, the Galerie de Montpensier on whose northern end the Palais Royal theatre lay, in the north, the Galerie de Beaujolais. The splendid garden of the Palais Royal was in the form of a parallelogram and was surrounded by 186 arcades. In the immediate proximity stood the theatre of the Comédie Française.

Before and during the Revolution the Palais Royal developed into that gay and colorful centre that has found so many excellent descriptions by travellers from all countries. Casanova described how it looked before its reconstruction in 1750: "Curious as I was about this so famous place, I looked closely at everything. I saw a very pretty garden, walks surrounded by great trees, reservoirs, tall houses, throngs of men and women walking about, stalls here and there selling books, perfumes, tooth-picks and other small articles. I saw great numbers of straw-chairs that were rented for a sou, men and women eating alone or in company, waiters hastening to and from the foliage concealing steps." An *abbé* named for Casanova all the prostitutes who were walking around.

In the year 1772 Marquis de Carraccioli remarked that the Palais Royal was the place for elegancy, the Luxembourg for dreamers, and the Tuileries for "all the world." But after the burning of the Opera (1781) and the consequent reconstruction of the Palais Royal all the night life of Paris gathered in this latter place. Here took place during the Revolution and Directory all those horrible scenes which we have partly already described. The Palais Royal became the *Hall of Prostitution* and the *Sewer of Paris* as Mercier in his *The New Paris* and Rétif de la Bretonne in his great work on the Palais Royal have described. Rétif investigated the night life in the Palais Royal as a doctor would the "anatomy of a corpse." He wrote in *Monsieur*

Nicolas in 1796: "It is well-known that the Palais Royal is the general rendezvous for all the passions and enterprises of vice, prostitution, gambling, swindling, crime, etc., and hence has become the center of all observation. This famous bazaar enticed me not by its sights but by the pleasures I found there."

Mercier gayly desired that Lavater, the famous physiognomist, might be present at the Palais Royal on a Friday evening so that he could read in the faces of those present everything that is usually kept in the deepest recesses of the heart. There were to be found prostitutes, courtesans, duchesses, and respectable housewives: they did not delude themselves there. But perhaps with all his science this great doctor might have been deluded. For there were distinctions and very fine nuances which must be very carefully studied. "I assert that Dr. Lavater would have great difficulty in distinguishing an ordinary prostitute from a respectable woman and that a shop-girl can without his great knowledge point out the fine points of differentiation." Such unconstraint, unceremoniousness, and free and easy ways has never existed in the world except in Paris and there only in the Palais Royal. All were familiarly addressed, words were bandied to and fro, remarks were made about the woman's lover in the presence of her husband, and vice versa, couples were caught up in a mad whirl, laughter and frank talk resounded everywhere. Lavater should by all means have made his physiognomical studies in the Palais Royal.

"The weather may have been fair or rainy but every evening at five I would walk along the Palais Royal. I am usually alone around the Bank d'Argenson. I converse with myself on politics, love, gastronomy or philosophy and give myself up to the complete freedom of the Palais Royal. One sees the young rakes in the *Allée de la Foi* follow the footsteps of a courtesan who walks along unashamedly with laughing gestures and joyous eyes. But immediately they leave her for another, banter her in common and attach themselves to none. My thoughts are my prostitutes." So wrote Diderot in the beginning of *Rameau's Nephew*.

These nightly promenades in the Palais Royal were famous throughout the whole world and was the first sight that tourists flocked to see in Paris. Here piquant adventure was sought—and found. It often happened that men looking for pleasure in the nightly promenade at the Palais Royal surprised their own wives with the same purposes. The women in the Palais Royal were all whores whether they belonged to the profession of prostitution or not. Whoever made nightly visits there was stamped with that name.

The famous Street of Sighs (*Allée des Soupirs*) was the promenade for the prettiest and most enticing girls and women recruited from all classes of life. Respectable ladies, the theatrical world, the higher demi-mondes and the better-class prostitutes were the goal of the rakes seeking for plunder. But also in the other streets, in the *Allée de la Foi*, the *Allée de Club*, under the colonnades and arcades there gathered untold numbers of dispensers of lust followed in close numbers by young and old roués from all parts of the world. This was the El Dorado of prostitution. Here were hidden corners, secret nooks, and lurking places in the form of numerous shops, beer dens, gambling halls and theatres. Here Rétif de la Bretonne learned from his friend, the notorious charlatan Guilbert de Préval, who was well versed in the secrets and kinds of passion in the Palais Royal, "how best to amuse women and how women can best satisfy the desires of men." Rétif could recite from memory the names of the prostitutes of the *Street of Sighs;* he also knew well the huris, the exsunamites, the *berceuses,* the *chanteuses,* the *converseuses,* as well as many other sexopathologic types. Rétif in his work on the Palais Royal wrote: "We will write a moral book about immoral affairs which has to do with foals, asses and other animals. The beauties of the Palais Royal are very pretty, especially the young ones. What happens to the old ones is the same all over the world: an old animal is never pretty. We will tell of remarkable and unbelievable morals. But first we would like to give an idea of the features, the age, the general appearance, the morals and talents of these beauties under the name they have assumed, *noms de guerre.*" Here Rétif described thirty-two prostitutes of the *Allée des Soupirs.* He then told the history of each of these girls, throwing many interesting side-lights on the state of morals during the Revolution. The second volume of his work treated of the famous "circus" of the Palais Royal. "The majesty of this hall, the charm of the orchestra, the proud movements of the dancers, the beauty, the elegance of the spectators, all contributed in giving a magical appearance to this subterranean retreat. Later attention was excited by the drinks, the gambling and the private rooms serving all kinds of tastes for love. We noticed that after nine o'clock, the hour when respectable women go out to eat, only prostitutes remained. We observed them very curiously in our capacity as an investigator." One of the girls served as cicerone for him and pointed out the others, the so-called "sunamites."

The sunamites received their name from the concubines of King David who was kept alive in his old age by the heat of their bodies which aflamed anew his powers. There were many in the Palais Royal who kept a number of girls just for this purpose. Six girls were furnished to act as a cure for a single man. The first time the matron herself was present to superintend his wants. He was given an aromatic bath and a thorough cleansing of his body. Then a heavy muzzle was placed on him and he was placed in bed with a sunamite close to each side. Two girls could serve him in this manner for only eight days, then they were replaced by a fresh pair. The first pair then rested for fourteen days so that in all there were three alternate pairs. The patient had to pay the girls three louisdors all told. Each girl received six francs, the matron twelve. Careful protection was given that the virgin modesty of these sunamites went untasted. Otherwise the cure would have been harmful rather than useful. Indeed if the patient wrought a miracle, proved again that the Lord is all-powerful, he would have to pay heavy damages to the girl; as a precaution the sum was placed on deposit with the matron before the cure. A girl lasted in this business three years, counting from the time she reached womanhood. A girl who was used every day could last at the utmost one year. The period of sunamite service amounted practically to the novitiate in the order of prostitutes. When the first was finished the girl automatically entered the higher rank.

Marquis de Sade also had Justine do this nightly heating service to a hoary old monk (Justine II, 228).

The third volume of Rétif's *Palais Royal* treated of the "Colonnades" and introduced the *converseuses* or exsunamites, 43 in number, whose work it was to entertain respectable ladies in diverse ways.

Mercier tells of another specialty of the Palais Royal. During the evening meal in a restaurant, which also served as a bordello, at a given signal from the proprietor there stepped down from a balcony, to the accompaniment of soft music, a nude nymph, who pirouetted about the tables presumably to aid the digestion of the diners.

At the hours from eleven to twelve one could see along the galleries of the Palais Royal the four and forty famous *figurae Veneris*, lascivious positions classified by a contemporary French author and very popular at the time.

In the Reign of Terror the Palais Royal became the scene of the maddest orgies and a favorite meeting-place for the dregs of prostitution and for the soldier-girls. The gardens, the galleries and other public places of the Palais Royal "were the most notorious gathering places for prostitutes and soldiers. They boldly transacted the most lewd practices on the streets and blocked all respectable people from passing. Obscene pictures of men and women, scribblings as well as paintings were drawn all over the streets and walls. In the nooks hidden by trees and fountains the freest practices were indulged in by the soldiers and prostitutes." Almost all the soldiers in the guard were pimps. Indeed many of them had only enlisted so that they could live on the proceeds of their staff.

We will close our description of the Palais Royal with the words of one of the best connoisseurs of Parisian corruption in the eighteenth century. Mairobert cried out in *The English Spy:* "All the bulwarks of vice and depravity, all the passionate and voluptuous orgies, wild abandonment and free and easy familiarity, all are to be found on the nightly promenades in the Palais Royal!"

All other amusement places paled before the Palais Royal yet there were a great number nearby. As fast as one died out another took its place. A similar condition, though far milder, exists in the present nightclubs. Of the others the Vauxhall *d'été* and *d'hiver* and the Colisée were the most popular. Admission cost from one to three livres but ensured the entrant pleasures of every imaginable kind.

An Italian artist Torré opened the Vauxhall *d'été* in the year 1764 in the Boulevard Saint Martin. Fireworks, lantern-shows and elaborate plays were held. From 1768 on dances and balls were added.

The Vauxhall *d'hiver* was in the western part of the city district of Saint Germain, near rue Guisard. It was built in 1769 and opened on April 3, 1770. Ballets with very pretty dancers were mainly given.

The Colisée was a building with gardens for dancing, song, play, festival, fireworks, etc. It lay in the western part of the Champs Elysées, near the Avenue Neuilly and was opened at the marriage of the Dauphin, later Louis XVI.

According to Dulaure the public purpose of these establishments was to amuse the Parisians. But the secret purpose was "to corrupt and plunder them." The managements winked at the number of prostitutes in their places and entered into arrangements with them and the police.

Onanism

We proceed from the description of prostitution and amusement places to an investigation of the chief aberrations of the sexual life and begin with the most common, onanism.

The *branler*, as it is technically called by de Sade, occurs almost on every page. In the very beginning of *Justine* as she was sorrowing for her parents, Juliette showed her how to satisfy herself by manustupration, a practice she had learned in the convents. This passionate excitation, which can be done every moment without the aid of another, was the best consolation for sorrow, for onanism caused all pain to disappear with safety (Justine I, 5). Delbène, the superior in the convent, to whom Juliette was entrusted, was a very passionate woman and had from the age of nine "used her finger to satisfy the wishes of her mind." (Juliette I, 3). In the *"Society of Friends of Crime"* there even existed a *Room for Masturbation* (Juliette III, 65). The Duke of Chablais also praised the *French method* of onanism as the best (Juliette III, 292). Madame de St. Ange, who in the beginning of *Philosophy in the Boudoir* imparted to Eugenie an entire course in the arts and technical expressions of love, does not forget to acquaint her with this comfortable kind of self-pleasure (Philosophy in the Boudoir I, 43). Havelock Ellis has also noted the use of masturbation for driving away pain.

Mairobert had Madame Richard express herself in characteristic fashion on the enormous spread of onanism in France. This so very refined art which she learned from a member of the French Academy became more and more the fashion in this century of passion and—philosophy. In the famous bordellos of Paris, Gourdan, Florence, and Brisson these arts were practiced. "Many also practiced simple and mutual onanism to escape children and the danger of syphilis" *(The English Spy)*.

The number of poems and brochures on the "voluptuous fingers of the libertines" were very numerous at this time. Many prostitutes indeed even preferred onanism and practiced it with their clients.

Tribadism

This chapter is perhaps most notable for the sexual life of France in the eighteenth century from an historical viewpoint. We do not believe that ancient Lesbos saw such conditions as ruled in France at this time. Here too de Sade's works truly mirror the picture of his age and inform us on the frequency of *amor lesbicus* or sapphic love.

Juliette immediately opens with a description of the passionate tribadic scene among the nuns of the Panthémont convent (Juliette I, 43, ff.). Mondor entertained himself by peeping at a lesbic love scene (Juliette I, 283). A decided type of tribade was drawn in the man-hater, Clairwil (Juliette II, 106), who promptly organized an orgy with Juliette and four other women (Juliette II, 138-150, also III, 157). The highest tribadic arts were to be found in Bologna (Juliette III, 306 ff.). The Princess Borgia (Juliette IV, 100 ff.), Queen Charlotte of Naples (Juliette V, 259, VI, 12 ff.) are tribades. This specialty of love has a great number of adherents in Venice (Juliette VI, 156 ff.).

In *Justine* there are also to be found as many, if not more, lesbian scenes, e.g., between Dorothée and Madame Gernande (Justine III, 285); Seraphine was a worshipper of the sapphic art (Justine IV, 116).

De Sade also did not lack allusions on the explanation

of tribadism. A tribadic orgy between Juliette and Durand surprised a young and an old woman, the latter in the autumn of her life and resigned to her own sex as a substitute. But perhaps she was predestined to this by the extreme length of her clitoris. De Sade mentioned this expressly as being the case of another tribade, Madame de Volmar (Juliette I, 34). Only twenty years old, she was the passionate companion of Delbène and had a *clitoris de trois pouces,* thus being able to play the rôle of a man and pederast. The Venetian tribade Zatta was a similar woman with masculine allurements (Juliette VI, 194). De Sade asserted that nearly all tribades practiced paedicatio.

Mirabeau described in *My Conversion* a tribadic orgy of thirty court ladies. The descriptions of this author, whom Diderot and numerous other authors have followed, did not transgress reality. Mairobert in his *English Spy* furnished us with many highly interesting documents that afford astounding insights into the activity and organization of the Parisian tribades of the eighteenth century. His already often mentioned *Confessions of a Young Girl* unrolled a picturesque panorama of the mysteries of the notorious *Secte Anandryne* which celebrated its orgies in the *Temple of Vesta.*

A young girl from the town Villiers le Bel, daughter of a peasant, was recruited by Madame Gourdan for her bordello. One day the father met her as a prostitute at the Tuileries. A great public scandal grew from this. But the daughter had already been promised to the Imperial Academy of Music so that the father had to return home emptyhanded. In addition she became pregnant. Mairobert had the girl, who called herself Mademoiselle Sapho, tell him the story of her life. It can certainly be assumed that Mairobert, the imperial censor in all the secrets of Parisian society, has woven in his own experiences in the *Confes-*

sions of a Young Girl. At any rate this strange report is one of the most famous and important contributions to the cultural history of France in the eighteenth century. We give a detailed discussion of the case and book.

From youth Sapho was inclined to coquetry, fond of finery, vain, lazy and with an insatiable desire for pleasure; in short, all the attributes of a prostitute. At fifteen she was already very lascivious and often gazed in admiration at her own nudeness and lasciviously caressed all parts of her body. This circumstance is very instructive and shows how sexual perversity comes to the fore. Sapho would never have been seduced by Gourdan no matter how she was kept at home by her parents unless the girl had found an opportunity for intercourse with a man; it is clear that such a fiery nature went of her own accord on the path of tribadism due to the necessity of her nature. The mode of life, the interplay of contrary sexual feelings play the main rôle. We look very skeptically at her heredity.

One day Sapho was surprised at these caressings of her body and was severely punished by her mother; she decided to flee from her parents. We have already mentioned that Madame Gourdan had a branch of her Parisian bordello at Villiers le Bel; Sapho had often seen the inmates prettily dressed, laughing, singing and dancing in the village. She determined to go there and was naturally received with joy and sent to Gourdan in Paris where she was turned over to an accomplice who took charge of the first prostitutions of Gourdan's novices. But after this accomplice had examined the girl she forgot about her usual course and sent the following characteristic letter to Gourdan:

You have found a pearl in this child; she is, on my honor, pucelle, if she is not a vierge. But she has the clitoris of a devil. She will be hence more useful for women than men. Our dear tribade must pay you the weight in gold for this acquisition.

Gourdan immediately let this discovery be known to Madame de Furiel, one of the most famous tribades of Paris, by the following letter:

Madame:
I have discovered for you a king's—or better—a queen's piece that will suit perfectly your depraved taste—for I cannot judge otherwise inclinations so contrary to mine own. But I know your generosity which causes me to relax my rigorousness and beg to inform you that I have secured for your services the prettiest clitoris in all France, a virgin, at most, 15 years. Just try for yourself and I am certain that you will be unable to thank me enough. If not send her back to me, understanding, of course, that you will not have maltreated her. She will always be the choicest piece of virginity for the finest of connoisseurs.

The business was completed and Sapho was sold to Furiel for 100 louisdors.

There now follows a description of the luxurious house of Madame de Furiel. First Sapho had to take a bath, eat a rich supper and then go to bed. On the following morning Furiel's dentist investigated Sapho's mouth, fixed her teeth, cleaned her and gave her aromatic mouthwash. Then followed another bath, careful manicuring of fingers and nails, removal of superfluous hair and a thorough cleaning of all parts of her body. She was next sprayed with a great amount of essences and perfumes, her hair was curled into great locks and let fall loose on her breasts, bright flowers were placed in her hair. A slip, *à la tribade* (cut wide in front and back) was carefully adjusted so that nothing was really hidden. She was then brought to Madame de Furiel.

Madame de Furiel, reclining on a sofa, received her. She was a woman of about thirty years, brunette with very black eyebrows, somewhat corpulent and masculine *(homasse)*. It took two hours for Sapho to be initiated into all the mysteries of lesbian love. After the love-bout

Madame de Furiel called two chambermaids by whom they were washed and perfumed. Then they sat down to a delicious supper at which Furiel told Sapho all about tribadism in Paris and that they were organized as the *Secte Anandryne* and held their festivals in the *Temple of Vesta*. Not every woman was admitted. There were examinations for those who desired entrance to the sect. They were especially severe for married women and only one out of ten passed. The parties were shut up in a boudoir, which contained a statue of Priapus *"dans toute son énergie."* There were besides different groups of males and females in the most obscene positions. The wall-frescoes displayed similar pictures. Numerous representations of the male member excited the senses; books and pictures of an obscene content lay on the table. At the foot of the statue was a little fire that had to be continually fed with inflammable material, so that the postulante had always to take care that there was sufficient fuel on the fire; if but for a moment she forgot to watch the fire in the entrancement of so many objects of masculine passion, the fire went out and gave proof of her weakness and destruction. These examinations lasted three hours daily for three days.

After this tale Madame de Furiel promised our Sapho pretty clothes, hats, diamonds, theatres, promenades, instruction in reading, writing, dancing and singing if she would only be true to her and never have intercourse with men. Sapho readily agreed to this.

Then on the next day began the great metamorphosis. Modists, manicurists, and other shop-girls arrived and surrounded Sapho in all comfort, she was then brought to the opera and was joyously admired by the other tribades.

On the following day Sapho was introduced into the mysteries of the anandryne sect with great solemnity and notable ceremonies. In the middle of the Temple of Vesta

HIS AGE

stood a cylindrical room that received light from a glass cover on top and on the sides. A small statue of Vesta was in the room. The goddess was represented standing majestically on a globe as if just stepping down to preside at the meeting. She seemed to sway in mid-air.

About this sanctuary of the goddess was a small corridor, in which two tribades paraded up and down during the meeting so that all the entrances were watched. Between the entrances stood a marble plaque on which were inscribed golden verses, at each side were altars with the necessary vestal fires. Next to the most resplendent altar stood a bust of Sappho, the protector of the temple, the oldest and most noted tribade. Next to the other altar stood a bust of Mademoiselle (alias Chevalier) d'Eon, "the most famous modern tribade." Around the niches in the walls stood the famous Greek tribades sung of by Sappho: Thelesyle, Amythone, Cydno, Megare, Pyrrhine, Andromeda, Cyrine, etc. In the middle of the room stood a great cylindrical couch on which rested the Lady President and her scholars. Pairs of tribades sat all around in Turkish fashion on small footstools, each pair interlaced and composed of mother and novice, or in the mystical terminology, incuba and succuba. The walls of the room were decorated with hundreds of reliefs, showing the various private parts of the woman as shown in Venette's *Tableau of Conjugal Love*, Buffon's *Natural History* and in the *cleverest* anatomical plates.

The reception of our Sapho was in the following manner: all the tribades sat in their places in their festival clothes. The *mothers* wore a red levite with a blue girdle, the *novices* a white levite and a red girdle and no underclothes. As Sapho entered she first saw the holy fire that burned with a pleasant and aromatic flame upon a golden pan; it was continually fed by two tribades with pulverized fuel. Sapho had to kneel at the feet of the president, Mademoiselle Raucourt, a noted actress at the Comédie Française; her *mother*, Madame Furiel said: "Dear president and dear companions, here is a postulante. She appears to have all the desirable properties. She has never had intercourse with a man, is wonderfully built, and has shown fire and zeal at the *trial* I gave her. I beg that she be taken in under the name *Sapho*." After this speech both had to withdraw. Shortly thereafter one of the guardesses of Sapho informed her that she had been admitted to a test without a dissenting vote. Sapho was then completely undressed, given a pair of white slippers, covered with a light mantel and brought back to the assemblage. Here the Lady President arose, gave Sapho her own seat and uncovered her mantel. Sapho was then put to a thorough examination by all the tribades as to how many of the thirty charms of women inscribed on the marble plaque she possessed:

Then one of the oldest of tribades read the following old French poem:

> *Let her who claims the honor of being beautiful,*
> *Of reproducing in herself the superb model*
> *Of Helen who once set the universe aflame*
> *Spread in her favor thirty diverse charms!*
> *That covering her thrice each in turn,*
> *White, and black, and red intermingled*
> *Offer as many times to the marveling eyes*
> *The changeful hues of a single color.*
> *Since nine times to this masterpiece of love*
> *Nature, prodigal and miserly turn by turn,*
> *In opposed extremes, with an ever-sure hand*
> *Traces for her the measure of her dimensions:*
> *Three little trifles still, she will have in her features*
> *The perfect contrasts of a divine combination.*
> *Let her hair be blond, her teeth like ivory,*
> *Let her skin surpass the freshness of a pure lily,*

So that the eye, the eyebrows, but of a blacker shade,
That the lashes emphasize its whiteness.
Let her nail, her cheek, her lip be vermillion;
Her hair, her waist, her hand long;
Her teeth, her feet short and also her ears.
Let her brow be high, and her breast broad;
Let the nymph above all, with rounded buttocks
Present well-rounded forms to her lovers;
Let her be so at the waist that her lover without hurting her
Can firmly encircle her with two hands;
Let her sweet mouth with infallible augury
Announce the narrow painful access to pleasure.
Let the anus, the vulva and the belly
Be gently swelled and never flat.
A little nose pleases greatly, also a little head.
A teat which resists the kiss that it invites;
Fine hair, thin lips, and very delicate fingers
Complete this beautiful whole which one never meets.

Of these charms somewhat more than half were needed for admittance, i.e., at least sixteen. Each pair of tribades decided separately and whispered their opinion into the ear of the Lady President, who counted them and announced the result. All had decided in favor of our novice. This result was then corroborated by a kiss *à la florentine*. Sapho was then dressed as a tribade and had to swear an oath never to have intercourse with men or to betray the secrets of the order. Then Madame Raucourt gave an inaugural address whose content in short was:

"Ladies, receive me in your ranks, I am worthy of you." These words are to be found in the *Lettres of Mlle. d'Eon*. This d'Eon was a model for tribadism. Her expression can well stand as a motto for the address.

Next Raucourt spoke of the origin of the *Secte Anandryne*. Lycurgus had started a school for tribades in Sparta. The convents in modern Europe, an emanation of the colleges of vestals, embody the constant priesthood of tribadism. How gratifying it is that a woman can find her pleasure so much easier than a mere man. For any suitable instrument in the boudoir or toilette is sufficient for the purpose.

Tribadism must spread everywhere the cult of Vesta and furnish zealous propaganda for it. The best known tribades were then named. Duchess of Urbsrex, Marquise de Terracenes, Madame de Furiel (the protectress of our Sapho and wife of the general-procurator), the Marquise de Téchul (who dressed as a chambermaid, cook or modist to satisfy her passion), Mademoiselle Clairon (famous actress of the Théâtre Français), the actress Arnould, the German tribade Sonck (kept by a brother of the Prussian king). Poulet-Malassis has solved the puzzles of these names in his edition of *The English Spy*: "Furiel" is Mme. de Fleury, "Urbsrex" is the Duchess of Villeroy, "Terracenes" is the Marquise de Senecterre and "Téchul" is the Marquise de Luchet.

Mlle. Julie, a young tribade, is mentioned; she has been initiated into the lesbian art of love by Arnould and Raucourt. In conclusion the joys of tribadism are extolled. Intercourse between the opposite sexes is fleeting, short and illusory. Only that between women is true, pure and lasting and has no remorse. Are defloration, pregnancy and childbirth pleasures?

"Tribadism leaves no remorse and is the *sauve-garde* of our young girls and widows, it increases our charms, holds them longer, is the comfort of our old age when no man wants us, a real rose without thorns throughout our whole life."

After this effective speech the holy fire is allowed to go out and all depart for the banquet in the vestibule; there is an abundance of wines, especially those of the Greeks; a number of passionate verses are sung from Sappho. When all were intoxicated and could no longer restrain their passions, the fire was again lighted in the sanctuary, and a wild orgy began. The two heroines who held their "lovebout" longest received as a reward a golden medal with the picture of Vesta and the pictures and names of the two heroines. On this day the winners were Madame de Furiel and Sapho.

Thus we leave our happy Sapho in the arms of her victrix.

Pederasty

Marquis de Sade sang the song of pederasty in all refrains. The most finished and expert pederast was Dolmance in the *Philosophy in the Boudoir*. "There is," says Dolmance, "no other pleasure in the world comparable to this. Oh, there is nothing more delightful than the back of a sweet young boy!" (*Philosophy in the Boudoir* I, 99). He described in detail all the joys of this vice. Although Dolmance felt more drawn to the male sex he was not abashed at undertaking pædicatio with a woman and indeed introduced young Eugenie to this pleasure. On the other hand Bressac, whom Justine surprised in the act of intercourse with his lackeys, was a thorough homosexualist and had a deep hatred for the feminine sex (Justine I, 145). As far as we recall, he was the only character whose sexual perversion de Sade ascribed to heredity. All the others had gradually acquired sexual perversions during their formative years. We are certain that de Sade who showed himself to be a profound *savant* of patho-sexual personalities here described from reality. And so it is in real life. Pederasty by heredity is the exception; pederasty by seduction, by vicious degeneracy and last but not least by mental illness, is the rule. Bressac develops the theory that the pathicus, of whom he was one, was destined by Nature to be an entirely different man from all others (Justine I, 162-164). He explained that this inborn passion rested upon a construction *toute différente*. It would be a *stupidité* to punish them for what was not their fault. Dolmance, however, gave an entirely different explanation that suffices for most pederasts. "If the purpose of nature was not such then why did she make the openings to the exact proportions of our members. What other reason could there be for nature to have made round openings."

The tribades, too, in de Sade rejoiced at Grecian love, whether by artificial instruments or by the aid of a clitoris. The spread of this vice is described as tremendous by contemporary authors. Duvergier tells that the pederasts are much sought after and are well paid. Numerous scenes of pederasty appear in the pages of *Justine* and *Juliette*.

Since the sixteenth century pederasty had found an increasing horde of devotees in Paris. Mirabeau assures us that during the reign of Henry III "men were found in mutual embrace under the portals of the Louvre," and that under Louis XIV pederasty was governed under strict laws and statutes. Henry III was himself a homosexual. Henry IV was very much opposed to it but could not prevent the reappearance of homosexual intercourse in court under Louis XIII. Philipp Orleans, brother of Louis XIV, became a homosexual; the story of his unhappy marriage with

Elizabeth Charlotte von der Pfalz, due to his preference for men, is well known. It is reported on contemporary authority that nobles in the court of Louis XIV tried to turn him from his perverted path so that they could rule him by a mistress. But the young king exhibited a deadly hate toward the men who so sought to influence him. One of the Gentlemen of the Chamber of the king reports in his *Memoirs* that in 1652 after a dinner with the fifteen year old king Cardinal Mazarin had sexual intercourse with him.

In an old work *Galant France* (1695), which is the second part of the *Amorous History of the Gauls* of Prince of Bussy-Rabutin, there is a chapter on the founding of a pederasty club by the Duke of Grammont, Sire de Tilladet, Manicamp and Marquis de Biran. All members were investigated on the strength, health, potency, vitality and beauty of their bodies. Celibacy from women was a cardinal rule. Every member had to undergo a rigid regime to fit himself for the arduous duties and demands of his lay-brethren. If one of the *brothers* married he had to explain if it had happened because he was forced by his parents, by reason of an inheritance, dowry, etc. He had at the same time to swear never to love his wife and to sleep with her only until she bore him a son. For this grace, special permission was also necessary and this was allowed him only once a week. The brothers were divided in four classes although the father-priors could possess anyone. Those wishing to enter the order were examined in a series by the four father-priors. A strict silence over the affairs of the club was enjoined and only those whose inclination for Greek love were known could be admitted to the test. The pederastic orgies took place in a country house. The participants wore over their official robe a cross on which was represented in relief a man stepping on a woman. The club did not last long for a royal prince joined the ranks and the club was summarily banned by the king.

At any rate the cult of pederasty was still prevalent in the French court in the eighteenth century. It would have been a miracle if that lascivious *roué*, Louis XV, had not fallen a victim to pædicatio and other homosexual practices. So it is reported that he often showed himself nude to a handsome boy that he was fond of and often embraced him.

The Revolution also brought this vice to the highest point. We have already given many illustrations of pederasty. In the year 1798, Dupin, the Commissioner of the Department of the Seine, reported: "For some time there has spread a yet more shameful kind of immorality. The reports of the police-agents on pederasty have increased to a horribly enormous sum. Sodomy and sapphic love have also appeared with the same boldness until they are as prevalent as prostitution."

In his *Porter of Chartreux* of 1789, Rétif de la Bretonne declared that "pederasty, bestiality and other forms of immorality degraded France continually for five or six generations."

Flagellation and Phlebotomy

Flagellation, that mighty assistant of vice, was thoroughly described in all its branches by Marquis de Sade in all his seven works. We mention only the great scenes of flagellation in *Justine* and *Juliette* (Justine III, 129; Juliette II, 138-150), between women; (Juliette V, 335). Juliette with three young modists visits the home of the Duke of Dendemar in St. Maur; his sexual monomania consisted of whipping the girls until they bled; he had to pay great sums for his pleasurable sacrifices (Juliette I, 344 ff.).

Marquis de Sade had also made extensive literary researches on this subject. He mentioned the most important writings of his time on flagellation by Meibom and Boileau (Juliette V, 169). These studies had taught him that it was the man who at all times took the active role in flagellation. He was surprised that the active whipping found little preference in women with their natural cruelty and had Dolmancé hope for the time that women would also show themselves masters in this specialty (Philosophy in the Boudoir I, 157).

Interesting details are given by Cooper in his *Flagellation and the Flagellants in the Eighteenth Century*. Voltaire often mentions the whip especially when he wants to make the jesuits look ridiculous. The whip is also often mentioned in the memoirs of the time.

The blows were often imparted on even small children. It was asserted that thereby the muscles and skin were "strengthened." In all French convent schools the rod was the usual punishment for the young girl, as it was the favorite instrument for flagellation with the nuns. The holy sisters whipped their students with delight in the same manner that the holy fathers absolved their penitents.

During the Reign of Terror the nuns were waylaid and ignominiously flogged. The tragic case of Théroigne de Méricourt is well known. She was flogged by a band of women and as a consequence lost her reason. After the downfall of Robespierre the young girls on the street were disrobed and beaten by the anti-terrorists.

Shortly before the Reign of Terror there existed a *Whipping Club* whose feminine members "delightfully laid on the whip." Many respectable ladies belonged to this club of whose sexual tendency there can be no doubt.

There has already been so much written about Jean Jacques Rousseau's preference for this kind of sexual excitation that we refer to Krafft Ebing for the story of his chastisement by Mademoiselle Lambercier. Cooper is full of stories of battles in which the fair sex took a prominent part. His reports on some *causes célèbres* of this kind are very interesting.

England is well known today as the classic land of sexual flagellation. One of her most famous flagellants was Theresa Berkeley in London, 28, Charlotte Street, who obtained great wealth and fame through her art. She possessed untold numbers of instruments of all kinds for excitation and enrichment of passion, "Thus, at her shop, whoever went with plenty of money, could be birched, whipped, fustigated, scourged, needle-pricked, half-hung, holly-brushed, furse-brushed, butcher-brushed, stinging-nettled, curry-combed, phlebotomized and tortured till he had a belly full." She also had prostitutes, a Negress and a gypsy for active flagellation. She invented a machine which caused the man fastened in it to experience voluptuous sensations (The Berkeley Horse). "There is a print in Mrs. Berkeley's memoirs, representing a man upon it quite naked. A woman is sitting in a chair exactly under it, with her bosom, belly and bottom exposed: she is manualizing his embolon, whilst Mrs. Berkeley is birching his posteriors. The female acting as frictrix, was intended for Fisher, a fine, tall, dark-haired girl. Everyone who visited Charlotte Street at that day must recall her as well as the good humored blonde, Willis; the plump, tight, frisky and merryarsed Thurlow. Grenville with the enormous bubbies: Bentine, with breadth of hip and splendour of buttock; Oliver, the gypsy, whose brown skin, wicked black eyes, and medicean form would melt an anchorite; the mild and amiable Palmer with luxurious and well fledged mount, from whose tufted honors many a noble lord has stolen a sprig; and Pryce, the pleasing and complaisant, who, if birch was the question, could both give and take." Berkeley died in 1836, having amassed a fortune of £10,000 sterling in eight years. Her correspondence containing letters from both sexes and from the highest classes in Europe were destroyed.

We gave this small description because we have found no description of the Institution of Mrs. Berkeley in modern works on flagellation and because there are to be found in de Sade's works similar machines in which the victims are tied.

Phlebotomy also plays an important part with de Sade. In the third volume of *Justine* there appeared a Prince Gernande, who could excite himself only by bleeding the veins of women. There were many such scenes in his works. Particularly horrible was the scene in which the prince bled his own wife and then satisfied himself sexually on her unconscious body (Justine III, 253).

Phlebotomy in the eighteenth century was an operation also practiced by the clergy. Brissaud stated that there were definite periods for blood-letting in convents. With the Carthusian friars, for example, the rule was five times a year, with the premonstrates once a year. The feasts of St. Matthew and Valentine were special seasons for blood-letting.

Raulin was accustomed to cure the frequent hysteria of women by phlebotomy. Brierre de Boismont reported the case of a man who had infusions made in the genitals and posteriors of his wife. As soon as he saw the blood, he became extremely excited and satisfied himself on her person.

Aphrodisiacs, Cosmetics, Abortions and Quackeries

De Sade gave special attention to "sexual medicines" (in the widest sense) in his works. Here, too, will plainly be seen that his descriptions had in almost every case an exact counterpart in the actual world.

It is no wonder that the many and unnatural debaucheries wore out the *roués* of de Sade and that they needed sexual stimulants to a great degree. There was no scarcity of aphrodisiacs of all kinds to enliven anew the impotent cravings of de Sade's characters. Delmonse had to rub very vigorously the scrotum of the impotent merchant Dubourg. This unfortunate had also to continually take bouillons *composés d'aramotes et d'épins* (Justine I, 62). Cornaro has whiskey used there. Oil of Wintergreen burns like the very devil. But Durand rubbed the member itself with a *terribly exciting activity*. The ancient Persians' use of asafoetida was also powerful. The odor of jasmine was also popular. De Sade also knew internal as well as external aphrodisiacs. Juliette used wine, liqueurs, opium (the opinion today is that opium has the negative result) and "other aphrodisiacs that were openly sold in Italy" (Juliette IV, 104). Durand has a regular business with aphrodisiacs and anti-aphrodisiacs (Juliette III, 229).

We have already mentioned that the bordello of Madame Gourdan was richly furnished with sexual stimulants. The *Pastilles à la Richelieu* were also alluded to. Since the latter are of importance in relation to Marquis de Sade and their main ingredient, cantharides, "played an important rôle in France in the eighteenth century" a few words on these cantharidic stimulants may not be amiss. The cantharides mentioned by Dioscordies (Materia Medica, Lib. II, Cap. 65) have been used for a long time as sexual stimulants. The Roman poet Lucretius is said to have died as a result of an aphrodisiac containing cantharide. Ambroise Paré reports many such cases. In Paré's time the use of *pastilles* or *bonbons* was the fashion in France. The home of these *bonbons* with their aphrodisiac effect was Italy, from where they were introduced to France by Catherine de Medici. The courts of Henry III and Charles IX found employment for them. In the eighteenth century Richelieu made very prolific use of the seemingly innocent *bonbons*. His propaganda for the *pastilles* named after him had as a result their adoption as the fashion in the last year of the reign of Louis XV. At this time occurred the affair of Marquis de Sade in Marseilles, the *bonbons* playing a fatal rôle. The *Secret Tablets of Madame du Barry*, the *Powder of Joy*, the *Seraglio-pastilles* were all very probably cantharidic.

The cantharides were a dangerous method for they very easily caused inflammation of the kidneys, urethra and skin. The erections produced by them came by the excitation of the mucous membrane of the urethra and bladder. An advancement of sexuality can best be observed at the beginning of the action.

Cosmetics enjoyed an especially wide use. Charlatanry

was at its height in this field. Thus in 1769 a society received the privilege of renting parasols on both sides of the Pont Neuf so that persons wishing to cross the bridge and protect their delicate skin from the ravages of the sun might hire a parasol at one end of the bridge and return it at the other. The aids for beauty were so numerous that Casanova had perfect right—he also liked to play the charlatan from time to time—in forbidding the use of all cosmetic applications to the Duchess of Chartres who suffered from acne. He prescribed a mild purgative and the constant cleansing.

For depilation Marquis de Sade mentioned *Rusma,* the Turkish depilatory. "Rusma" is an old and favorite depilatory of the Orientals. The *Depilatory Paste* or *Rusma Turcorum* or *Nurék Persarum* is composed of 2 parts auripigment, 15 parts calcaria and 2½ parts of wheaten flour. That is the prescription of J. J. Plenck, a famous dermatologist of the eighteenth century. It may be noted here, that Marquis de Sade had a great interest in all medical and anthropological matters. He studied by himself all the available scientific works of his time. We shall later mention how his wife had to continually supply him with books when he was in prison.

A notable anomaly in the eighteenth century was the so-called *false virginities;* its great frequency brought it into special prominence. The remainder of the hymen was sought and brought together artificially by astringent means, mainly by narrowing the *introitus vaginæ*. This attempt had a long history in France. In the thirteenth chapter of the surgery of Henry de Mondeville, a physician of the fourteenth century, there are instructions on the deception of virginity by the use of astringent plants. A number of other methods to draw blood at the touch are also given. Such practices were ordinary occurrences in the France of the eighteenth century. We have already noted the virginity-water of Madame Gourdan. De Sade knew other methods for the restoration of the hymen. Delbène praised her pomade and wanted to repair the already deflowered Laurette (Juliette I, 171) and gave to Juliette, victim of the same fate, a myrthus extract, which she had to rub in for nine days in order to arise on the tenth a virgin (Juliette I, 179). Duvergier also used a similar virginity salve (Juliette I, 187).

In general this whole century was a golden age for toilette aids. It is notable that all important cosmetic aids of modern times were employed in the eighteenth century. There were hundreds of essences, pastes and salves, toilette waters and astringents. Especially important was, of course, the rouge. An anecdote of the Reign of Terror told by Mercier illustrates the high opinions of rouge by women:

> *Marton:* Dear Lady—
> *Marquise:* Marton, I am just arising—
> *Marton:* Here I am, dear lady—
> *Marquise:* My child, what's new?
> *Marton:* Dear lady, there is talk of a rebellion that is supposed to have broken out this morning—
> *Marquise:* And why not?
> *Marton:* There is talk of destruction, of pillage, of rape, yes, even—
> *Marquise:* Even rape—O child, you're joking—heavens, if one—
> *Marton:* Oh! I have heard everywhere that the monsters will kill all the women, and, it is said, that those that please them will fall victims to their lust—
> *Marquise* (very sprightly): I tremble—Marton—dress me—Marton—my rouge! Quickly, my rouge! Heavens! How I look—pale—I must look dreadful—they will kill me!

The men likewise used the same toilette articles, rouged themselves, spilled "artificial tears" and depilated their entire body at the request of their mistress. A great achievement in the eighteenth century in the cosmetic field was the bath. In the latter half of the year they became an immense luxury and were mostly used for cosmetic baths. The heroines of de Sade after their full day's or night's work take their cosmetic bath.

The writings of Marquis de Sade afford a frightful picture of the frequency of abortion and contraception which had a definite connection with cosmetics in the eighteenth century. The statistics of Galliot which began with the year of 1789 show what a horrible decline there was in the birth rate. "The state must go further: it must not only protect the infant but also the foetus." All the means used today were known then; every possible means was used to hinder conception or to force away the foetus. Highly characteristic is the discussion in *Philosophy in the Boudoir* in which Madame de St. Ange, upon a question from Eugenie, told of the means of prevention: of *éponges,* which served the women, *condoms* which served the men and pædicatio which was an excellent method for both parties. But if this "misfortune" had happened, the heroes and heroines of de Sade knew means and ways of killing the fruit in the womb (Juliette III, 204, 212).

A last group of sexual cures was the anti-venereal class, with which the country was flooded. For in spite of all the debaucheries there was a great fear of syphilis and the charlatans found a very gullible public for their lies. We are not certain whether the bordello with its emblazoned motto *Safe Love* fulfilled its promises. At any rate extreme precaution was certainly justified. Casanova had a cardinal principle never to sleep in a strange bed. Juliette always investigated her clients for syphilitic symptoms. A man tainted with syphilis received short shrift with Juliette. It is told in *The English Spy* how a man voluntarily got syphilis so that he could infect his mistress who would pass it on to his rival. A similar idea was carried out by de Sade in *Philosophy in the Boudoir*. There a syphilitic servant is brought in and before the eyes of the triumphant monster infected the unhappy Madame de Mistival, whereupon Dolmance called out: *Parbleu, voici une inoculation, comme Tronchin n'en fit de ses jours* (Philosophy in the Boudoir).

Medical preventatives against syphilis were mainly fashioned in the cellars of the Palais Royal. There were also many who made their wares known by means of fugitive papers and posted advertisements of their wares on the streets and walls.

We have previously mentioned the charlatan Agirony and the "specificum of Doctor Préval." The latter was perhaps the most notorious charlatan of the eighteenth century. It was indeed Guilbert de Préval who introduced Rétif de la Bretonne to the secrets of Parisian prostitution and the *artes amandi* of the Palais Royal. The history of this arch-charlatan is told in detail in *The English Spy*.

Préval studied from 1746 in Cannes, where he built up a rich practice, and then moved to Paris to take his doctor's degree in anatomical studies in Paris. He spent over twenty years on the therapy of syphilis and discovered at the end of this period an "infallible cure" against this disease, of which he cured more than eight thousand people! The specific also possessed the power of curing all the other "blood and skin diseases." This cure was also a trustworthy prophylactic for syphilis. It was claimed to be a so-called *eau fondante* but really consisted of a sublimate of limewater. It finally also served for a diagnosis of syphilis for which purpose it was, for example, used by Madame Gourdan. The announcement of this cure made an extraordinary sensation and "there was a tremendous riot in the old court when all the *roués* came storming at his door." Préval was received with the honors scarcely accorded to the discoverer of a new part of the world but was asked to perform his miracle in the presence of witnesses. Préval assented. In the June of 1772 there occurred the unbelievable. In the presence of respectable gentlemen our charlatan completed coition with an unfortunate prostitute who had already been under observation in the hospital of the Compassionate Sisters. He first, of course, had taken his infallible cure. He remained healthy but it was not investigated whether this immunity was the result of a previous but indiscernible syphilis. Parent Duchatelet "could still name the witnesses of this remarkable scene, but the high circle in which they moved prevented the disclosure of their names."

Since we are not in the position of Parent Duchatelet we can name the gentlemen. There were the Duke of Chartres, Count de la Marche, Richelieu, Duke of Nivernois, and other "cavaliers." Préval was ordered by a Parisian magistrate to try his cure on the syphilitics in Bicêtre. Six men and four women were given him for this purpose. These affairs came to the knowledge of the Parisian Medical Faculty and at a notable meeting on August 8, 1772, the name of Préval was stricken from the lists of their members. He started action against the faculty and brought the suit before the Parliament. The decree of the faculty was lifted early in 1777 but in August 13, 1777, it was again confirmed and Préval in addition had to pay a penalty of 3000 francs. The arguments for the decision of the faculty were of a questionable character. We quote from the charges: "It is a matter of morals to investigate to what degree may be permitted a remedy which has no other purpose but the enhancement of pleasure in vice and removal of all restraint and punishment. We believe it would be a calamity to allow any such purpose for destruction of morals." Even Girtaner, a vigorous moralist, noted: "The discoverer of such a method earns the thanks and not the hatred of the human race for thereby in a short time syphilis throughout the entire world could be destroyed. And what friend of man does not desire so fortunate a revolution!"

The main preventative in the eighteenth century for venereal diseases was the same as today's—the condom. We have pointed many times to the wide use of condoms of which there was a whole arsenal in every bordello. The prostitutes in business for themselves also used these *redingotes d'Angleterre*. When Casanova came to Marseilles and according to his custom sought his first relaxation from the trip at a prostitute's where he expressed fear of disease, the girl offered *english caps*. But he did not care for them because they were of poor quality. Thereupon the beauty offered "better quality at 3 francs apiece and which were sold only in dozen lots." Casanova bought a whole dozen and had a few specimens adapted for the use of a fifteen-year-old servant girl.

The condom was discovered by a London doctor in the court of Charles II, named Dr. Conton; hence it should really be called *conton*. According to the plan of the doctor it was to be prepared from ceaca of lambs. For this purpose the desired length of the intestine was cut from the lamb, dried and then well oiled to make them soft and pliable. Proksch in his *Prevention of the Venereal Diseases* gives a complete history of this discovery and believed that in modern times "the hyper-moralistic ravings against the condom have almost entirely ceased." All doctors recognize the high value of the condom as a method of protection against venereal disease. Most of the recognition of the protective value of the condom came involuntary from sources one never expected. In 1826 there appeared a Papal

Bull by Leo XII in which he damned this discovery "because it hindered the arrangement of providence." The moralistic attacks against the condom hold no water with those who know that everything in this world is misused and that the health of society must be considered more important than the caprices of an individual. The doctor who protects the health of the family cannot take the stand of the theologian.

After detailed physical and chemical examination of forty-eight varieties of condoms Proksch came to the conclusion that those made of india-rubber were the best and withstood the greatest amount of pressure.

We finally come to the last group of aphrodisiacs. They were the substitutes for man; the artificial apparatus by which women compensated for the absence of man. They were the leather phallus, *godmichés*, the *consoler* or as in English *dildo*. These artificial penes have been in use since ancient times. During the eighteenth century they became very prevalent in France. De Sade described the workings of an automatic *godmiché* (Juliette V, 328) as well as other sharp pointed instruments that were used by the tribade Zatta (Juliette VI, 124). The engravings in *Philosophy of the Boudoir* show that the dildos used in the eighteenth century were similarly constructed to the ones found in France today. Garnier gives the following description: "Here in Paris they make perfect imitations of hard red rubber; they are sold secretly at the known addresses to all the interested parties. The mechanism is most ingenious. They can be blown up and filled with milk or any other liquid. They heat up in contact with the vagina and the liquid flows out at the psychological moment to give the proper illusion."

These things were not only used in lesbian bouts but also between male and female; Madame de St. Ange used it for pædicatio of Dolmance (Philosophy in the Boudoir II, 31).

Garnier believed that the *Japanese Balls* which were used in Japan, China and India from the earliest time by nymphomaniacs, first reached Europe in 1819 and were then written up in the *Dictionary of Medical Science*. This is entirely wrong. We have shown that these *Pommes d'Amour* were already well known in France in the middle of the eighteenth century.

Gastronomy and Alcoholism

Sine Baccho et Cerere friget Venus. Good food and drink are also aphrodisiacs not to be despised. Marquis de Sade knew this well. In the very beginning of Juliette, Delbène called out after the orgy: "*Déjeunons près amils, restaurons-nous; lorsqu'on a beaucoup déchargé il faul réparer ce qu'on a perdu*" (Juliette I, 10). "Good plentiful food makes one efficient for physical love," said Noirceuil (Juliette II, 151). "Let us drink," said Rodin, "I love to prepare myself for the joys of love by a good drink" (Justine I, 332). Ambroise described "the powers that Bacchus lend to Venus" (Justine III, 126). The participants in the horrible orgy at Minister Saint Fond's prepared themselves by "splendid wine and opulent food (Juliette II, 15). Juliette and Queen Charlotte of Naples drank two flasks full of champagne between their love scenes (Juliette IV, 18). A horrible *gourmée* was Count Gernande who had for a motto: "Intemperance is my goddess, her image stands next to that of Venus in my temple." He prepared himself for the joys of love by drinking 12 flasks of wines of different kinds, 2 flasks of liqueur, 1 flask of rum, 2 glasses of punch and 10 cups of coffee! (Justine III, 231-232).

The eighteenth century was "in truth the age of great chefs and cuisines." Everyone was at that time a gourmand, especially among the aristocracy where "very excellent meals were prepared." Indigestion was often the punishment of the glutton. The Field Marshal, Prince Soubise, was "more famous for his opulent dinners than his battles." The prince had an especial preference for a sumptuous omelette that cost one hundred thalers. Voltaire spoke very sharply against gastronomic excesses which he held were ruinous both for mind and body. The alcoholic parties which under the regency took place every evening in the Palais Royal, were again adopted under the rule of Louis XVI. According to Brillat Savarin the chevaliers and the abbés were the greatest connoisseurs of transcendental gastronomy. *Déjeuners littéraires et philosophiques et soupers célèbres* were the fashion throughout all France. Casanova, de la Bretonne and many others have often described such feasts.

Reichardt has well described how the alcoholic debaucheries served to enkindle the masses in the Reign of Terror. He concluded that the unaccustomed strong drinks were in the main responsible for that bloody September Day.

It is notable that Marquis de Sade delineated the vegetarian and the anti-alcoholic types in his novels. The first code of modern vegetarianism was the work of J. Newton, *Return to Nature and Defense of the Vegetable Regime,* which appeared in London in 1811. De Sade described in Bandole a typical vegetarian and prohibitionist who refrained for sexual grounds. He ate little, and then only vegetables, and drank only water. A number of such characters and beliefs appeared in *Justine* and *Juliette*.

Crime and Murder

The fact that prostitution and crime go hand-in-hand was clearly stated in Marquis de Sade's novels. Fatíme, the sixteen-year-old friend of Juliette, had as her *specialty* stealing from her customers, for one of the most famous thieves, Dorval, of the suburb La Villette. The latter had reported to him by spies through all Paris the arrival of every stranger, whom he had seduced and robbed with the help of his prostitutes. He experienced intense sexual pleasure if he were present at the execution of such robberies. We shall later speak of his theory and justification of robbery. The chief passion of the Venetian tribade, Zanetti, was also robbery. Such personalities to whom robbery was a delight, appeared very often in de Sade.

The greediness for money at this time in France was very enormous. We read in *Rameau's Nephew*: "There is no longer a country. I see only tyrants and slaves from one end of the country to another. Gold is All, and he without gold is Nought." Gold, as Madame de Hurset has it, was the *universal motor* of the age. The robbers and thieves who flooded the pages of de Sade's novels formed the real framework of the Revolution and were closely connected with prostitution in the city and provinces. Since 1789 robbery and murder took a sharp climb and became daily occurrences during the Revolution. The first half of the year 1792 proved most prolific in robberies and murders. The prisons and guards had to be increased almost double. August the 10th and the September Day both gave a dreadful impulse to all kinds of crimes.

Paris drew more and more to itself the swarms of criminals from all over the country. The first few months of the year 1796 saw armed bands of thieves openly parading down the streets looking for plunder. They would search for well-to-do houses, break in, terrify and murder the inhabitants and then proceed at their leisure in despoiling the house.

The reasons for this criminal state of affairs in Paris and the vicinity were drawn up in an official report: the number of public places of depravity, the degeneration of morals, the hiding places of prostitutes and robbers, the schools of vice, the balls, the gambling dens, the impotency of the police force because of politics, numbers, etc., etc.

All conversation in Paris turned on murders and robberies. The impunity of crime called forth more and more disrespect for the law and for continual imitations of the latest crimes. It meant the citizen's life to be found on strange streets in the dark. Even the respectable streets had to be patrolled by a body of citizens at night. Jaded Paris certainly received its morning quota of thrills when it heard the latest recitals of the crimes of the night before.

Poisoning

Poisoning ever follows in the wake of prostitution and sexual debaucheries. Even in Ancient Rome, Suburra, the residential and business section of prostitutes, was the gathering place for poison-makers and sellers. It was no accident that the notorious poisoners like Brinvilliers and Voisin, were sexually passionate women. De Sade with his profound knowledge of all relationships of the sexual life, thoroughly understood this connection and brought it out in the description of his characters. In a highly intuitive manner he painted the mood and passions of the poisoners who received tremendous sexual satisfaction from their profession (Juliette III, 214). Poisoning was also given the preference over other kinds of killing because of its quietness. Verneuil said: "No forceful act! under your very eyes death surprises the victim, without noise or scandal. O Justine! Justine! Poison is a splendid power! How many services has it performed! How many people enrichened! Of how many useless beings has it freed the world!" (Justine III, 235.)

The poisoner Durand living in the Faubourg was an erotic monster *par excellence* (Juliette III, 220 ff.). De Sade plainly described her as a sickly degenerate individual. He displayed an hysteric fit of Durand that represented a panorama of classic poisoning with her cold, calculated cruelty, her cynical atheism and her colossal sexual excitability. She had an entire garden full of poisonous plants and a great number of prepared poisons, emmenagogs, aphrodisiacs and anti-aphrodisiacs. Her main poisons were: the *poudre du crapaud verdier* which when given to a girl in coitus gave the other party the greatest of pleasure in seeing her moribund contractions and sufferings; the *chair calcinée de l'engu, espèce de tigre d'Ethiopie*, by which a young man was removed from the world; the *poison royal* by which, according to de Sade, many members of the royal family of Louis XV were poisoned. There were also poisoned needles and arrows and various snake-poisons, Cucurucu, Cocol, Polpoc, Aimorrhois, etc.

Minister Saint Fond carried on a wholesale poisoning. Likewise Noirceuil sang a hymn of praise to Brinvilliers (Juliette II, 31 and 85); Juliette poisoned Count Lorsange with the *poison royal* and mixed strammonium in the chocolate of the monstrous cannibal, Minski (Juliette III, 285 and IV, 15). When Durand and Juliette opened a bordello in Venice, the poison-trade was a profitable sideline (Juliette VI, 251).

Since the seventeenth century, which had a real epidemic of poisoning under the rule of Louis XIV and the aristocracy, poison became the ever-increasing favorite of the land. At that time the notorious Abbé Guibourg, the organizer of the *Devil's Masses*, supplied the entire aristocracy with poison and love-philtres. Poisonings indeed became so numerous that the King had to organize a special tribunal, the *chambre royale de l'arsénale or chambre ardente* which dealt exclusively with cases of poisoning. The poisoner best known was Marie Madelaine Marquise de Brinvilliers, very often mentioned by Marquis de Sade. It is interesting to note that this female devil reveled in sexual debaucheries from earliest youth. An insatiable sexual appetite was her lot throughout her whole life. She early learned the art of making poisons and devoted herself zealously to this field. She poisoned her father, two brothers, sisters and many others. Upon discovery of her crime she was beheaded. The corpse was then burned and scattered to the four winds so that as Madame de Sévigné wrote in her letters: "All Paris ran the danger of breathing in the atoms of this little woman and thereby becoming infected with the same poisonous desires."

And this infection actually spread. The poisonings increased in dreadful fashion. The most notorious poisoners of the seventeenth century, Voisin, Vigouroux, Oeillets and Delagragne were also active in the field of prostitution. Both trades developed hand-in-hand in the eighteenth century. The most famous poisoner was Desrues and his wife, whose one desire was to get rich at any price, and who poisoned all who stood in their way.

De Sade had this Desrues serve as hangman of the great robber Cartouche at an orgy (Juliette VI, 323). Rétif de la Bretonne described the whole affair in the fourth volume of *Gentle Ladies*.

Public Executions

The works of Marquis de Sade drip with the blood of his century. No one before or after him has described with such monstrous fidelity that dangerous union which ruled steadfastly and securely throughout the century: the union of the century—Vice and Blood! He brought his age to eternal life in the pages of his novels. Hence his works have such horrible effects upon the reader. The terror and fear, the horror and dread, the vice and blood, all have their living corpse in the novels of Marquis de Sade: *Justine* and *Juliette*.

The executions in the eighteenth century were public. Before the Revolution the executions had a horrible effect upon the populace; during the Revolution the guillotine had an even more powerful influence for cruelty and ferocity.

Montesquieu in his *Spirit of the Laws* as well as Voltaire and many others, described the public executions and declared that they were making the people more cruel in spirit, regarding the executions as pleasurable spectacles.

Until the Revolution the principal kinds of death penalties in France were quartering, the wheel and the gallows. The less stringent decapitation was so seldom practiced that even the executioners forgot the methods as was shown by the execution of Count de Lally in 1766. The usual form of execution was the wheel, often met with in de Sade. The unfortunate delinquent was stretched out on a wagon-wheel. The executioner with a heavy iron band broke the upper and lower bones of the victim with great dexterity so that he might be awarded the approval of the spectators. The criminal was then fastened to the spokes of the wheel and exhibited to the spectators in his dying convulsions.

The punishment at the gallows is well known. We shall become acquainted with quartering at the later description of the horrible execution of Damiens.

An execution was always "a great festival for the populace" which was extremely curious to see all the morbid details. Most of the executions took place on the Place de Grève. The most famous were those of the robber Cartouche and his band (November 27, 1721), the robber Nivet and his accomplices (1729) by the "wheel," Deschauffonis, who was first strangled and then burned (1733), the wife-murderer Lescombat by the gallows (1755), Desrues and his wife by the wheel (1777). The day and hour set for the execution were cried throughout the streets, printed accounts of the trial were hawked by street-urchins. In this tumultuous and often passionately moved mass, women and children were not those least impatient. Each followed *avec ardeur* all the dramatic points of the execution which often lasted for more than an hour.

The executioner, surrounded by his servants, bore the expression of a *seigneur* on display; he was barbered and powdered, clothed in while silk and looked about very proudly. His every movement was jealously watched. The condemned soon learnt whether the crowd was in a good or bad mood according to the expression of sympathetic or curse words on the part of the spectators.

The most horrible execution, perhaps of all time, was that of unfortunate Robert François Damiens who made an attempt on the life of Louis XV and on March 21 of that year was tortured to death. Thomas Carlyle in his *The French Revolution* cries out: "Ah, the eternal stars look down as if shedding tears of compassion down on the unfortunate people." We believe that a thousand executions by the guillotine cannot balance the terrible execution such as that of poor Damiens, who merited the sympathy of heaven and the stars. This shameful deed of the *ancien régime* could not have been washed away by all the blood that fell during the Revolution.

And when the individual details are given, the cruelty in

Marquis de Sade's works seems entirely conceivable and heralds the passionate bloodthirstiness of the Revolution.

We possess the following account of the execution of Damiens by an eye-witness, de Croy, which we follow in the main. The same judgment was carried out on Damiens as on the murderer of Henry IV, François Ravaillac, on May, 27, 1610. On the morning of March 28, 1757 Damiens was put on the rack; with glowing hot forceps his breasts, arms, legs and calves were torn out and in the wounds were poured molten lead, boiling oil, burning pitch mixed with red hot wax and sulphur. At three o'clock in the afternoon the victim was first brought to Notre Dame and then to the Place de Grève. All the streets that he had to pass by were packed with people who showed "neither hate nor pity." Charles Manselet reported: "Wherever one turns one's eyes one sees only crowds in Rue de la Tannerie! The crowds at the intersection of Rue de l'Epine and Rue de Mouton! The crowds in every part of the Place de Grève. The court itself was a compact mass, consisting of all possible classes, particularly the rabble."

At half past four that dreadful spectacle began. In the middle of the court was a low platform upon which the victim, who showed neither fear nor wonder but asked only for a quick death, was bound fast with iron rings by the six executioners so that his body was completely bound. Thereupon his right hand was extended and was placed in a sulphurous fire; the poor fellow let loose a dreadful outcry. According to Manselet, while his hair was burning, they stood on end. Thereupon his body was again attacked with glowing tongs and pieces of flesh were ripped from his bosom, thighs and other parts; molten lead and boiling oil were again spilled on the fresh wounds, the resulting stench (declared Richelieu in his *Memoirs*), infected the air of the entire court. Then four horses on the four sides of the platforms pulled hard on the heavy cables bound to his arms, shoulders, hands and feet. The horses were spurred on so that they might pull the victim apart. But they were unused to acting as the handmaids of executioners. For more than a hour they were beaten to strain away so that they might tear off the legs or arms of the victim. Only the wailing cries of pain informed the "prodigious number of spectators" of the unbelievable sufferings that a human creature had to endure. The horses now increased to six, were again whipped and forced to jerk away at the cables. The cries of Damiens increased to a maniacal roaring. And again the horses failed. Finally the executioner received permission from the judges to lighten the horrible task of the horses by cutting off the chains. First the hips were freed. The victim "turned his head to see what was happening," he did not cry but only turned close to the crucifix which was held out to him and kissed it while the two father-confessors spoke to him. At last after one and one-half hours of this "unparalleled suffering" the left leg was torn off. *The people clapped their hands in applause!* The victim betrayed only "curiosity and indifference." But when the other leg was torn off he started anew his wailing. After the chains on his shoulders had been cut off his right arm was the first to go. His cries became weaker and his head began to totter. When the left arm was ripped off the head fell backwards. So there was only left a trembling rump that was still alive and a head whose hair had suddenly become white. *He still lived!* As the hair was cut off and his legs and hands collected and dropped into a basket, the father-confessors stepped up to the remainder of Damiens. But Henry Sanson, the executioner, held them back and told them that Damiens had just drawn his last breath. "The fact is" wrote trustworthy Rétif, "that I saw the body still move about and the lower jaw move up and down as if he wanted to speak." The rump still breathed! His eyes turned to the spectators. It is not reported if the people clapped their hands a second time. At any rate during the length of the entire execution none moved from their places in the court or from the windows of adjoining buildings. The remainder of this martyr was burnt at a stake and the ashes strewn to the four winds. "Such was the end of that poor unfortunate who it may well be believed—suffered the greatest tortures that a human being has ever been called upon to endure." So concluded the Duke de Croy, an eye-witness, whose report we have almost literally translated. We will give a few more accounts by eye-witnesses of that fateful day when an entire populace greedily waited through four hours for the most dreadful tortures that the world had ever seen.

"The assemblage of people in Paris at this execution was unbelievable. The citizens of near and far provinces, even foreigners, came for the *festival*. The windows, roofs, streets were packed head on head. Most surprising of all was the dreadful impatient curiosity of women who strained for closer views of the torturings." Madame du Hausset tells in her memoirs that gambling went on during the execution and that wagers were made on the length of the duration of the tortures by Damiens.

Casanova, one of those who came from a foreign country to see the execution, reported a scene that was an excellent if terrible example of the theory of de Sade, that the tortures of another spur on real pleasure. He writes: "On March 28, the day of the Martyrdom of Damiens, I called for the ladies at Lambertini's and since the carriage could scarcely hold us all, I placed my charming friend on my lap without much difficulty and so amused ourselves until we came to the Place de Grève. The three ladies pressed as close to each other as they could so that they could all look through the window. They rested on their arms so we could see over their heads.

"We had the patience to maintain our uncomfortable position for four hours of this horrible spectacle. The execution of Damiens is too well-known for me to write about it. Also because the description would take too long and because nature revolts at such atrocities. During the execution of this sacrifice of the jesuits (his execution was said to have been done by order of the jesuits), I had to turn my eyes and hold my ears so that I might not hear that heart-rending cry when he had but half of his body. But Lambertini and her old friend made not the slightest movement; was that because of the cruelty of their souls? I had to pretend that I believed them when they said that his crime had prevented them from feeling sympathy for his plight. The fact is that Tiretta occupied herself during the execution in a most peculiar manner. She lifted her skirt high because, she said, she didn't want it dirtied. And her friend obliged her in the same way. Their hands were busily engaged during all the tortures."

Commentaries to Casanova's account are superfluous. That it was not an isolated case of satyriasis but one of the phases accompanying the horrible execution and calling forth passionate ecstasies was shown clearly by the fact that this charming sexual maneuver lasted two hours as expressly mentioned by Casanova later. "The action was repeated and without a resistance." That Louis XV told the embassies all the details of the execution with great satisfaction is not strange. The execution of the poisoner Desrues who, on May 6, 1772, was placed on the wheel and then burnt alive, was also "well attended by a distinguished crowd."

The Revolution hence found a ready public for executions. We have mentioned a number of times that de Sade witnessed all the atrocities of the Reign of Terror since he was freed from prison in 1790 and was a prisoner again only from December, 1793 to July 28, 1794. The first forerunners of the September murder, the storming of the Bastille (July 14, 1789), the drive to Versailles (October 5, 1789), the bloody events in Avignon in 1790 and 1791, showed what roles the women played in the executions and murders. In Avignon the fight between the Papal Aristocrats and the Patriotic Brigands for the possession of Avignon flamed to white heat. Thomas Carlyle has well described the open street murders and the role of *l'escuger* in Bk. V, Chap. III of his *The French Revolution*. "A hundred and thirty corpses of men, nay of women and even of children (for the trembling mother, hastily seized, could not leave her infant), lie heaped in that *glacière;* putrid under putridities: the horror of the world!"

Ethnological and Historical Examples

Marquis de Sade was a keen observer. He had besides become very well acquainted with contemporary literature during his stay in prison. It is therefore no wonder that we find the signs of both properties in his work. What seems to us most characteristic is the great rôle that ethnology plays with de Sade. That was no accident. The first pretences to folklore started in France. Lafitau wrote the first important work of this kind in 1724 on the American savages. The great interest in the wild races was increased by the number of expeditions of French *savants* in the eighteenth century. We name only such well known figures as Bouguer, La Condamine, Bougainville, La Pérouse, Marchand, d'Auteroche, Duhalde, Charlevoix, Savary, Le Vaillant, Volney, Dumont. In a tentative fashion comparative analyses of morals and customs of primitive races and the development of humanity were essayed. The glorification of European civilization thus started from these early ideas of ethnology. Lafitau says: "I have read with great irritation the usual works on savage races; they are described to us as people who have no religious instincts, no knowledge of a God, no personality, neither laws, justice nor organization; men who have only the form in common with us. They indeed differ but little from animals." This conception of savage races is also found in de Sade.

He justified all the vice and cruelty found in the savage races. James Cook found pederasty rampant in the South Seas. Therefore it was good (Philosophy in the Boudoir I, 201). The cruelty of women was the same all over the world. Zingua, Queen of Angola (often mentioned by de Sade), the "most cruel of all women" sacrificed her lover after her pleasure, had battles fought for her and gave herself to the victor and had all pregnant women under thirty years of age stamped to death in a huge mortar. (Philosophy in the Boudoir, 1856.) Zoë, the wife of the Chinese Emperor, found the greatest pleasure in having criminals executed before her very eyes, and had all slaves sacrificed in the bed chamber where she was engaged with her husband. The greater the cruelty, the greater the pleasure. She found her greatest enjoyment in watching men roasted alive! Theodora amused herself by castrating men (ib., p. 157). De Sade also told the well known story of Amerigo Vespucci, that the women of Florida had their men place small poisonous insects in their members which swelled up tremendously at the contact and caused an insatiable libido accompanied by dreadful pain and ulcers (Philosophy in the Boudoir I, 157). De Sade had ethnological examples in plenty for poisoning, prostitution, anthropophagy, sexual degeneration, Malthusianism, atheism, etc. The Bible for one, gave him a number of examples. Then the Africans, Asiatics, Turks, Chinese, etc., etc. De Sade had all the facts. He had all the available material and quoted that in Lapland, Tartary and America it was "an honor to prostitute one's wife," that the Illyrians celebrated remarkable mass orgies, that adultery flourished among the Greeks, that the Romans borrowed one another's wives, that his beloved Zingua had made a law that proscribed *vulgivaguibilité* of the women. Sparta, Formosa, Otaheiti, Cambodia, China, Japan, Peru, Cucuana, Riogabor, Scotland, etc., afforded him a mass of convincing examples on the justification of his theories.

All bizarre ideas, all remarkable cases of notorious erotic monsters were made use of by de Sade. Noirceuil declared that he would marry twice in one day and indeed at ten o'clock dressed as a woman he married a man; at twelve o'clock, dressed as a man, he married a boy who was married as a woman. Juliette also wanted to marry in the same church and at the same time, two tribades, one dressed as a woman and another dressed as a man. This, of course, was an imitation of the double union of Nero who married Tigellinus as a woman and Sporus as a man (Juliette VI, 319). Juliette, who did not want to fall behind Noirceuil in imitative talent, took an example from the Empress Theodora. She sprinkled barley in her most secret part and had the geese peck there, thus affording her continued pleasure (Juliette IV, 341).

De Sade made continual mention of Marshal Gilles Laval de Rais throughout *Justine, Juliette* and the *Philosophy in the Boudoir*. This "bluebeard" was a man of elegant appearance and great learning. At the age of 27 he left the court and army, cast off his wife and child, disappeared to his lonely castle, delved in mystical studies, alchemy, devil-craft and similar pursuits, finally gave himself up to sexual debaucheries and became a pederast, kidnapper, murderer, sadist, caprophiliac, etc., etc. This monster systematically murdered over 140 children in his castle. The victim was thrown on the floor, his throat cut deep and Gilles de Rais drank in his pleasures in watching the convulsive movements of the body. Then the extremities were cut off, breast and stomach opened and the entrails ripped out. At times he sat on the body of the victim to feel the death struggles. He also beheaded the corpse, took the head in his hands, looked at it closely and kissed it passionately. He often said to his accomplices: "No one in the world understands or can understand what I have done in my life. There is no other person who could have enacted my deeds." The heroes of de Sade spoke with similar pride of their crimes.

But the very age of Marquis de Sade was full of similar figures! "How many secret privileged criminals were there," asked Michelet, "who were not prosecuted? How many murders were set down as simple disappearances?"

De Sade also mentioned very often Count Charolais (1700-1760) who "committed murder for pleasure." This Count combined a raging cynicism with an unbelievable boldness. He loved to see blood flowing at his orgies and executed the courtesans who were brought to him in a dreadful fashion. "In the middle of his debaucheries with his mistress he would suddenly shoot a roof-thatcher. The rolling of the body from the roof afforded him infinite satisfaction." Abbé de Beauffremont is also said to have shot down people on the roofs. De Sade indeed placed this monomania in his register of sexual perversions. Juliette shot her father, while satisfying herself sexually with another man, in order to increase the pleasure (Juliette III, 115).

According to Michelet, Charolais loved the fair sex only "in bloody condition." His father, Prince Condé, had derived his pleasure from poisoning people as, for example, the poet Santeul, and had willed to his sons, the Duke of Bourgogne and Prince Charolais, these perverse inclinations. Both served as accomplices at the orgies of Madam de Prie. One day, there appeared a Madame de Sart S . . . who when undressed by the princes was lightly browned in a servette. In spite of this experience the victim again came to the house of de Prie and this time was "roasted like a bird." Michelet expressly mentioned that the Duke of Bourgogne had this horrible idea. This monster was described in *Juliette* as Duke Dendemar, who poured burning oil on the naked bodies of four prostitutes (Juliette I, 352).

The notorious anthropophagist, Blaize Ferrage, called Seyé, seemed to have served the Marquis as a model. This man terrorized the Pyrenees, killed men, women and especially young children; he ate men only when hungry; he used the women sexually before he murdered them; it was reported that he especially satisfied his passion in the most brutal manner on children. On December 12, 1782, he was condemned to death by the wheel; on the following day, only 25 years old, he was executed. De Sade described such an anthropophagist in Minski, the "Hermit of the Apennines" (Juliette III, 313).

Brunet mentioned additional sadistic types of the eighteenth century. A respectable Pole, author of many historical works, Count von Potocki, committed crimes "of the kind of Marquis de Sade." In Lyons the morals before the Revolution were so degenerate that "a number of sadistic outrages took place within a short time." Michelet rightly said in his *History of the French Revolution* that "not without justice did a notorious writer find a number of his episodes in his horrible novels in Lyons."

Jean Paul Marat, undoubtedly the most bloodthirsty person among the great Revolutionaries, gave the Marquis many ideas that are to be found in his novels. "He behaved like a drunkard who had washed himself in blood and was greedy for the flow of more blood." He advised mass-murders in his *Friend of the People* and returned again and again to this favorite topic of his. We will encounter this idea of mass-murders more than once in de Sade's novels.

Conditions in Italy

In the year 1772, after the Marsellais Scandal, Marquis de Sade and his cousin fled to Italy where they remained for six years. The result of this story was the description of Italian conditions which occupy more than three volumes of *Juliette* (from the end of the third volume to the end of the sixth volume). The Marquis made it clear that he knew Italy from his own experience and said (Juliette III, 290): "Those who know me are aware that I went to Italy with a very pretty woman whom I, by a unique principle of obscene philosophy, introduced to the Grandduke of Toscana, the Pope, Princess Borgia, the King and Queen of Naples. They may be assured that I have truthfully described the actual morals of these persons. Had the reader himself been an eye-witness he could not have described them more truthfully. The reader may also be assured that I have faithfully described my journey with the greatest accuracy."

Italy was undoubtedly the breeding-ground of real modern and refined immorality. We have but to mention Pietro Aretino, Pope Alexander VI, Lucrezia and Cesare Borgia, Giulio Romano and Agostino and Annibale Carracci, those great artists of passion. In comparison how innocent and naïve sound the love-adventures in Boccaccio's *Decameron!* The Renaissance and the jesuits started a new era in the sexual life of Italy.

Marquis de Sade described the growth of prostitution in Italy as enormous. All the cities that Juliette visited overflowed with prostitutes of all kinds who bore themselves proudly and were in no way ashamed. According to the glossary of the Pope a real *whore* was one who had sinned at least 23,000 times! What an enormous amount of sins Italy had on its poor head!

Venice was especially degenerate in its sexual life and Marquis de Sade had some horrible things to tell (Juliette IV, p. 144 ff.). The courtesans, for centuries the "pestilence of the city," were glorified in Venice. "Where in the world were there so many charms and pleasures as in Venice? Where were the courtesans prettier, better formed and more accomplished as priestesses of Cytherea? To

Venice on the first train came all the *roués* to taste every sin they could imagine and to find many they had never dreamed of. Only one purpose led all to Venice. This was the significance of the city of lagoons: The metropolis of absolute freedom for sexual delights. The prostitutes enjoyed the especial protection of the authorities."

Italy was very famous for its pederasty. Marquis de Sade, in this point certainly a true observer, cried: "The back is the best part of Italy" (Juliette III, 290). This was the inheritance from Greece and Rome. Dante even mentioned the great spread of homosexualism in the fifteenth and sixteenth stanza of the *Inferno*. Pope Sixtus IV (1471-1484) swore allegiance in the widest sense to pederasty and was said to have raised his Ganymede to a cardinalship. A few cardinals asked the Pope to be allowed to practice pederasty and the Pope is said to have granted it. The following verse found its adherent in Pope Sixtus IV.

Since Rome (Roma) delighted in inverse love (amor),
Love took its name from inverse Rome.

In the eighteenth century pederasty was the daily fare in Italy. Indeed one ran the danger of being attacked by pederasts in the open streets. Casanova told of such an attempt that a man made upon him. Cardinal Brancaforte, one of the greatest *roués* of the world, according to Casanova, "when he went into a bordello he went in to stay," was especially fond of pederasty. At a stay in Paris a young girl of Padua confessed to him that some men had taken certain freedoms with her that were strongly forbidden in the codex. Before he granted her absolution he desired to hear every detail of the crime. At each recital he would cry "but this is monstrous! Oh, my dear, you have committed a horrible sin—but it's a very pretty story." Casanova gave many similar anecdotes.

Even today masculine protection in Italy is more general than in any other country. "In Naples, today, on the Via Toledo young men offer themselves to passersby and the pimps proudly describe their masculine as well as feminine wares." Moll, who tells this in his *Perversions of the Sex Instinct* believes that Italy has always been more disposed to homosexualism than all other countries of Europe.

It is unnecessary to add that the Italian clergy of the eighteenth century played a great part in these sexual debaucheries. The enormous number of the clergy that overran the entire country speaks for itself. Joseph Goroni, whose interesting *Memoirs* have been verified as historically accurate, estimated that the Kingdom of Naples (without counting Sicily) had 60,000 monks, 3,000 lay brothers and 22,000 nuns in a population of 480,000. These clergy were of an "unheard of ignorance" and of a monstrous *débauche crapuleuse*. The convents were scenes of most depraved orgies. The clergy was in addition so rich that it possessed one-third of all the property in the country. Casanova was escorted in all the Italian bordellos by the clergy. The horrible abuse of castrates for spiritual purposes is an additional proof of the extreme depravity of the Italian clergy.

Zoophilia and sodomy were also more rampant in Italy than in other countries. Marquis de Sade saw in the house of Princess Borgiose a regular parade of turkey-cocks, a great bull-dog, one ape and a goat used as *Maîtres de plaisir!* (Juliette IV, 262.) The shepherds in Sicily were one and all said to have preferred goats. Cardinal Bellarmin after 1624 had "immoral intercourse with women and four pretty goats." Casanova was replete with information on sexual affairs and conditions in Italy. In his own words "there was no kind of depravity that was not practiced in Italy, especially among the clergy." Marquis de Sade's description of Pope Pius VI and Queen Charlotte of Naples will prove interesting.

According to de Sade this Pope was a great *roué* (Juliette IV, 26 f.); Juliette had a long conversation with him on the immorality of the Popes (IV, 270, ff.) and called him "an old ape" (IV, 285). Later His Holiness held an equally long discourse and his conclusion was that murder was the "simplest and most legitimate action in the world" (IV, 370) and did not fall behind this assurance in his numerous orgies (V, 1 ff.).

Was Pope Pius VI such a man? History assents only partly. Pius VI (1775-1798), previously Giovanni Angelo, Prince Braschi, was one of the most beautiful men of his times, "tall, of noble appearance and rudulent complexion." He carried his royal wand coquettishly, liked to show his well-rounded lines and laid great emphasis on his barbering.

He had the clergy and the faithful worship him with a stupid veneration, but which often concealed an ironical attitude. Pius was regarded in the Vatican as a much bespotted man, outside, as a god. When he stepped into the street, the women cried: *"Quanto è bello, quanto è bello!"* Cardinal Bernis called him a lively child who had always to be watched. According to Casanova, he approved of prostitution; according to Gorani, he had many mistresses and even committed incest with his natural daughter. In all, a handsome man with too many vanities that he could not help but succumb to.

Marquis de Sade described Queen Charlotte of Naples

as the perfect tribade (Juliette V, 258) and wrote of her charms "according to nature." She, as well as her husband, King Ferdinand IV, were distinguished by their high degree of passionate cruelty and often expressed themselves with a cold fervor on the great Neapolitan festival, at which 400 persons were killed (Juliette VI, 1).

Here Marquis de Sade actually described "according to nature." Gorani and Coletta as well as other authorities, agree that Charlotte was an actual Messalina and Ferdinand a suitable consort.

The relation of Charlotte to the famous Lady Emma Hamilton, the huntress of Nelson, was especially notorious. Coletta's judgment on tribadic liaison is confirmed by all scientific investigators.

De Sade's description of orgies celebrated in the ruins of Pompey actually occurred (Juliette V, 34 ff.). The great mass-murder of which de Sade wrote is also an historical fact. On October 18, 1794, there was a great streetfight in Naples, thirty men were killed and many hundreds were wounded.

All other Neapolitan conditions were actually as bad as represented in *Juliette*. According to Gorani the Roman Empire had never seen such moral corruption as in the court of Naples, no such Messalina as Queen Charlotte. Nelson said of Naples: "Not a woman is virtuous, not a man deserves but to be hanged on the gallows." Again according to Gorani, King Ferdinand IV's main passion was the torturing and killing of conies, cats and men; his next preference was his countless love-adventures, leaving Acton and the Queen to go on with their orgies without him.

We have seen that Marquis de Sade presented in the main a true account of the condition of cultural and sexual life in France and Italy and that his works have high value in regard to historical, literary, and philosophical purposes. In a later section we will give detailed analysis of his works.

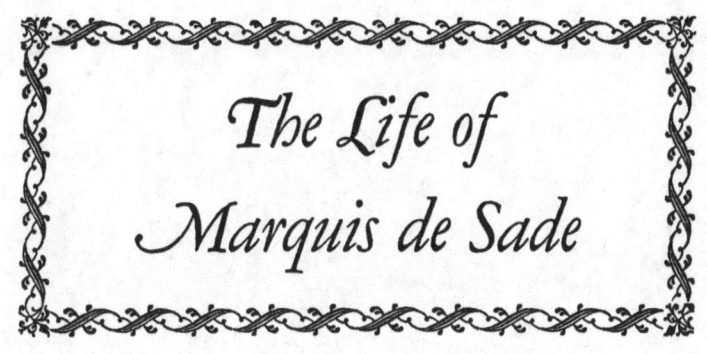

The Life of Marquis de Sade

His Ancestors

It was the day when the sun's heavy rays
Grew pale in pity of his suffering Lord
When I fell captive, lady, to the gaze
Of your fair eyes, fast bound in love's strong cord.

Who does not know this famous verse in praise of the first meeting with Laura, Madonna Laura, by Francesco Petrarch in his most famous Sonnet? What has this symbol of tender feeling to do in a book on Marquis de Sade? Laura, whom Petrarch met on that memorable Monday in the holy week in 1327 in the Church of Santa Chiara at Avignon, daughter of Audebert de Noues, was the wife of a Hugo de Sade, the ancestor of the family of de Sade. A strange and cruel jest in the history of literature: in the beginning a light from heaven, in the end, the darkness of hell!

Hugo de Sade, the husband of Laura, called the "old

man," left many sons, one of whom, Paul de Sade, became the Archbishop of Marseilles and the confidant of the Queen, Jolande of Aragoine. He died in 1433 and left his wealth to the Cathedral of Marseilles.

Hugo, the third son of the first Hugo de Sade and the beautiful Laura, was the progenitor of the three branches of the house, Mazan, Eiguières and Tarascon. His oldest son, Jean de Sade, was a learned jurist and was named president of the first parliament of Provence by Louis II, King of Anjou. His brother, Elzear de Sade, was so powerful that Emperor Sigismund allowed him to use the imperial eagle on his coat of arms.

Pierre de Sade, of the branch of Eiguières, was the first governor of Marseilles (1565-1568). He cleaned the city of all evil elements.

Jean Baptiste de Sade, Bishop of Cavaillon, wrote many pious religious works. He died in December 21, 1667.

Joseph de Sade, Seigneur d'Eiguières, born in 1684, was a very famous general and had notable victories both on land and sea. He held many important posts and received many decorations and honors. He died on January 29, 1761.

Hippolyte de Sade was also noted for his amazing sea exploits. Voltaire sent him a poem on the occasion of his marriage and Hippolyte replied using the same intricate verse scheme. He died in 1788.

Jacques François Paul Alphonse de Sade, the uncle of our Marquis de Sade, had a great influence upon him and hence must be described in more detail. He was born in 1705 and was the third son of Gaspar François de Sade. He devoted himself to the study of theology, became the general vicar of the Archbishop of Toulouse and Narbonne (1735) stayed for many years in Paris, where he experienced very profane and happy days at the side of the beautiful Madame de la Popelinière, the mistress of the Marshal of Saxony. He was an elegant writer, a spirited man, who gave himself up to "all frivolous pursuits of the century" and knew when to say farewell to "the vices of Paris" and return to the solitude of Vaucluse, where he pursued his studies on Petrarch and Laura and wrote many famous works on them as well as an excellent translation of all of Petrarch's works.

If one thinks in terms of hereditary influence it is clear that Marquis de Sade inherited the properties of his uncle and not his father. It so happened that the uncle undertook the education of his nephew for some time. At any rate the nephew had both his main characteristics: a love for frivolity and for writing. For Marquis de Sade was an ardent bibliophile. And if the uncle cared for love only in his youth, the nephew made his life work the theory and practice of vice.

The father of Marquis de Sade, Count Jean Baptiste François Joseph de Sade, was born in 1700, entered the military service and became the ambassador to Russia (1730) and London (1733). He allied himself with the Bourbons by marriage with Marie Eléonore de Maillé, niece of Cardinal Richelieu and court lady of Princess Condé. The great Condé had also married a Maillé. Comte de Sade was appointed in 1738 the general-lieutenant for Bresse, Bugey and Valromey; he bought the property of Montreuil at Versailles and returned to private life. He died on January 24, 1767, and left many manuscripts of anecdotes, moral and philosophical ideas, as well as a large correspondence on the war during the years 1741-1746.

We would here like to mention the eldest son of Marquis de Sade, Louis Marie de Sade, born in 1764 at Paris. He was a famous army officer and fought in many campaigns. He was also noted for his writings, especially his *History of the French Nation* (1805), a scholarly investigation. He was killed by brigands in Otranto on June 9, 1809.

The Childhood of Marquis de Sade

On the second day of June in the year 1740, one of the most remarkable men of the eighteenth century, indeed of modern times, was born in the home of the great Condé. Donatien Alphonse François, Marquis de Sade, Philosopher of Vice and *professeur de crime,* as Michelet and Taine call him, received the title of Comte after his father's death, but since he became notorious even before then the name Marquis de Sade clung to him. At the age of four he was sent to his grandmother at Avignon in sunny Provence, then a few years at Ebreuil with his uncle who carefully gave him his first lessons and prepared him for admittance in 1750 to the College Louis le Grand in Rue Saint Jacques in Paris. This institution was deemed the best in all France and gave the students the opportunity of a well-grounded and diverse education. They had to give public speeches, present plays, debate, etc. More care was taken of the mind than of the body which became defensively inured to the blows and floggings of the teacher.

There are many descriptions of the personality of de

Sade at this tender age, but all are not well-founded. According to Uzanne he was at this age an "adorable boy with delicate, pale face from which two great black eyes gleamed." But already there was an atmosphere of evil about the entire environment around him and was even more dangerous because of his almost "feminine charm" which inspired involuntary sympathy. Lacroix gives him a "graceful figure, blue eyes and blond, well-kept hair." A German author indulges himself in the following phantasy: "The young Vicomte was of such startling beauty that even in his early youth all the ladies that saw him stood stock still in rapt admiration. He also had a charming voice that pierced into the hearts of all women. He was always dressed in the latest of fashions, bright, colorful clothing that set off his appearance perfectly."

At any rate Marquis de Sade made as a youth a striking appearance. There exists unfortunately no authentic portrait of him. There are, of course, many pictures of him, mostly poor lithographs, but all have been proven to be false.

We also do not know in what mental condition Marquis de Sade left the College Louis le Grand. He is said to have been "an inveterate bookworm from earliest youth and early established a philosophic system on epicurean principles. He was also devoted to fine arts and was a proficient musician, dancer, fencer and sculptor. He spent many days in the art-galleries, especially those in the Louvre, Fontainbleau and Versailles." That de Sade loved music is confirmed by Lacroix and that he often visited art galleries is proven by his description of the collection of paintings in Florence (Juliette IV, 19 ff.).

Janin believes that when de Sade left school he was already a "fanatic of vice." De Sade left school in the same year (1754) that Maximilian de Robespierre entered.

Youth

The young Marquis then entered the regiment of Cheraux-Legers, became a sub-lieutenant in the king's regiment, lieutenant with the Carabiniers and finally captain of a cavalry regiment, serving in the seven-year-war with Germany. According to Lacroix he returned to Paris in 1766 where his father reproached him with "many youthful follies," but in 1763 de Sade was already in Paris. In May, 1880, a letter of the Marquis dated Vincennes, November 2, 1763, was found giving the date of his marriage, May 17, 1763. This is supported by the circumstance that the oldest son of the Marquis, Louis Marie de Sade, became a lieutenant in the Soubise Regiment in 1783. Since it is quite improbable that a boy of 16 could become a lieutenant Marquis de Sade must have returned to Paris to be married in 1763.

The history of the marriage has been described in detail by the bibliophile Jacob from contemporary accounts. Marciat is inclined to place great value from a psychological standpoint on this marriage for the moral deviations of Marquis de Sade. We cannot agree. De Sade's moral decline had already started. The "youthful follies" his father threw up at him, were a part of the general depravity of the French Army as a result of the seven-year-war. His father wanted the son married to rescue him from "the evil practices that flourished in the army during the war."

Montreuil, president of the *Cour des aides,* long a friend of the father, Marquis de Sade, had two daughters, 20 and 23 years of age, both pretty and well educated but differing in character and external figure. The elder, a brunette with black hair and dark eyes, was very majestic in appearance, very pious and *passionless.* The younger, a blue-eyed blonde, in spite of her youthful age appeared mature, was very intelligent, "of a heavenly disposition and charm" and was of a very passionate nature.

It had been agreed by the fathers that Marquis should marry the elder daughter and as luck would have it, he saw at his first visit to the home of President Montreuil only the younger daughter since her sister was ill. He immediately fell passionately in love with the younger who entranced him with her musical enthusiasm, her sweet voice and excellent technique at the harp. When de Sade met the older sister at his second visit, he felt only distaste for her and made known that he wanted to marry the younger. The president flatly refused and the Comte de Sade gave his son the choice between submission to his will or return to the army in an obscure post and disinheritance. So the Marquis, whose appeal "to the heart of the mother of the two girls found only a cold reply" was forced to marry the older sister. The younger had already returned de Sade's love and had sought in vain to move her parents by cries and prayers. Lacroix declares in detail that de Sade had married the older sister only in thought of committing adultery with the younger and that he very probably had come to an understanding with both sisters. Madame Montreuil, who understood the nature of her son-in-law from the very beginning, placed the younger daughter in a convent to escape the threatening scandal.

It is undecided whether this marriage is the chief origin of the demoralization of Marquis de Sade, as Marciat believes. It assuredly explains the hatred of marriage that is found in all of the works of de Sade. That his wife gave him no cause is shown by Ginistry's *Letters of Marquise de Sade*. She is revealed in these letters as a good wife, always tender and loving to him, stood by his side in all the scandals that surrounded him, helped him in a thousand ways during his stay in prison, assisted him in his flight from prison, in short, showed him all the care and regards of a loving wife. Women were said to have been irresistibly drawn to him by the "air of vice" that surrounded him. Ginistry has shown in detail how the Marquis evaluated his wife's love. We give one of the letters from his wife: "You know the world much better than I and do what you will. I am only the servant for your commands. You know that you can count on me as your best and dearest friend." De Sade wrote on the margin of this letter: "How can one lie so shamelessly?"

It is not strange that in the first year of the marriage after vain attempts by the Marquis to find the younger Montreuil, that he broke out into wild debaucheries, threw away his health and wealth with the assistance of the most notorious *roués* of his time and the "Coryphée of perfumed orgies" of the Duke of Fronsac and Prince Lamballe and did not disdain to use lackeys in wild saturnalias.

Initiated in the "secrets of the *petites maisons* and bordellos" he sought to outdo his companions by devising new, refined vices. Indeed there is a contemporary report that describes the idea of the Deer Park to Marquis de Sade. Even a few months after his first marriage de Sade, but 23 years old, was imprisoned in Vincennes because of great excesses in a *petite maison*. Here he was very retiring and quiet and made no trouble, only asked for a servant and for permission to enjoy some fresh air at intervals. In a letter dated November 2 he asked that his wife be informed of his imprisonment, without giving any reasons, and desired a priest to be sent to him. He closed with the words: "As unhappy as I am, I do not bewail my fate; for I desire divine punishment; to repent for my errors, to repair my wrongs will hence be my only desire." He must already have written an obscene book about this time. For he wrote in this letter of the "unfortunate book" which he wrote the preceding month. Which of his writings de Sade referred to is not clear. Cabanès believes that he referred to *Justine* but this is not borne out by present literary evidence and data.

Perhaps Marciat is correct in saying that this letter to the governor of the prison is written in a hypocritical style and intention, but it is also possible that this was one of the religious seizures that are so frequent with the perverse and libertines. There is at hand a letter to the prison chaplain, Griffet, on November 4, 1763: "We have a new prisoner at Vincennes who wishes to speak to a priest and has immediate need of your services although he is not sick. The person is Marquis de Sade, a young man of 23 years. Please visit him as soon as possible and I will be grateful if you report to me."

His Prison Life

*P*aul Verlaine has written that the Marquis de Sade spent a great part of his life in prisons. Counting from his last sentence at Charenton he spent 27 years in 11 jails: of these 27 years 13 were in his old age. In the solitude of the prison he worked on the material for his books. We can describe the entire manhood of Marquis de Sade as an interrupted prison life of dramatic proceedings that spread his name and "fame" throughout the world.

The reason for his second imprisonment was one of the most talked of contemporary proceedings. It was the Keller Affair.

We have many different accounts of the Keller affair. The most important is that of Madame du Deffand in a letter written ten days after the incident to the English writer and statesman, Horace Walpole. She wrote: "Here is a tragic and very strange story. A certain Comte de Sade, nephew of the *abbé* and Petrarch-student, met on Easter Tuesday a tall, well-built woman of 30 years who asked him for alms. He questioned her at length, showed much interest, promised to free her from her misery and make her the superintendent of his *petite maison* near Paris. The woman eagerly assented and was ordered for the next day. When she appeared the Marquis showed her all the corners and rooms of the house and finally brought her to the attic. There he ordered her to undress completely. She threw herself at his feet and begged him to spare her since she was a respectable woman. He threatened her with a pistol that he drew from his pocket and so forced her to obey. Then he bound her hands together and whipped her savagely. When she was completely covered with blood he applied salve to all her wounds and had her lay down. I do not know whether he gave her food and drink. At any rate he first saw her again on the following morning, looked at her wounds and saw that the salve had worked effectively. Then he took a knife and made cuts on her entire body, again placed salve on all her wounds, and left. The victim succeeded in tearing her bonds and to free herself by means of a window to the street. It is not known whether she was injured by the fall. A great outcry arose. The police-lieutenant was informed. De Sade was imprisoned. What will happen further is not known; it may be that this will be all the punishment since he comes from highly respectable people. It is said that the reason for his dreadful action was to prove the value of his salve."

On the following day (April 13) Madame du Deffand wrote: "Since yesterday I have been informed of further details of this affair. The place in which he had his *petite maison* was Arceuil. He whipped and cut her on the same day and poured *balsam* on her wounds. Then he untied her hands, covered her and placed her on a good bed. As soon as she was alone she made a bold escape through the window. The police-lieutenant had de Sade imprisoned. The latter had the audacity to claim that his crime was a noble public service because he had thus shown to the public the miraculous working of a salve that immediately cured all wounds. She received a large sum of damages from him and he was therefore freed."

This is the most trustworthy report of the affair. The

other accounts of the notable case deviate so greatly from one another that they befog rather than clear the details of the event. Janin wrote that Marquis de Sade had in Arceuil a *petite maison* where he held his orgies. The windows were covered with double shutters and the house was padded *(matelassée)* inside so that no sound or sight was granted the passerby. On an Easter morning, April 3, 1768, his servant and confederate brought there two common prostitutes; the Marquis himself, on his way to Arceuil, met a poor woman, Rosa Keller, widow of a certain Valentine, who was trying to earn her bread by prostitution. De Sade spoke to her, promised her food and sleep, addressed her very reservedly and tenderly, so that she rode in the carriage with him to Arceuil. The Marquis brought her to the second story of the dimly lighted house, where both prostitutes, drunk and decorated with flowers, sat at a richly laden table. She was here gagged, entirely undressed, bound and beaten until she was "only a single wound" whereupon the orgy with the two prostitutes began. Then Janin described the flight of the victim, the riot, the imprisonment of the criminal who was found dead-drunk in a pool of "wine and blood."

Eulenberg gives practically the same account and adds that the sadism was evidently a preparatory act to incite de Sade for the girls.

Lacroix reports that Keller was whipped under obscene circumstances which Madame du Deffand did not describe in her letters to Walpole but that even the "greatest prudes told to each other all the scabrous details without any feminine modesty." He adds that Keller was cut in many places with a knife and that the wounds were sealed again with Spanish wax.

Rétif de la Bretonne, who knew the Marquis since 1768, gave in his *Nights of Paris* an entirely different account of the history of the "*femme vivante disséquée.*" Marquis de Sade is said to have met Keller on the Place des Victoires, brought her to his house, placed her in an anatomy-room, where a great number of people were assembled, and made preparations to vivisect her. "Who wants this unfortunate being in the world?" said the Marquis in a grave voice. "She can do nothing and will serve to reveal to us the mysteries of the human structure." At a lull in the vivisection the woman is supposed to have freed herself and escaped. In her later story she claimed she saw a number of corpses in the house.

According to Cabanès, it was much simpler: Rosa Keller took one look at the room and company and fled to the street, nude as she was.

Finally there is an account by Brierre de Boismont which Marciat relates to the Keller affair but which we believe to be another case. Some years before the Revolution some people in a lonely street of Paris heard weak cries coming from the ground-floor of a house. They broke into it and found a nude girl, white as wax, upon a table. Blood streamed from cuts in all parts of the body. When the victim was revived she said that she had been enticed, beaten and cut by Marquis de Sade after which he satisfied himself on her. According to Brierre de Boismont this affair was hushed up, the victim receiving damages.

The Keller affair went off quite easily for de Sade. He was first imprisoned at the castle in Saumur but was released in six weeks after Rosa Keller had received damages of 100 louisdors.

He then again started on his debaucheries in the lowest spheres of the theatrical and literary world, associated with people of all sorts of callings, surrounded himself with prostitutes and gave free rein to his perverse inclinations. Montreuil finally had the police forbid the Marquis entrance to his castle, La Coste, when he was informed of the vices of his son-in-law by an actress (probably Beauvoisin of the Théâtre Français).

His wife who had asked for permission to visit the Castle Saumur in order to be near him, was foolish enough to inform him that her sister had finally left the convent. De Sade, whose desire for the younger sister had never diminished, hypocritically pretended indifference to his wife. But the first chance he was alone with his beloved, he fell at her feet, swore that he loved only her and that all the crimes had been the result of his unfortunate love. He threatened to take his life if his plea was not heard and he understood from the features of the silent young girl that he would receive a favorable answer. So, according to Lacroix, he conceived the plan of committing a strange crime, dazzle his sister-in-law with a suicide and thus get her to flee with him. The execution of this plan is the Marseilles Scandal (The Cantharidic Bonbon Orgy).

Bachaumont's secret memoirs has the following report under the date July 25, 1772: "I am told that Comte de Sade, who in 1768 caused great disorder by his crimes with a prostitute on whom he wanted to test a new cure, has just played in Marseilles a spectacle at first amusing but later horrible in its consequences. He gave a ball to which he invited many people and for dessert gave them very pretty chocolate pastilles. They were mixed with powdered 'spanish fly.' Their action is well known. All who ate them were seized by shameless ardor and lust and started the wildest excesses of love. The festival became an ancient Roman orgy. The most modest of women could not restrain themselves. The Marquis de Sade abused his sister-in-law and then fled with her to escape the threatening penalty of death. Many persons died as the result of the excesses and many others still suffer recurrent pains."

This account is plainly exaggerated. According to Lacroix who received his information from a trustworthy eyewitness, Marquis de Sade left with his servant for Marseilles. He had provided himself with cantharidic bonbons which he distributed in a public house. One prostitute sprang from a window and killed herself. The others, half nude, gave themselves to the most infamous debaucheries even in the midst of a great crowd. Two girls died as a result of the poison. De Sade read a letter from the council announcing the judgment of death upon him, showed this letter to his sister-in-law, called himself a monster and threatened to kill himself. She pleaded with him to flee and he enticed her to accompany him. After an hour they departed.

According to the Universal Biography this account is also false because no one died and only a few persons were "lightly harassed." Rétif de la Bretonne places the scene of the action in Paris in the Faubourg St. Honoré. This is important since Rétif, who hated the Marquis, declared no one died as a result of this orgy.

It is hence quite certain that the affair did not lead to any deaths. Marseilles often saw such scenes which were part of the extravagant life of the *ancien régime*. According to authentic documents discovered by Cabanès the only actual facts in this famous affair were the visit of Marquis de Sade to one or a number of bordellos at Marseilles and the distribution of innocent bonbons to the prostitutes.

Marquis de Sade was sentenced by the Parliament in Aix on September 11, 1772, to death on account of sodomy and poisoning *in contumaciam*. The severity of this sentence was ascribed to the Chancellor Maupeou who wanted to make an example of de Sade. The death sentence was finally lifted on June 30, 1778. The Marquis had to pay a penalty of 50 francs; according to the author of *Contemporary Biography* he received only an admonition.

He had in the meantime fled with his sister-in-law to Italy where he led a quiet life with her until after a short, severe illness she suddenly died and he fell back into his old habits. He was then seized in Piedmont and imprisoned in Fort Miolans on December 8, 1772. He conspired with his fellow-prisoner, the well-known de Songy (Baron de l'Allée), and they escaped on the night of May 1, 1773, with the aid of the Marquise and 15 men. They went to Geneva and from there to Italy where he met his wife. He soon changed her company for that of a mistress. He returned in 1777 to France where his wife and mother-in-law occupied themselves with his rehabilitation.

Imprisonment in Vincennes and in the Bastille

After a short stay in Provence where he led a vicious life, de Sade was seized, brought to Paris and imprisoned in the chief tower of the fortress at Vincennes. In a letter to the governor he implored him to allow him to see his wife. Somehow he got in touch with her and through her efforts he secured a reversal of judgment. De Sade was brought to Aix where Counselor Siméon brilliantly defended him and brought about an annulment of judgment on June 30, 1778. But by the influence of his mother-in-law, who rightly feared de Sade's freedom more than his imprisonment, the judgment was made retroactive and he was brought back to Vincennes. He was guarded by Inspector Marais, already well known to us. At a stop in Lambesc in July 5, 1778, he succeeded in escaping, again with the aid of his wife. But he was shortly thereafter (September 7) discovered by Marais at his castle and this time brought back without mishap to Vincennes. In 1784, he was transferred to the Bastille.

From 1774 to 1790, in the flower of his manhood, Marquis de Sade sat in prison. There is no doubt that here he made the first outlines of his works.

In his first year at Vincennes he was placed in a cold, damp room containing only a bed. No other furniture. His food was pushed through a small hole. Books and writing materials were withheld. This he found extremely painful.

His wife, who clung to him with patient love, finally got permission to send him books, writing materials and some other useful items. She later received permission to visit him. But every visit started a scandal. The Marquise had to be protected from the anger and wild fits of her husband. Hence police-lieutenant Le Noir denied her visits on September 25, 1782. Not until July 13, 1786, was she again allowed to see the Marquis. As a precaution there were always people present to protect her from the violence of her husband.

Marciat finds in the life of Marquis de Sade before his imprisonment a tendency to be cruel, a hatred for all women and an untamable sexual lust. He rightly concludes that thirteen years of imprisonment, from his twenty-eighth to fifty-first year, must have wrought terrific havoc on his body and mind, since confinement made every satisfaction of his mighty sexual inclination impossible.

This is seen in his increased irritability due to his illness. It is proven by the endless mistrust of his wife as shown by the notations on his wife's letters, which ascribe sexual motives to all her actions. The prison made a deep impression on de Sade. In the solitude of the cell his phantasy roamed free in images of passion and cruelty. It could be his only substitution for reality. As soon as he received books he sought in them all the possible examples and models for his vicious presentations which he placed as a record in his many manuscripts. This also was plainly a means of escape for his tired mind and body. He wrote and read incessantly while in prison.

Unfortunately the diaries kept by de Sade from 1777 to 1798, 13 books, were burnt so that an important aid for knowledge of his mental state was lost forever. He had marked down in his diaries everything that he had "said, done, heard, read, wrote, felt, or thought for 13 years." Only his works are left for a judgment of his personality.

It is interesting to note that while in prison the Marquis kept a correspondence with some of his former mistresses. There recently came up at auction some of these letters, filled with passionate remembrances.

By chance, Mirabeau was imprisoned at Vincennes at this time and, curiously enough, he also wrote his obscene works there. A strange effect of prison life!

There exists a remarkable letter by Mirabeau on his relations with the Marquis. "De Sade yesterday set the prison in an uproar and without the slightest provocation called me most infamous names. I was permitted by Rougemont (the governor of the prison) to walk about the court, while his request to do the same was denied. He asked me for my name so that at his release he could cut off my ears. I lost my patience and told him: 'My name is that of an honorable man, who never was imprisoned for strangling women.' He was silent and since then has never opened his mouth to me. It is dreadful to be in the same place with such a monster."

Participation in the Revolution and Literary Activity

The first scenes of the Revolution took place before the imprisonment of Marquis de Sade, who from youth had great sympathy for the movement. On July 2, 1789, before the storming of the Bastille, he halted the passersby on Rue Saint Antoine by means of a speaking trumpet, and soon had a great crowd listening to his loud insults of the governor of the Bastille. As the result of this incident Marquis de Sade was imprisoned at Charenton on July 4 and so missed the storming of the Bastille which took place on the fourteenth. He was freed from Charenton on March 29, 1790, by demand of the people. His first act was to hasten the separation from his wife. He also became estranged from his family; his sons left the country at the beginning of the Revolution. According to Lacroix he took a mistress who acted the hostess at his home. He lived first in the Rue Pot de Fer, near Saint Sulpice, later in Rue Neuve des Mathurins, Chaussée d'Antin, No. 20. According to most reliable reports the Marquis was in a bad way as far as material wealth went. There exists a letter written in the year III of the Revolution, in which de Sade asked for a position as librarian or museum-conservator because he was completely without means, having lost his literary property at the storming of the Bastille, his lands at Marseilles by confiscation. There is another letter written in the year VI of the Revolution in which he asked payment for a poem he wrote and the return of a comedy. Soon after his release from Charenton he began to write a great number of comedies which he sold to the numerous theatres. For a couple extra louisdors he himself would play a part.

During the Revolution de Sade's chief works appeared one after the other in quick succession. A year after his release, 1791, there appeared *Justine*, which was written for the most part in prison. The first edition is just erotic; those later, especially the last edition of 1797, contain all the bloody details. Marciat rightly believes that the influence of the milieu, the mighty events in the Revolution, called forth these later changes. Another novel written in the Bastille was *Aline and Valcour* which appeared in 1793. Then followed in 1795 *Philosophy in the Boudoir* and in 1797 as a crowing glory the double publication of *Justine and Juliette*. His *120 Days of Sodom* was also written in the Bastille in 1785 but was not discovered until 1904. Until 1804, the year of his new imprisonment, the Marquis' pen was sterile, a fact which will later be explained.

Much has been made of the fact that Marquis de Sade at times denied the authorship of his works. But that signified nothing. It was a common practice of contemporary writers; for example, Voltaire and Mirabeau. Again, de Sade probably did not care to sit in prison any longer. At any rate he acknowledged to his personal friends that he was the author and presented to them a de luxe edition of *Justine* and *Juliette* in ten volumes.

We are scantily supplied with information on the private life of Marquis de Sade during the Revolution. One can only conclude from his earlier affairs that he resumed his previous vicious life. When Marquis de Sade was again seized in 1801 his bedroom was found full of large pictures representing the "principal obscenities of the novel, *Justine*." Many stories are told of finding instruments of torture in his bedroom. He had his walls decorated with pictures of all sorts of *enemas* and nude figures in all kinds of postures.

Especially notable is the political activity of Marquis de Sade during the French Revolution. He had clearly and early foretold its appearance. He said in *Aline and Valcour*, written in the Bastille in 1788: "A great Revolution is being prepared in this country. It has become tired of the crimes of our rulers, their cruelties, debaucheries and stupidities. It is tired of despotism and is getting ready to break its chains." In the solitude of his cell he had time to develop systematically all the Revolutionary principles, especially the fight against God, empire and priests.

The "martyr of the Bastille" also took a lively part in the leading incidents of the Revolution. He became secretary to the Section des Piques, also called Section de Place Vendôme and Section de Robespierre. In the disorders of September 2, when everyone remained at home, he thought he would be safest in the bosom of his section. So he left his home in Rue Neuve des Mathurins and went in the evening to the Place Vendôme. The friends of Robespierre were not there but in the Jacobin club. De Sade was recognized only as a man who had been in prison under the *ancien régime*. "Would you like to be our secretary?" "Gladly." He took the pen.

De Sade was an enthusiastic admirer of the bloodthirsty Marat and after his murder by Charlotte Corday, delivered his funeral oration, all filled with revolutionary phrases and celebrating "holy and divine freedom" as the only goddess of France. But all are agreed in saying that the Marquis was secretly despised and hated by the members of his section as well as by the other revolutionaries. According to Cabanès he was still called Marquis by his companions and adds that he was the only living Marquis under the rule of Robespierre and Fouquier. He was probably a republican not from political conviction but rather from his war against justice and law in general, because of his *théorie du libertinage*. He was the philosopher of vice but not a passionate politician. He developed a theory of absolute evil but in life he was very gentle, prudent, and full of virtuous phrases, which did not fail to please the great terrorists. A paradoxical action gave them the excuse of proceeding against him. He saved his wife's parents from the scaffold, for which he was condemned as a "moderate" and on December 6, 1793, upon the command of the Comité de la Sûreté Générale he was imprisoned in turn at Madelonnettes, Carmes and Picpus; he, after a year of prison, finally received his freedom through Rovère, to whom he sold his property at La Coste. He had money for a while, once more.

De Sade went back to his literary activity which was hindered under the Directory. Indeed he had presented to each of the members a special de luxe edition of *Justine* and *Juliette*. At that time all the notorious works of Marquis de Sade were publicly sold. They were found in all bookstores and catalogues. A great capitalist financed the sale. This lasted until 1801. In the preceding year Marquis de Sade had published a novel *Zoloë and Her Two Acolytes*, a pamphlet against Josephine de Beauharnais (Zoloë), the ladies Tallien (Laurenda) and Visconti (Volsange), Bonaparte (Baron d'Orsec), Barres (Vicomte de Sabar), a senator (Fessinot), etc., all carrying on the most shameless infamies in a *petite maison*.

On account of this diatribe de Sade was seized on March 5, 1801. Without being legally tried he was brought to the prison of Sainte Pélagie, because a "trial would have provoked great scandal," and because the punishment was "even too mild for the crime." The prefect complained that de Sade seduced the young people in Sainte Pélagie and he was sent to Bicêtre. Upon the pleas of his family he was brought to Charenton on April 26, 1803. All his manuscripts and books were again confiscated.

The practice of setting people in prison without trials was common in the rule of Napoleon. The poet Desorgues who wrote a chanson against Napoleon with the refrain:

> *Oh, the grand Napoleon*
> *Is a grand chameleon.*

was interned in Charenton where he died in 1808. Many other authors met the same fate. De Sade indeed came off lucky. Buckle cites many similar fates in his *History of Civilization in England*.

We possess many interesting accounts of Marquis de Sade's stay in the insane asylum at Charenton. The most notable is the report of the famous Dr. Royer Collard on the Marquis in 1808. We give it verbatim:

Paris, August 2, 1808.
The Chief Doctor of the Hospital at Charenton
   to his Excellency, the Senator and Police Minister:
Sir:
   I have the honor to appeal to your authority for assistance in an affair that threatens the entire order in my house.
   We have here a man whose bold immorality has made him only too well known and whose mere presence attracts the greatest evils. I speak of the author of that shameful novel Justine. *This*

man is not mentally ill. His one delirium is that of vice—and this cannot be aided in an insane asylum. He has to be placed in the severest isolation to protect others from his outbreaks and to separate him from all circumstances that might increase his horrible passion. Our place at Charenton does not fulfill any of these conditions. De Sade enjoys too great freedom here. He can have intercourse with a great number of patients and convalescents either in his or their rooms. He has the right to walk in the park and often meets patients there. He preaches to them his criminal theories and lends them books. Finally we received a report that he is living with a woman whom he claimed was his daughter.

That is not all. They were so improvident at the asylum that they had a theatre erected for the performance of comedies and did not think of the harmful effects of such a tumultuous proceeding upon the mind. De Sade is the director of this theatre. He presents the plays, hands out the rôles and directs them. He is also the asylum poet. For example, at the dinners of the director he writes an allegorical piece in his honor or at least some couplets in his praise. I ask your excellency to remedy such a horrible condition. How can such things be in an insane asylum? Such crimes and immorality! Will not the patients who daily meet this man be also infected by his corruption and does not the mere thought of his presence in this house awaken the phantasy of those who do not see him?

I sincerely hope that your excellency will find these reasons imperative enough to find another resort than Charenton for de Sade. An order for him not to associate with the patients will not be sufficient as it will be only a temporary aid. I do not ask for him to be sent back to Bicêtre but I believe that a strong castle would be better fitted for him than an asylum with its many opportunities for the satisfaction of his degenerate desires.

ROYER COLLARD, M.D.

This report had no results. Marquis de Sade remained in Charenton. There is a justification for the conjecture that he preferred this to a prison. He was the especial favorite of the director of Charenton, Abbé Coulmier. He was thus allowed the greatest possible freedom. Royer Collard's repeated complaints on the theatre finally resulted in its removal. But in its place were substituted concerts and balls! This he also made many protests against, but it was not until May 6, 1813, that they were stopped.

We have many impressions of the personality of Marquis de Sade during his stay at Charenton but they are none too trustworthy. Janin describes the perverted influence he had on the patients and the tender sympathy he showed to young and pretty girls. Lacroix writes that all the persons he met gave the best reports of him. Nodier recalls that he "spoke politely, solemnly and respectfully of all that was deserving of respect." But the "grace and elegance" were not borne out by his appearance for he was enormously fat. His tired eyes, though, would at times suddenly light up in excitement. According to the *Universal Biography* de Sade retained his perverted habits until his death.

His Death

Marquis de Sade died at the age of 74 on December 2, 1814, at 10 o'clock in the evening, easily and quietly as a result of a long illness which had nevertheless not impaired his vigor. De Sade wrote of his illness in a letter to Napoleon dated June 17, 1808. He bitterly complained that he had led a most unhappy existence for 20 years in three different prisons. He was 70 years old, almost blind, suffered from gout, and had very severe pains in the breast and stomach. This could be confirmed by the doctors at Charenton. He therefore begged His Majesty to release him. The archives at Charenton state that the Marquis had been ill for some time from "liver trouble as a result of asthma." The end was sudden: he became severely ill two days before his death. His son, Armand de Sade, was present and burnt all the "dangerous papers" of his father. He was scarcely dead when "his skull was seized as an invaluable booty as if with one stroke the secret of the strange constitution would be discovered." The skull was like all others. It was a notable mixture of vice and virtue, of crime and honor, of hate and love. It was small, well formed and very like a woman's.

After his death the following testament was found:

> *I forbid my body to be dissected under any pretext whatsoever and desire most stringently that it shall remain in the room in which I died for 48 hours in a wooden coffin to be made only after the expiration of this time. The timber merchant, Lenormand, in Versailles, shall be ordered to come with his wagon and take my body to the forest on my property near Epernon where without any ceremony I should be buried on the first coppice that is seen from the great path in the old part of the castle. The grave should be dug by the tenant at Malmaison under the direction of Lenormand who shall not leave until all the arrangements are completed. My friends and relatives who wish to show me this last mark of love for me may be present. The ground over my grave should be sprinkled with acorns so that all traces of my grave shall disappear so that, as I hope, this reminder of my existence may be wiped from the memory of mankind.*
>
> *Written at Charenton Saint Maurice in sound mind and health on January 30, 1806.*
>
> D. A. F. SADE.

The Works of
Marquis de Sade

"Justine" and "Juliette"

The main works of Marquis de Sade, to which he owed his "herostratic eternity" were *Justine* and *Juliette*, later amplified to *Justine or the Misfortunes of Virtue* and *Juliette, her Sister, or the Fortunes of Vice* (Paris, 1797, 10 volumes, 18mo, 4 vols. of *Justine* and 6 of *Juliette*).

The plan for *Justine* dates back to the imprisonment of Marquis de Sade. According to the *Universal Biography* he wrote both, *Aline and Valcour* and *Justine* in the Bastille. After he was freed in 1790 there appeared the next year two editions of *Justine,* one with a frontispiece by Chery, the other revised edition having twelve obscene pictures by Texier. The third edition, printed in 1792, is even more cynical than the first two; for example, Bressac practices his monstrosities on his mother instead of as in the earlier editions, on his aunt. A fourth edition appeared in 1794.

Juliette appeared for the first time in 1796. All these plans are essential for the study of Marquis de Sade since the great combined edition of *Justine* and *Juliette* in 1797 was not only the most exhaustive but the one which had the ideas of the author developed to the highest degree. In this combined edition *The History of Justine or the Misfortunes of Virtue* by the Marquis de Sade was in four volumes. *The History of Juliette or the Fortunes of Vice* by the Marquis de Sade, was in six volumes. *Justine* contained 40 obscene illustrations, *Juliette* 60; there are in addition 4 frontispieces. The motto for the work was printed on the titlepage:

> *To portray the desires*
> *That perverse nature inspires*
> *Is a criminal act?*

The Preface

It is found in the first volume of *Justine* and declared that the work was conceived in 1778, that the author was dead and that the false friend to whom the manuscript was entrusted had printed many faulty editions of the work. The present was a true copy of the original. Their bold thoughts would cause no shock in a "philosophic century," and the writer, to whom all "affairs of the heart" were open, had made use of all possible situations and cynical pictures. "Only fools will take offense. True virtue fears not the pictures of vice. She finds only a firmer conviction than before. Perhaps some people will cry out against this work. But what people? The *roués*, as once the hypocrites cried out against Tartuffe. No book will awake so pleasant an expectation and hold the interest so grippingly. In no other book are the passions of a libertine so cleverly executed and their phantasies so realistically described. There has never been written anything like this present work. Have we not then reason to believe that this work will last to the dimmest future? Even Virtue, though she tremble a moment, should forget her tears in her pride that France can own so piquant a work in which the cynical expressions are bound with the strongest and boldest system of immoral and atheistic ideas."

We see that Marquis de Sade himself was convinced of the uniqueness of his work and he indeed declared that he wanted to outdo all other similar works in cynicism. We shall now give a detailed analysis of *Justine* and *Juliette* since the first is very difficult to procure and the second has never been translated.

Analysis of "Justine"

*I*t is the *Misfortunes of Virtue* that are described in *Justine*. Virtue, embodied in the heroine, Justine, always meets misfortune, and is strangled by vice and evil. This is the plot of the novel.

Justine and Juliette were the daughters of a very rich Parisian banker and were brought up in a famous convent of Paris until their fourteenth and fifteenth birthday, respectively. At the sudden bankruptcy of their father, followed by his death and that of the mother, they were notified to leave the convent and shift for themselves.

Juliette, the older, "lively, frivolous, malicious, wanton, and very pretty" was jubilant at her golden freedom. Justine, the younger, was naive and more interesting than her sister, a tender nature, inclined to melancholy, who bewailed her unfortunate state. Juliette tried to comfort her by showing her the joys of sexual excitements and how she could earn much gold by her bodily beauty. But her proposals were repulsed by the virtuous Justine and the two parted, later to meet one another under anomalous circumstances.

Then the fate of the virtuous Justine is told. She turned to the friends of her late parents but they insolently showed her the door. A priest even tried to seduce her. Finally she came to a great merchant, Dubourg, whose greatest sexual pleasure consisted in making children cry and who was naturally delighted at the wailing complaints of Justine. But when she later repulsed his ardent sexual advances she was thrown out. Meantime a certain Madam Desroches, at whose house Justine put up, opened her chest in Justine's absence and stole all her belongings so that the poor girl was entirely in the hand of this megaera. Finally Justine became acquainted with a demi-mondaine, Madame Delmonse, who gave her a lengthy lecture on the advantages and joys of prostitution (Justine I, 28 ff.). "Our virtue is not taken, only its mask. Hence I, like Messalina, am a whore; but I am also esteemed as modest as Lucretia. I am an atheist like Vanini; I am esteemed as pious as the holy Theresa. I am as false as Tiberius; I am esteemed as truthful as Socrates. I am believed to be as temperate as Diogenes; but Apicius was less immoderate than I. I love all the vices and hate all the virtues. But if you ask my husband or my family they will tell you: Delmonse is an angel!"

Justine was now being assailed by both women and was finally led by them again to old Dubourg, but again she successfully resisted him. She was then locked in the house of Delmonse where Dubourg for the third time was to try his luck and where Justine had to defend herself against the tribadic attack of the wanton Delmonse. Finally the old impotent Dubourg arrived and was first prepared by Delmonse who gave him magnificent bouillon and rubbed him all over until he became heated. At the critical moment Justine for the third time gave him the slip by creeping under the bed. Poor Dubourg was again disappointed and swore revenge on the disobedient girl. Delmonse accused Justine of having stolen a golden watch from her and the poor girl was sent to prison.

Here she made the acquaintance of a certain Dubois who had committed every possible crime. She and Justine were condemned to death. Dubois started a fire in the prison and 60 persons were burnt to death. Justine and Dubois escaped and allied themselves to a band of robbers in the forest of Bondy. As Justine hesitated to follow the path of crime of her companions she was threatened to be put to death if she did not join. She was forced to be a witness and assist in a wild orgy of the four men with Dubois. The brother of Dubois, *Coeur de Fer,* then greatly praised pederasty, which was loved especially by the priests (Justine I, 88-89). After many crimes of this band Justine escaped with a merchant Saint Florent whom she had saved from death and who pretended to be her uncle. They stopped on the way at an inn. It was soon apparent that Justine had leapt from the frying pan into the fire. For Saint Florent revealed himself as a thorough *roué*. He even waited to catch Justine during the satisfaction of a natural need. At the break of night they left the city and came to a forest. Here Saint Florent struck her in the face so that she fell down unconscious and satisfied himself on her, and left her unconscious in a truly sad state. When she awoke Justine could trust only in prayer. At dawn she hid herself in the thicket since she feared the return of Saint Florent and there she became an unwilling witness of a pederastic scene between a young noble, de Bressac, and his lackey, Jasmin. Justine was discovered by them, bound to a tree, but again freed and made chambermaid of the mother of de Bressac. She was a woman of severest virtue who held her son within bounds. Hence relations between the two were very strained. Madame Bressac sought to rehabilitate Justine in Paris. Delmonse had sailed to America so the affair was not discovered. In a notable fashion Justine was seized by Bressac, a complete degenerate and misogynist. He used Justine only to make known to her his evil principles, and to poison her character. He also started in her presence a sexual orgy, even overpowering his own mother. He told Justine that he wanted to do away with his mother because she had for a long time been in his way. Justine, who had refused to be a party to the murder, was to have been killed but fled to the City Saint Marsel to a house, supposedly a school kept by a certain Rodin. He received the now 17 year old Justine very warmly and introduced her to his daughter, Rosalie. Rodin was 36 years old, a surgeon, and lived together with his 30 year old sister, Celestine. The latter was a tribade and as erotic a monster as her brother. There was also a 19 year old governess in the house. Rodin had a *pension* and school for both sexes, 100 boys and 100 girls between 12 and 17 years. Ugly children were not admitted. Rodin instructed the boys, Celestine the girls. No stranger was admitted to betray the secrets of the house. On the very first day Justine and Rosalie observed the secret conduct of the brother and sister. Rodin appeared to be of the same taste as Saint Florent since he watched from a mirror Justine relieving herself. Later when Justine refused to obey the degenerate orders of the couple and sought to flee with Rosalie, Rodin determined to murder them both with the aid of a colleague, Rombeau, first performing a physiological experiment on them. A *sectio cæsarea* was performed on Rosalie amid a wild orgy. Justine came off luckily, being only branded, and was then driven away.

In her flight she reached the neighborhood of Sens. As she was sitting at the bank of a pond in the evening twilight she saw a child thrown into the water. She saved it but was surprised by the angry murderer who threw the child back into the pond and led Justine to his castle, where this monster lived alone. He had the peculiar mania of abusing each woman only once for the sole purpose of child-rearing. The children were raised until 18 months and were then thrown by him into the pond. At the moment he had thirty girls in his castle. He was a vegetarian and anti-alcoholist and also gave the girls plain fare so that they would be better fit to bear children. He also bound them to a machine before coition and had them afterwards lie in a bed for 9 days with their heads bent and feet high. That was his method of aiding conception. He conducted his own operations and took especial pleasure in the Cæsarean. Just as the choice fell upon her she was freed by *Coeur de Fer* whom she had let into the castle and who gave her her freedom.

She next entered a Benedictine abbey, Sainte Marie des

Bois, whose Prior Severino, a relative of the Pope, turned out to be a dangerous *roué* and pederast who practiced the vilest things in the underground halls with his lecherous monks. Two "seraglios of girls and boys were kept in the monastery and were watched by a Messalina by the name of Victorine." Descriptions of the orgies are then given and diverse sexuo-pathologic types appear. One received pleasure from boxing the ears of the women; another, menstruations; a third, the odor of the armpits. The monk Jerome said: "I would like to swallow them (the women), I would like to eat them alive, I have for long eaten no woman nor drunk their blood." Justine made friends with a young girl, Omphale, and was informed by her of the affairs and rules of this monastery-bordello. The monks preferred to give death penalties in the form of roasting, cooking, wheeling, quartering, strangling and beating. Between the numerous orgies great orations were given to justify them. The horrible Jerome then told his bloody, passionate life story. In the beginning of his career, after getting much pleasure from the seduction of his own sister, he induced sisters to be seduced by their brothers. He was also in Germany in 1760 and had practiced his crimes in Paderborn and Berlin (Marquis de Sade had also been in Germany at this time). Then he went to Sicily where poisoning was at its height and the clergy led the most degenerate life. He became acquainted with the chemist, Almani, who was very fond of goats and who had an orgasm at the eruption of Mt. Etna. With the help of a certain Clementia, Jerome practiced the cruelties of a Gilles de Rais. From Sicily Jerome went to Tunis and then returned to France when he had an opportunity to study the corruption at Marseilles before he entered the Convent again.

This account enthused the monks so much that they

executed some more girls. Justine also was selected, for her only protector, Severino, had been called away from the Convent. In the nick of time she succeeded in fleeing. She met on the way Dorothée d'Esterval, a canny hypocrite, the wife of an innkeeper who plundered and bestially murdered all his guests. Dorothée begged Justine to go with her and protect her. But Justine again fell into a trap. The wife was as degenerate as the innkeeper. Justine had to serve both their lusts besides enticing and ensnaring travellers. Many such horrible scenes are described. One day there came an old friend of Justine, de Bressac, a relative of d'Esterval. All four went to Count Gernande, another relative. He was a real glutton and satisfied his passion by making incisions and wounds on his wives; he was on the sixth. Such scenes are presented in the most horrible fashion. Dorothée later seduced Madame Gernande to tribadism. Then there came another branch of that honorable family, de Verneuil, his wife, his son Victor, and his daughter Cécile. Old Verneuil also had a peculiar specialty of sexual pleasure. He stole from poor women and gave to rich women! He immediately started an orgy upon an *Ottomane Sacrée* over which hung a picture of God. There then followed many similar scenes. Bressac delivered an oration on the eternity of the soul and murdered the wife and daughter of Verneuil. Justine then fled to Lyons where she again met Saint Florent whose specialty was the seduction of virgins and then subsequent sale to the madames. He wanted Justine to be his accomplice but she indignantly refused. He imprisoned her and forced her to consume his spittle. After an orgy Justine was released and on her way from Lyons met a beggar who asked for alms and then robbed Justine of her purse. In her pursuit Justine came upon a band of beggars in a cave. The chief participants in the sexual debaucheries were the pederast and jesuit Gareau and the tribade, Séraphine, whose history is told in detail. She escaped from the cave and on her way found a man named Roland who had been left for dead by two cavaliers. This Roland was the head of a band of forgers and hid in a castle high up in the mountains. Poor Justine soon found out that she was in the hands of a dangerous libertine. In a subterranean cellar of the castle were numerous skeletons, weapons of all kinds, crucifixes, etc. Here he enjoyed his sexual sport: *jeu de coupe corde*, the hanging of women; since this was an unspeakably passionate death. Roland himself proved this to Justine who released him before it was too late. Later she was placed in an abyss filled with corpses by Roland; as soon as he left the next day she was saved by his attendant, Deville. One day the whole band was seized, brought to Grenoble and hanged. Justine, however, was saved by the devoted work of an attorney at Grenoble, S . . ., who also made a collection for her.

Justine now met an old friend, Dubois, who had promoted herself to a baroness. She tried to get Justine to aid her in a plan to rob a young merchant, but instead, she betrayed her, but it was too late as Dubois in fear had poisoned him. Justine was then seized by three men in the street and brought to the home of the Archbishop of Grenoble where the vengeful Dubois presided. This Archbishop was naturally a paragon of vice and cruelty, a "faun from the fables," a monomaniac for the head. He had his own execution room "in which before the eyes of the shuddering Justine a girl was beheaded." Justine fled but was again found by Dubois, denounced as a pyromaniac and murderess and placed in the prison at Lyons from where she was brought by the ubiquitous Saint Florent to the judge, Cardoville. In his castle a society of anthropophagists celebrate their orgies with the assistance of twelve Negroes. Justine was flogged on the wheel for a time. Then two girls made the operation of infibulation on her. Then she had to run between two aisles of men who beat her with rods. Then many participants lay themselves down upon a cross set with iron points and which excited them terribly, and gave occasions to wild outbreaks. Then Justine was led back to prison and condemned to death by fire. The prison guard, who had her commit a robbery for him, let her escape.

In her wanderings she noticed one evening an elegant lady with four gentlemen. It was her sister Juliette, who upon recognizing her cried out: "Oh, poor girl, do not be amazed. I had told you all that would happen. I have walked the path of vice and found only roses. You were less of a philosopher. You see to what you have come." Justine was provided with clothes and food; one of the cavaliers pointed to her and said: "There you see the Misfortunes of Virtue!" And pointing to Juliette: "And, my friends, the Fortunes of Vice!"

Analysis of "Juliette"

The *Fortunes of Vice* is the theme of the six-volumed *Juliette* which appeared in the combined edition of 1797 as a continuation and completion of *Justine*, and described the triumphs of vice in truly ingenious pictures.

Justine and Juliette were, as has been mentioned, educated in the Panthémont convent from which came the "prettiest and most immoral women of Paris." For five years Madame Delbène was the abbess of this convent, a thirty year old tribade who initiated Juliette and her fifteen year old friend, Euphrosyne, into the secrets of lesbian love. She later met them in a bordello. She had *le tempéramente le plus actif*, 60,000 livres income, and was of a "delicious perversity." She developed quickly and at 15 years of age formulated her materialistic and antimoral system of philosophy, studied Holbach and La Mettrie, defined conscience as a "prejudice implanted by education," discoursed on electrical fluid, objective existence of God, the soul, etc., etc. She started a great tribadic orgy in which participated the 20 year old Madame de Volmer, the passionate companion of Delbène, a true hermaphrodite, the 17 year old Saint Elme, the 13 and 18 year old Elizabeth and Flavia as well as Juliette. All were held by the world to be modest and chaste. Here they were of an "energetic indecency." Nevertheless their virginity was very anxiously protected. Juliette was deflowered much later by Delbène with the aid of the dildo. The entire society climbed into the catacombs of the convent by means of a grave in the church. There was an artistically arranged room in the catacombs in which the 10 year old Laurette awaited her defloration at the hands of two monks, the 30 year old *abbé*, Ducrez, main vicar of the archbishop of Paris, who was entrusted to the Panthémont convent and the 36 year old Father Télème, a franciscan and father confessor for the novices and pensionaries of the convent. With cynical plainness Delbène explained to the astounded Juliette that there the nuns assembled with the monks for the purpose of sexual debaucheries and atrocities. Here the great "crimes" were planned and carried out. In the following orgies natural and artificial pædicatio played a great rôle with the men and women. It was especially recommended to the unmarried girls with the argument: *point d'enfants, presque jamais de maladies, et des plaisirs nuls fors plus doux.* Juliette had to deflower Laurette who was bound fast to the table. A rich meal was then spread and Laurette, nude, had to serve all the persons who were sitting at the table. Volmer manustuprated the monks over a punchbowl in which Juliette relieved herself whereupon the other women drank from it. Suddenly the lights were extinguished by the flight of a frightened owl and the orgy came to an end.

After the bankruptcy and death of her parents Juliette was immediately released by Delbène who advised her to enter a bordello of a certain Duvergier where she would also find her friend Euphrosyne. Juliette followed her advice and separated herself from her sister, Justine. Juliette went from convent to bordello where she had all kinds of adventures. The isolated position of this bordello has already been described. Juliette here had intercourse with princes, nobles, rich merchants, etc., and encountered all kinds of possible ways for satisfying desires. She became friends with Fatima, a 16 year old prostitute, whose specialty was robbing her clients. She was instructed in this art by one of the most famous thieves of Paris, Dorval, who received reports from his spies of all new visitors in Paris. These were seduced and robbed by his prostitutes while he watched and received great sexual excitement. He already owned thirty houses. His sexual perversion consisted in *cunnilingus post coitum.* He delivered a long lecture on the theory and justification of robbery, the "main pillar of society." He thereupon had Fatima and Juliette thrown into a dark torture chamber where they were undressed and told they were going to be put to death on the gallows, Dorval receiving great pleasure from their distress. A mock execution was performed, Dorval satisfied his lust on the quasi-dead and then had them brought back nude to Duvergier in a wagon.

Juliette was then sent to the archbishop of Lyons in the quarter of Saint Victor in Paris. This shepherd of God practiced pædicatio with the assistance of another woman and as a conclusion was beaten by a third woman with rods.

After Juliette had luckily escaped the danger of infection with a man having a bad case of syphilis, she made the acquaintance of a certain Noirceuil, a rich *roué* and a grandiose scoundrel. Noirceuil had the strange complex; his wives—he was up to the 18th—had to be witnesses of all his orgies. He moreover desired only virgins. Two naked boys had to beat, bind and cut his own wife during his orgies. She had then to undress and serve him and his mistress at the meal following their intercourse.

Noirceuil made a surprising disclosure to Juliette: "I knew your father very well. I was indeed the cause of his bankruptcy. I ruined him. I cast an eye on his property, I could double it if it were in my hands. So according to my principles I took the money from him. He died in ruin and now I have an income of 300,000 livres." "Oh! horrible creature! no matter if I am a victim of your vice, still I love you! Nay more, I even embrace your principles." "Oh! Juliette, if you knew all!" "Try me!" "Your father, your mother!" "What of them?" "If they went on living they might betray me. . . . I had to sacrifice them. . . . I mixed some poison in your father's food one day; and shortly thereafter in your mother's." At this dreadful revelation Juliette cries: "Monster, you make me shudder but I love you!" "The murderer of your family?" "What of it? I judge everything *par les sensations*. Your victims never excited such a sensation in me, but your confession that you are a murderer inflames me and makes me burningly passionate," exclaimed Juliette.

Noirceuil highly rejoiced at finding such a delightful companion, and kept her in his home. But she also always visited the bordello of Duvergier. She had a special section for respectable ladies and young girls who were seized with some degree of nymphomania and so spent part of their lives in the bordello. Many sexuo-pathologic types were to be found there. The Duchess of Saint-Fal gladly sold her *pucelage antiphysique* and another loved intercourse only with priests. Every evening a virgin from Duvergier was sent to Noirceuil who, in the presence of Juliette, the two children and his wife deflowered them. Once Duvergier had Juliette and six other girls participate in an orgy of a millionaire, Mondor, a decrepit old man of 66 years who needed infinite patience and excitation to attain his desire. He had to be made potent by a tribadic scene of six girls, artificial pædicatio and *defaecatio in os*. Juliette stole 60,000 francs from him but after his return to the home of Noirceuil she found the money gone but Noirceuil hypocritically pretended that Juliette's chambermaid stole the money and had her thrown into the prison at Bicêtre. After the heroic deed he delivered an oration on the profits of intelligent crime. Juliette then went with three young modistes upon an order by Duvergier to a Duke Dendemar in St. Maur whose mania was flagellation of women, especially those who were not prostitutes, and paid great sums for his victims. Juliette was bound to a cross, and burning oil was spilled over the bodies of the four naked girls. Juliette stole a great sum of money from him, departed from Duvergier and lived for a year in the house of Noirceuil, had adventures from time to time, until later, a servant of Dendemar, saw her on the street and had her thrown into jail. But she was freed by the intercession of State Minister Saint Fond at the request of Noirceuil who declared that one of the girls who accompanied Juliette must have been the thief. Noirceuil told Juliette that the monster was delighted with her criminal talents and had presented her with a great sum of money. They then had supper with the minister.

Saint Fond was a man of about fifty years of age, a treacherous and cruel libertine, traitor and thief. He had on hand many *lettres de cachet* and more than 20,000 people were thrown into prison on his orders; "none of whom," he said, "were guilty." There were present at a dinner, the President of Parliament D'Albert, four virgins, Juliette and Madame Noirceuil. They were served by six nude boys. Each libertine received two boys for his disposal. D'Albert promised Juliette an omnibus decree which would protect her from prosecution for any crime whatsoever; Saint Fond also assured her of the same but asked that he should always be regarded with the highest respect and to address him as "monseigneur" as befitting his wealth and station. He had an extreme case of megalomania and thought more of himself than the king did. He hated the entire world with the exception of Noirceuil, d'Albert and a few others. In sexual affairs he cared only for the backside and its products which he devoured with joy. He was then described as a handsome, powerful and healthy man. In the course of the following orgy the wife of Noirceuil was killed in a horrible manner. Her whole body was rubbed with spirits, burning candles were placed in all the openings of her body. She was finally poisoned in the presence of the others. Juliette was then selected by Saint Fond to arrange his private orgies; a great hotel in Rue du Faubourg Saint Honoré was then erected by her with his money; she also procured a pretty country house near Sceaux and a *petite maison* near the Barrière Blanche for his delectation. There were four chambermaids, a reader, two night-watchmen, a housekeeper, a hairdresser, a cook, two servants, three carriages, ten horses, two drivers, four lackies and twelve tribades, all at her disposal. The minister made her the head of the "Department of Poisonings," since he dealt in wholesale murder. He explained to her the necessity in which a state often found itself of removing some objectionable character. Juliette was to poison these persons and receive 30,000 francs for each murder. There were at least fifty a year, giving her an income of 1,500,000 francs a year. The sacrifices of the secret orgies—two girls usually twice a week— brought her 20,000 francs apiece. Juliette hence received 12,000 livres from her personal enterprises, a monthly pension from Noirceuil, a million from Saint Fond for the general costs of the festivals, 20,000 or 30,000 francs for each victim, altogether a yearly income of 6,734,000 francs. Saint Fond added 210,000 livres for his *menus plaisirs*. He was easily able to afford this for he paid the money not from his own pocket but from that of the state which he plundered.

The amusements at the *petits soupers* and in the boudoir at Barrière Blanche started anew and were managed most excellently by Juliette. Saint Fond, who had also brought an imperial prince to taste these pleasures, had Juliette poison his own father. He then, together with Norceuil, brought his own daughter, with whom he had long incestuously lived, to his moribund father and openly practiced pædicatio. Noirceuil followed suit. What pleasure for Saint Fond! He cried out triumphantly: "I have all at one time committed parricide, incest, assassination, prostitution and sodomy!"

There then followed a luxurious meal; a burning candle was placed in the backside of the little girl to provide light: she was eventually burned to death. Other girls were then placed upon a spit and roasted alive. Juliette desired a younger girl to assist her and was introduced to Lady Clairwil, a cold, heartless English beauty, who was a passionate tribade and hated all men. All her cruelties and atrocities were practiced against men. She delighted in both passive and active flagellation, and proved it at a tribadic orgy with Juliette and four women. Saint Fond engaged the services of a professional executioner, Delcour. The idea of being together with a veritable executioner aroused the greatest passions in Juliette. She had herself flagellated and Delcour practiced *cunnilingus*. Then with the assistance of Clarwil and Delcour the greatest cruelties were begun. Cloris, a relative of Saint Fond, who owed his whole career to him, was hence selected for the victim, and especially because his wife and daughter had not assented to the covetous desires of Saint Fond. The latter had slandered both women to Queen Marie Antoinette, who gave him three million francs for their murder. Father, mother and child were locked in prison and forced to practice the most horrible kinds of incest with one another. Then father, mother and child were murdered one after the other. The executioner, Delcour, had to cut the throat of the daughter of Cloris very slowly for Saint Fond was practicing pædicatio with her at the time. Juliette had draped a room in black and placed the heads of the corpses in niches along the walls, later to be brought to the queen. Moreover their buttocks were hung on the wall. A number of torture-instruments were then brought up. A girl, Fulvia, was placed on the wheel. Others had their eyes stabbed or their bones broken. A youth was placed in a huge machine, resembling a coffee-mill and cut into small pieces.

Some days later Clairwil and Juliette were seized by relatives of the murdered Cloris, but were freed by order of Saint Fond. The girls then killed the men while they were engaged in coition. Saint Fond strangled a girl in the same situation. Faustine and Felicitas, Dormon and Delnos, the two sisters of Madame Cloris and their fiancés were sacrificed after an "enormous dinner." Dormon was fastened "in a moment." Clairwil lacerated him with her teeth, and he was then flogged upon the wheel by two old women. Faustine, who was hanged from the ceiling by her hair, died from fright, Delnos was filled with nails by Juliette. Felicitas was "impaled" alive. The still-alive Delnos was then crucified like Jesus by Clairwil. As a conclusion a natural son of Saint Fond, Marquis de Rose, was poisoned. Saint Fond then had the mother of the Marquis killed so that he could come into possession of her immense wealth.

Juliette also practiced many atrocities in her country home. One day she rode about Sceaux and came to the hut of a brave peasant who was scared out of his wits at the visit of "so great a lady." She praised the cleanliness and order of the house, the pleasant countenances of the children, the proper conduct of the family and took advantage of the peasant's absence to place the hut on fire. At his return he found the house in flames and his children burnt alive, since Juliette had made sure that all exits were closed. She was greatly amused at the cries of the victims and then hurried to Paris to tell Lady Clairwil of her heroic deed. At the relating of the story Lady Clairwil wrinkled her brow like a university professor. For Juliette had omitted something. She should have accused the peasant of having burnt his own home so that he would have been hanged or placed on the wheel!

This excellent instructress introduced Juliette into the "Society for the Friends of Crime" to complete her education. Her initiation is described. After the reading of the forty-five statutes, from which one understood that only the greatest criminals and libertines belonged to this institution, Juliette was accepted. There followed the most unbelievable debaucheries. Defecations one over another, excitation by enemas, needles pierced into the genitals of men and women. All parts of the body are licked, sucked, bitten; hands and feet were vigorously used. Human blood flowed freely and was ardently swallowed. Testes were a favorite dessert. There were separate rooms for masturbation, flagellation, torture and execution. All four rooms were filled with their respective devotees. Incest of all imaginable kinds was the order of the day. Great argument ensued over who received the greatest pleasure, *coniste, bourge, masturbateur* or *f . . . en bouche*. But neither Saint Fond, Noirceuil, nor their half dozen lackies chosen from the strongest men, nor their twelve tribades, nor Clairwil, the numberless male and female victims, the festivals and harems of the "Society of the Friends of Crime" could satisfy the insatiable temperament of our heroine. She wanted more and more diversions. Clairwil and Juliette went to the Carmelite monk, Claude, for confession and discovered that this marvellous man had three testes! He informed them that he served his brother monks as Pathicus and that he was a confirmed atheist. He had a separate room in the Barrière de Vaugirard and the girls found there good wine, soft, snug sofas and a select library of pornography, besides *godmichés*, martinets and condoms. But the luck of this stalwart monk did not last. He was one day attacked by the girls in ambush and an ablation was made of his virile member which was used by Clairwil as a *godmiché*. He was then killed.

Shortly thereafter a certain Bernole, a dirty and ragged person, informed Juliette that he had important news for her. She found that the rich banker whom she had believed to be her father and who had been ruined by Noirceuil was her father only by power of law. Bernole was her real father and he showed her the proof. Immediately the idea of incest came into the mind of our sensitive heroine. She realized this idea and had herself made pregnant by her own father whom she later shot in the presence of Noirceuil, Saint Fond and Clairwil. She then undertook the education of Saint Fond's daughter, who we had seen was instructed by her father in all sexual secrets, and completed his omissions from a feminine viewpoint. They attended an orgy at a Carmelite monastery at which two "black masses" were read. They both learned much from Count Belmor, whose mania consisted in binding children on the shoulders of a pretty woman, beating them until they bled and to lick up the blood with his tongue from the woman's genitals. He was an excellent statistician and had estimated that a libertine could easily corrupt 300 children a year; in 30 years it amounted to 9000. If only a quarter of the seduced boys imitated him, a very probable event, and counting a generation for every thirty years, then each libertine would see after two generations nine million products of his vice!

Juliette, who had had her incestuously conceived child killed by a famous abortionist, visited with Clairwil the poisoner and card-reader, Durand, who could only prophesy after she had seen the flowing blood of the passersby. She prophesied that Clairwil would not live more than five years longer and that Juliette would fall into much trouble the moment she stopped her wicked ways. After an hysteric fit of this bloodthirsty poisoner, Clairwil and Juliette were introduced into the mysteries of poisoning; many poisons were described and the exotic methods of their growing were explained.

So two years passed; Juliette was now entirely bestial

and found pleasure only in the strangest and most extraordinary pursuits. She was almost 22 years old. Saint Fond informed her in a secret conversation that he had conceived his masterpiece. He wanted to depopulate all France and let two-thirds of the inhabitants starve to death. This made even the hardened Juliette shrink back. Saint Fond noticed it and grew very angry. Juliette then received a letter from Noirceuil saying that Saint Fond was very angry with her because of her "relapse into virtue" and that he was thinking of doing away with her and that she should therefore flee from Paris at one. Head over heels she ran from the house of Saint Fond and bewailed: "O damnable virtue! Again for a moment you have deceived me! But no longer do I fear that I will ever again be found at the feet of your shameful altar. Virtue only destroys people. And the greatest misfortune that can happen to anyone in this wholly corrupt world is to desire to protect oneself from the general corruption!" She took her money, jewels and tribades to Angers where she opened a bordello in the style of Duvergier's. Soon all the nobles and high-bloods flocked to her place. The rich forty year old Count of Lorsange, who had a yearly income of 50,000 livres, married her after she had revealed her entire life with mock-holy tears. The Count then sought to ensure the new-found virtue of Juliette by a virtuous discourse that even moved the speaker to tears. But "this pretty little talk" did not have much effect upon Juliette. After she had endured for a time her married life, her "reason" warred with "prejudice and superstition." She sweetened the two monotonous years with her "harmless man" by secret vices, especially tribadic pleasures, until, at a mass she met Abbé Chabert, an early member of the "Society of the Friends of Crime." The old splendor returned again. There followed a continuous stream of festivals and orgies, Juliette found some time in between to give birth to a child so that "the property of the man might be assured." She then became frightened that Saint Fond was looking for her and determined to leave France; she poisoned her husband who died in the arms of the hypocritical Chabert and took over his income of 50,000 livres a year. Provided with many letters of introduction of the Abbé Juliette left for Italy and left her daughter with Chabert.

How well she felt in the home of Nero and Messalina! She did not want to become a mere tourist and so planned to travel everywhere as a "famous courtesan" and announced herself as such. She first came to Turin, the "most proper city of Italy;" the pious superstitious people who had little care for pleasures, naturally failed to please her. Immediately after her arrival she had Signora Diana, the most famous *appareilleuse* of the city, informed that a young and pretty French courtesan was "for hire." Princes, counts and marquis came running. For as the Duke of Chablais said: "The story of all French girls: form and skin are enchanting. There is nothing here like it." Juliette learned from a certain Sbrigani, a Molierian figure, the secrets of cheating at cards and then took fabulous sums from a count and marquis in a gambling den. Sbrigani accompanied her on her journey as her husband. They went next to Alexandria where they plundered a rich duke. They found the tribadic art most highly developed; they participated in a few such orgies at a convent. On the trip over the Apennines they became acquainted with a seven-foot-three-inch anthropophagic monster, by the name of Minski, who lived in a lonely fortified house on an island. The chairs in this house were made from human bones; the house itself was full of skeletons. The victims set aside for consumption were placed in cells in the subterranean cellars of the house. Minski came from the grandduchy of Moscow and had made many voyages "to study and imitate the vices and crimes of all the world." He had retired to live in a little island of a pond as the "hermit of the Apennines" in order to give his criminal desires free rein. He ate chiefly human flesh and ascribed his strength to this practice. He lay in wait for the travellers who were to be served on his table as roasts and ragoûts. Juliette, her servant and Sbrigani were also doomed to this fate. But first he did the honors and showed them about his well-populated harem and the cellars with their enormous treasures. Enchanted by the loveliness of Juliette he finally promised to let her live if she would never attempt flight. They next went to eat. Minski, an extreme alcoholist, drank 60 flasks of wine! They were served on a living table! A row of naked women, one pressed on top of another, with bent shoulders and immoveable positions, formed the "table" on which they were served. No tablecloth was necessary for these pretty *croupes satinées*. Nor napkins, for the fingers were dried by the waving hair of the women. The food was excellent. Juliette, after tasting a very succulent ragoût asked what it was. She did not know whether it was beef or veal, venison or bird, that made such a delightful dish. "It's your chambermaid," answered the monster with a lovely smile. The poor tribade and true companion of her mistress had been turned into a ragoût! This charming cannibal then showed his guests a menagerie of wild animals, had some women brought from his harem and thrown between the lions and tigers for their meal. But the greatest wonder was a machine that hanged, stabbed and decapitated 16 men all at one time! Everything was indeed very amusing and Minski promised them more surprises on the next day, but Juliette was a little mistrustful. Sbrigani also shared her fears, so they decided to flee. They mixed a little strammonium in the chocolate of the cannibal but only enough to drug him to sleep for "such a monster should not be killed." They robbed all the treasures from his chests and took along two women, Elise and Raymonde. So they finally reached Florence laden with gold and silver.

Here they put up a gambling house, connected with a bordello and a poison-den. Gold, indeed, they had enough, but it still gave them pleasure to see the world, learn the family secrets and to become acquainted with the morals and customs. Leopold, grandduke of Tuscany, and brother of Marie Antoinette, ruled Florence. Juliette and her companion were soon invited to an orgy given by the grandduke and his father-confessor in Pratolino. Leopold, "the grand successor of the first prostitute of France," diverted himself by the artificial abortion of women he had made pregnant. But he had something special to show his guests that day. He entertained Juliette with an especial performance of decapitation with musical accompaniment! The heads were cut off in accordance with the musical beat and *à la ritournelle!* Juliette observed that in Florence the men dressed like women and the women dressed like men and hence there was nowhere as much inclination for the same sex as there. The prostitutes lived in an especial quarter of the city. Titian's *Venus* in the Uffizi gave occasion for a lecture on the obscene representations in painting. There are mentioned the *Venus of Medici, Hermaphrodite,* and *Caligula Caressing His Sister.*

After our adventurers murdered another tribadic mother and sister they left for Rome. There they were richly received, soon became acquainted in the best circles, were admitted to all the palaces, and won the high favor of the tribadic Princess Olympia Borgia, Cardinals Albani and Bernis, and Duke of Grillo. They soon commenced the usual debaucheries with these new-found companions. Bernis composed in cynical self-irony an *Ode to Priapus*. Borgia poisoned her father and Juliette did the same to the Duchess of Grillo.

Both noticed how priests, monks, *abbés*, etc., slunk into a bordello. Then Borgia got the brilliant idea of setting fire to all the hospitals and charitable institutions in Rome. She wanted it performed by police-director Ghigi and Count Bracciani, the first physician of Europe. Ghigi would rather have the people hanged because he received the greatest sexual pleasure in that manner. Bracciani, that great physicist, killed a girl "by artificial lightning." Finally the 37 hospitals of Rome were set afire and more than 20,000 people perished. Olympia and Juliette watched and got the highest sexual enjoyment from it. The conflagration lasted eight days. At the following orgy in the house of Borgia there appeared as participants in the feast a eunuch, an hermaphrodite, a dwarf, a woman of eighty years, a little boy of four years, a great bulldog, an ape, and a cock! Bracciani took the last-named and Borgia wrung its neck at the moment of ejaculation. The old woman had naturally committed many sins in her long life and so she was condemned to death and was immediately burnt alive on a funeral pyre.

Juliette was then presented to Pope Pius VI, whom she addressed by his former name, Braschi, and delivered a bold lecture on the prejudices of the church and the immorality of the pope, which was received with great applause by Pope Pius VI, who was himself described as a horrible atheist and as a sexual monster. At times he indeed tried to interrupt her, but he was abashed by a: "Shut up, old ape!" At the end of her lecture he cried: "O, Juliette, I was indeed told the truth when they said you had spirit. But I did not expect so much. Such hyperbolic ideas are indeed rare in women." The Holy Father would naturally have liked to possess such a woman. Juliette placed the most unworthy conditions for such a surrender. She was then escorted about the Vatican and shown the garden, making cynical remarks all the time. The meeting ended with a very intimate scene that gave the pope the opportunity of developing his materialistic and blasphemous principles. The next time a great orgy was celebrated in St. Peter's Church. The pope himself celebrated some "black masses" and had some people killed at its conclusion. Juliette emigrated to the bedroom of the Holy Father and used the opportunity of a sexual debauch in one of the galleries to rob the pope. Thereupon she rode with recommendations to the royal family at Naples. On the way she was held up by the robbers of the notorious Brisa Testa, to whose castle she was brought and with her companion thrown into a dark dungeon. They heard the bloodthirsty wife of the chief robber declare that they would be murdered on the morrow. Juliette recognized the woman as her old friend Clairwil, a sister of Brisa Testa living with him in incest. Brisa Testa then told the long story of his life that had led him to England, Sweden, Russia, Siberia and Turkey. He described in detail the perverse inclinations and cruelties of Empress Catherine II who gave herself up to tribadic pleasures in the winter palace, the knout being stoutly applied. After diverse enjoyments at the robbers' Juliette left with Clairwil for Naples. She was received by King Ferdinand in Naples; Juliette gave him, too, a lecture on the Kingdom of Naples and its affairs, on the moral depravity of the populace, the "half-Spanish nation," and spiced her discourse with severe attacks on his sister-in-law, Marie Antoinette. Queen Charlotte of Naples was a lusty tribade whose *charmes d'après nature* Juliette learned at the first meeting;

there followed a tribadic scene between the two and the *godmiché* as well as *defæcatio in os* played important parts. Ferdinand was a confirmed necrophile. He delighted practicing pædicatio on a page whom he had strangled. The splendid surroundings of Naples, also recalling the horrors of Nero, were profaned by orgies on Cap Misenum, Puzzoli, in the ruins of the Procida, on Ischia and Niceta. In the temple of Venus at Baiae, Clairwil, Juliette and Olympia gave themselves to fishermen, and then returned to more respectable pleasures at the house of Prince of Francaville, a confirmed pederast. He organized a luxurious festival in the garden where the splendid pavilions, kiosks, stimulating activity, mass-flagellation, and automatically working phallus-machines enflamed the senses. At a visit in the museum at Portici our travellers saw a painting depicting a satyr in the act of intercourse with a goat, a practice, according to King Ferdinand, much in vogue in Italy. The ruins of Herculanus and Pompeii served as abodes of vice. Vespoli, the father confessor of the king and guide for his orgies, had erected a house for secret executions and tortures in Salerno. He found his chief pleasure in crucification and intercourse with lunatics! In Paestum the three tribades lived at a virtuous widow's with three young and innocent girls. Naturally all were overpowered and killed after they had been abused.

They next visited Sorrento, Castellamare and the Blue Grotto. On Capri they found that the practices of its former resident, Emperor Tiberius, were still being imitated. They returned to Naples in time to see a great folk-festival at which 400 persons were killed. Charlotte and Juliette formed a plot against the king; the following contract was drawn up by the queen: "I will rob all valuables from my husband and give them to the person who provides me with the poison necessary to transport my husband to another world." The contract was sealed by a tribadic scene. The unsuspicious king pleased Juliette by two especially strange performances. He had two women bound to iron plates, and one was pounded upon the other with such great force that both bodies were squashed to pieces. But the most noteworthy was the *Theatre of Horrors* whose performances were of an unusual kind. Executions and again executions! That was the steady program for the productions. Each guest had his own loge in which hung seven pictures showing the seven different kinds of executions: fire, beating, gallows, wheel, impalement, decapitation, dismemberment. There were also in each loge 50 portraits of men, women and children. For each portrait and kind of execution there was an apparatus which was set in motion by the machinist in response to a press on the proper button by the guest. One bell denoted the appearance on the stage of the victim. The second bell announced the execution, performed by four executioners, as "naked and pretty as Mars." The guests tried to form all sorts of amusing combinations, and at one "performance" 1176 persons were executed. This spectacle inspired Juliette and Clairwil to an especially piquant crime. They agreed to destroy their true companion, Olympia Borgia. At an excursion which brought them to the top of Mt. Vesuvius, they seized the unsuspecting Olympia, undressed her and threw her into the crater; resulting in an intense sexual excitement that brought them to a tribadic orgy. There then followed an eruption of Vesuvius! "Ah," Juliette cynically cried, "Olympia wants her clothes!" and she threw them after her, first having removed all the valuables. Meanwhile Queen Charlotte brought all the millions of Ferdinand to Juliette and wanted to flee to France after the murder of the king. But Juliette denounced her to Ferdinand who had her imprisoned; Juliette meanwhile fleeing with all the treasure.

Clairwil and Juliette again met the poisoner, Durand, who hated Clairwil and finally convinced Juliette to poison her because she knew that Clairwil was plotting against her (Juliette's) life. After the murder Durand said coldbloodedly: "I lied to you. She was not thinking of murdering you. But her time was up. She had to die." They next came to a church where a merchant, Cordelli, was abusing the corpse of his own daughter. This blood-thirsty monster owned a castle by the sea from which he threw his victims into the ocean or placed them in a snake-box to be eaten by the snake. But his pleasures could no longer be possible. Durand and Juliette poisoned him and his companions and availed themselves of his great fortune. They rode to Venice where as we have previously fully described they opened another bordello in the style of Madame Gourdan. Again the usual round of debaucheries commenced. Poisoning, prophesying and prostituting; Juliette and Durand tried to outdo themselves in vice and crime.

But finally their splendor came to an end. The bordello was suspended; the properties of Juliette and Durand were confiscated. Juliette went to Lyons and informed Noirceuil of her proposed return to Paris. The Abbé Chabert informed Juliette that he was bringing her seven-year-old daughter to Paris so that she could be brought up as a "law breaker." The joys of reunion with Noirceuil were very great. He gave one of his usual long discourses and told Juliette that he was now a thousand times worse than when she had left him. They then celebrated their reunion with a murder. Juliette fixed up a bordello for men and women in Paris; six pimpesses selected, assorted and parceled the wares. Juliette and Noirceuil tried to outdo

Emperor Nero and Empress Theodora in debaucheries. Noirceuil then married in a church with regular prayers, blessings and witnesses his two sons, Juliette, her daughter, and a girl Fontanges seduced by her. The joys of this happy family did not last long. At an orgy, honored by the presence of the executioners Desrues and Cartouche, the sons of Noirceuil and Mademoiselle Fontanges were murdered amid horrible tortures. Juliette's daughter was thrown into the fire!

Here Juliette ended her story before the amazed hearers, after she had added that she had poisoned all the brooks and springs in the village where Noirceuil's home was situated and where she was reunited to Justine. Many peasants had, of course, died with horrible torments. Juliette closed her long report with a glowing apotheosis of vice:

> This is the fortunate position you see me in now, my friends! I understand and love crime passionately. This alone charms my senses and I will follow its principles until the last day of my life. Free from every religious fear, above the law because of my secrets and my wealth, I would like to see the divine or human power that can stand in the way of my desires. The past tires me. The present electrifies me. I fear the future very little and only hope that in the rest of my life I can surpass the debaucheries of my youth. For nature has created man to enjoy himself with all the possible amusements in this world. That is her highest law and will always be mine. So much the worse for the victims that must be provided. Every thing would collapse in the universe without the law of balance of power. Only through frivolities can nature regain her rights torn from her by virtue. We thus set things aright by compensating with evil. O, my friends, convince yourself of this fundamental principle from whose development all sources of human fortune spring.

Justine had cried more than once during this long story. Not so the Chevalier and the Marquis. At the return of Noirceuil and Chabert the sacrifice of this "incorruptible and perfect virtue" was determined. At the last moment Noirceuil decided on a sign of fate for there was a heavy storm brewing. Justine was brought into the open. And lo! she was immediately struck by lightning. The joy of the companions of vice was great. Nature had spoken. Vice was the only joy of man. As they still practiced their atrocities on the corpse of the unfortunate Justine, Durand suddenly appeared again. She had rescued a great part of the money confiscated in Venice. At the end Noirceuil was named minister, Chabert became an archbishop, the Marquis became an ambassador to Constantinople and the Chevalier received an income of 400,000 livres. Juliette and Durand followed their beloved Noirceuil to new splendors; after ten more years of remarkable successes in vice Juliette died.

"Whoever writes my history," she cried, "should title it: *The Fortunes of Vice!*"

Philosophy in the Boudoir

Philosophy in the Boudoir appeared for the first time in 1795 as a "posthumous work by the author of *Justine*" in two volumes with five pictures and for the second time in 1805 in two volumes with ten pictures and appeared frequently thereafter.

The book is an imitation of the *Education of Laura* by Mirabeau and the *Luisea Sigea* of Nicholas Chorier. The main theme, the rearing of a girl in vice, is told in the form of dialogues and long, instructive lectures, which from time to time are interrupted by practical applications of the philosophical principles of vice.

The preface is characteristic of the book: "Libertines of all ages and sexes! Only to you do I dedicate this work; feed on those principles which feed your passions. These passions, from which cold and weak moralists shrink back in fear, are only the means of nature in allowing men to come closer to her and recognize her purposes. Listen only to this joyous passion, its organ is the only one that can bring you good fortune.

"Lascivious women, whose model might well be the sensuous Madame St. Ange, follow her example and despise everything that brings you into opposition with the divine laws of pleasure and that stand in your way of a joyous life.

"Dear girls kept at home by ludicrous tenets of virtue, superstitious parents and mere circumstances, step on anything that prevents you from enjoying your bloom of youth. Allow no one to prevent you from seeing that every maiden wish of yours be fulfilled.

"And you dear libertines who know no reins but those which give free vent to your desires, know no other laws than your fancies; may the cynic Dolmance serve as a model for you! Go as far as he; so that when you have reached the end of your journey through a joyful land strewn with flowers and fruit you can look back and feel certain that this is the only purpose of life, the only reason nature, in her very prolificness, intended you to serve. Then will you cry indeed that this is the only way to pluck roses from the thorns of life."

We summarize very succinctly the main points. In the first dialogue appeared Madame St. Ange and her brother, Chevalier de Mirvel. The former was the Juliette type that poisoned everything it came into contact with. Her brother was more receptive and was pushed in the rear by the more powerful individuality of Dolmance. He was a perfect cynic who always ruled the entire situation with his brilliant and spirited sophistry. According to Mirvel's description he became hard through his early start in the path of vice and instead of a human heart had only animal passions. He was a pederast and never ceased to revel in it.

Eugenie de Mistival was a young girl whose mother was a bigot and whose father had an affair with Madame de St. Ange. The latter had already given her a theoretical discussion in vice, had thrown out all her ideas of religion and pure morals and so ensnared her that Eugenie trusted everything to her. So today—the whole plot takes place in one day—she was to be initiated into the mysteries of the service of Venus and sodomy. Eugenie came and betrayed her true nature by a confession that she hated her mother, the old bigot. Dolmance then appeared and instructed Eugenie, who at the beginning blushingly pretended modesty, in the anatomy and physiology of the male and female privates, not omitting practical demonstrations. She learned the arts of *amour physique et antiphysique*. She was later given Chevalier, the gardener-boy and an idiot so that she might learn the different kinds of obscene groups. Towards evening as Eugenie had turned herself into the most horrible erotic monster, her mother, Madame de Mistival, opportunely arrived. Under the eyes of the triumphant daughter she was overpowered and received a dose of syphilis from a servant, Lapierre; before they sat down to eat Eugenie had to consummate the infibulation.

This is the action of the play. More than three-fourths of the book is taken up by instructive excursions.

Other Works of Marquis de Sade

Justine, Juliette and the *Philosophy in the Boudoir* are the works to which Marquis de Sade owes his herostratic fame. All the others of his numerous works are milder imitations of the above-named. It is for this reason that Marciat named the class of erotic pleasures that the Marquis delighted in as *sadism*.

Aline and Valcour, a philosophic novel written in the Bastille and during the Revolution, first appeared in 1793 in four volumes and again in 1795. Girouard was entrusted with the printing of this work in 1792 by de Sade. But the printer became embarrassed in a royalist conspiracy, was condemned and guillotined. Meanwhile the novel was secretly printed and appeared in 1793 under the firm name of Madame Girouard. It found few buyers. In 1795 the title was changed. In the same year the bookseller, Maradan, procured the remaining copies, changed only the title and frontispiece. It is undoubtedly an original of *Justine* and *Juliette* for it described almost the same characters. Valcour, a virtuous young man, loved Aline, the noble daughter of the noble wife of the cruel and degenerate President de Blamont. The latter wanted to marry his daughter to the old libertine Dolbourg since he had earlier given to this old friend as a mistress, the virtuous Sophie whom he acknowledged as his daughter. When the marriage was to go through he wanted to give his wife also to Dolbourg and to receive in exchange Dolbourg's daughter and wife. The plan failed. Aline killed herself. Madame de Blamont was poisoned by order of her husband. Valcour entered a monastery, Dolbourg became virtuous and the president had to flee. Two degenerate females were pictured in Rosa and Leonore. Leonore, who everywhere found fortune, was evidently a counterpart to Juliette. The work is also rich in descriptions of other personalities. Until the poisoning and some flagellation scenes there are no descriptions of cruelty.

Quérard thinks that the author described himself as Valcour and at times told some of his own experiences.

The *Crimes of Love* (Paris, 1800) is a collection of romantic tales, as *Juliette and Raunai, Clarisse, Laurence and Antonio, Eugene de Franval*, etc., in which the struggle between vice and virtue is described. Virtue usually conquers.

As a preface to *Crimes of Love* de Sade wrote *Ideas on the Novel*, a survey of the novel in the eighteenth century, introduced by an historical sketch of the development of the novel, which he defined as "a painting of the morals of the century, that has to compensate history in a certain sense. Only a keen observer of human nature can write a good novel. This keen observation can be derived only from misfortunes or travels." At the end he called unjustified the attacks on the cynical expressions in *Aline and Valcour*. Vice in order to be shunned must be shown. The most dangerous works are those that beautify and describe vice in brilliant colors. It must be shown in its entire nudeness so that its true nature can be recognized.

We finally mention the pamphlet that brought the displeasure of Napoleon on de Sade. *Zoloé and Her Two Acolytes* appeared in Paris in 1800. Zoloé is Josephine de Beauharnais, the wife of Napoleon. She was described as a lascivious, avaricious American. Her friend Laureda (Madame Tallien) a Spaniard, was "all fire and all love," very rich and hence could satisfy all her perverse desires. She and Volsange (Madame Visconti) took part with Zoloé in an orgy of libertines. Among the latter one recognized Bonaparte in the Baron d'Orsec and Barras in the Viscomte de Sabar. One word is sufficient to discover the author. That is the word "virtue." He wrote in *Zoloé*: "You have to remember that we are speaking as historians. It is not our fault if your pictures are painted in the colors of immorality, perfidy and intrigue. We have painted people of an age that is past. May this age produce better ones and give to our brush the charms of virtue!"

Of the comedies of Marquis de Sade only *Oxtiern or the Misfortunes of Libertinage,* praising the joys of crime, and *Julia, or Marriage Without Women,* an idealization of pederasty, are worthy of mention.

Character of the Works of Marquis de Sade

Whoever wants to note the results of a complete preoccupation with the purely sexual functions and pursuits of man can find them in the works of Marquis de Sade. This can readily be assumed from the analyses that we have given of *Justine* and *Juliette*. But de Sade went further: he made cold and naked crime the climax and dénouement of the action of his works. This union of sex and crime and destructive processes of all kinds must have had the most fearful effects since it was varied a thousand times by an unequalled imagination. Janin recognizes that "de Sade possessed the most indefatigable imagination that has perhaps ever terrified the world." A mind that could have conceived such a gigantic work of pornography in ten volumes demanded a painstaking genius and an experience that had to cover every walk of life and every phase of the human mind. And yet the Marquis de Sade was great enough to transcend this; for he always interrupted the action or broke up an orgy with long philosophic discussions and dialogues, often more horrible in their effects than the actions he preached.

Finally to complete the terrifying picture, all the truly monstrous assertions and convictions, all the products of a hyperbolic phantasy of erotica, were given by specific incidents and characters. Minski, drinking 60 flasks of wine at one time (Juliette III, 332); the carmelite monk, Claude, with three testicles (Juliette III, 77); the theatre of horrors at Naples where 1176 people were killed at one time (Juliette VI, 22-26), etc., etc., etc.

The works of Marquis de Sade are extremely important and instructive for the history and culture of the human race. Yet they are still repugnant and repulsive and repellent to any person save the most degenerate libertine; and at that I believe it would be difficult to find such an absolutely corrupt person that he would not shudder at some episode or person in *Justine* or *Juliette*. The effect of the original to a casual reader is one of immediate horror. Napoleon had all the copies of Marquis de Sade's works that he could find burned in an immense pyre. It was not, in his opinion "fit for any human being to read." In fact the obscene pictures accompanying the text were less potent than the writing itself. In later times his works were indeed given the generic title *Opus Sadicum*.

The Philosophy of Marquis de Sade

Marquis de Sade was the first and only philosopher of vice. But his importance goes deeper than that. His works analyzed carefully everything in life that is related to sexual instincts which, as Marquis de Sade has shown with unmistakable clearness, influences in some manner or other almost all human affairs. "Love and hunger" do not equally "rule the world" for love is much more important and domineering in its rule.

The gross physical debaucheries and atrocious cruelties are covered with a resplendent mental veil because of the systematic exposition of the philosophic principles in all fields of vice. Its justification by logical method as well as by precepts and examples only makes vice more horrible in effect, both for degenerate and normal beings. Delbène, for example, recognized "sensations must not only be experienced but also exhaustively analyzed. It is at times just as sweet to speak of them as to enjoy them. And when one can no longer enjoy them it is divine to speak of them" (Juliette I, 105). Jerome said that the orgies in Sicily were interrupted only by philosophic discussions and that new cruelties were not attempted until they had been thoroughly "legitimized" (Juliette III, 45).

All the observations of de Sade were derived, as expected, from his materialism. He deified nature, which was for him the principle of the good in opposition to her enemy, virtue. The universe was moved by its own power and the eternal laws inherent in nature were sufficient to bring forth and explain everything that we saw without dragging in a "first cause." Why is a motor necessary for an object that is always in motion? The universe is a collection of diverse beings that alternately and successively act and react with one another. There are no boundaries. There is everywhere a continuous change from one state to another in relation to the individual essence which takes on, one after another, new forms (Juliette I, 72, ff.).

The movement and impact of molecules explain all

physical and mental phenomena. Hence the soul, as an "active, thinking" principle must be material. As an active principal it is divisible. For "the heart still beats after it is taken from the body." All divisible things are matter. Matter is further overcome by "dangers" (*periclité*). The "spirit" cannot be endangered. But the soul follows the impressions of the body, is weak in youth, depressed in old age, is overcome by all dangers of the body, and hence matter (Juliette I, 86). Bressac gave an easier proof. As the body of the dead wife of Count Gernande made its last convulsive movement he cried out delightedly: "You see! Matter needs no soul for its movement!" (Justine IV, 40).

The immortality of the soul is hence a chimera. This nonsensical dogma had made men fools, hypocrites and liars. There is only left virtue to which immortality is not ascribed. Juliette asked Delbène of immortality. "Have courage, believe in the universal law, resign yourself to the thought that you will return to the womb of nature and be reborn in another form. An eternal laurel grows on the grave of Virgil, and it is better to be entirely destroyed for ever than to burn in the so-called hell." "But," asked Juliette anxiously, "what will become of me? This eternal destruction frightens me, this darkness makes me tremble." "What were you before your birth? You will again return to the same. Did you enjoy anything then? No. But did you suffer? No. What being would not sacrifice all pleasure for the certainty that he would never suffer pain again!" (Juliette I, 83-85).

These doctrines of the soul are not the only possible ones for materialists. Durand, e.g., asserted that the soul was a fire that was extinguished after death and permitted its content to pass over into the world of matter (Juliette III, 247). Saint Fond constructed the world from *molécules malfaisantes.* Hence he only saw wickedness in the universe, evil, disorder and crime. Evil existed before the creation of the world and will exist after it. Virtue hence suffers great torments. Actually Saint Fond believed in a beyond, punishment and rewards. In order to prevent his victims from reaching heaven he concluded a bargain with them and had them sign their soul to the devil with their own blood on a piece of paper, which was sealed in a pederastic fashion; the victim was thereafter horribly tortured to death (Juliette II, 287, 341).

Following Holbach's methods, who characterized every religious impulse as a mental insanity, de Sade never tired of ridiculing the concepts of God and religion. His atheism was clothed in "a fanatic misotheism: 'if there isn't a God, I'll invent one' for the sole purpose of mocking and deriding the invented God." The idea of such a chimera and the erection of such a monster is the only injustice that Delbène cannot forgive mankind. "My blood boils at His very name. I think I see around me all the trembling shadows of the poor unfortunates whom this horrible superstition has sacrificed." Delbène then delivered a critique of the different theories of God. The Jews indeed spoke of a God but they did not explain this concept and spoke of him only in childish allegories. The Bible was written long after Moses by different people and "stupid charlatans." Moses asserted that he received the Commandments directly from God, Himself. Was not this preference for a God, Delbène declared, by a petty, ignorant people ridiculous? The miracles in the Bible were not reported by any historian. And how this God treated "the chosen people!" Scattered all over the world and hated by all the world. God need not be sought among the Jews. But perhaps among the Christians? And Delbène found even greater absurdities here. Jesus is even worse than Moses. The latter had God perform the miracles. The former made them himself! The religion proved the prophet and the prophet proved the religion.

Since the existence of a God cannot be proven by either Christianity or Judaism, we must fall back on our own reason. But this in both man and animal is the result of the coarsest mechanisms. If one tries to recall a thing as an absent object then memory becomes a reminder. If one tries to recall it, without being told of its absence, he sees it as an actually present object as the result of phantasy, the true cause of all our errors. The imagination consists of "objective ideas," which do not show us reality, and the memory consists of "real ideas," which actually show us existing things. God is the product of the imagination, the "stupid chimera" of a "debilitated imagination" which belongs only to an idea objective without real existence. God is a "vampire" who sucks the blood of men (Juliette I, 49-62). In actuality God does not exist since the eternally working nature finds herself in perpetual motion from her own power and not received from the creator as a present. For then one would have to believe in the existence of an indolent being who after he had made his gift went back to sleep. Such a being is ridiculous on account of its superfluity (Philosophy in the Boudoir I, 56).

And what a monster is this God! He drowned, murdered, tortured, harassed and did more damage to His people than any dozen Satans could ever dream of. His chief torment was His creation of a religion and a traveling salesman sent to earth amid a fanfare of angels and some thunder-bolts. But nay! He was conceived by a sinful Jewess in a stall! Let us follow him and see what he does and hear what he says! What divine mission did he fulfill? What secrets did he reveal?

We see first of all an obscure childhood, some work he

did for the Jewish priests of the temple of Jerusalem, then a fifteen year disappearance, during which time he imbibed the virus of the Egyptian cult, which he brought to Judea. He went so far as to reveal himself as the Son of God, and equal to His father in power: He created at the same time a third being, the Holy Ghost, and tried to make us believe that these three persons were not three persons but really only one! He said He took on a human form so that He could save us. This sublime ghost had to become matter and flesh to set the world ablaze with his miracles. He changed water into wine at an evening meal for some drunken men. He deludes some fools into thinking He knows the secrets of life. One of His companions plays dead for Him so that he can be "brought back to life." He climbs a mountain with two or three of His friends and performs some awkward legerdemain of which a thousand jugglers of today would be ashamed. He damns all who will not believe in Him and promises the kingdom of heaven to His believers. He left no written work, spoke little and did less. Yet He drew many by his rebellious talk and was finally crucified. In His last moments He promises his believers to appear as often as they call upon Him so that he might be eaten by them. He lets Himself be executed without His dear papa exerting the slightest effort to save Him from such an ignoble death. His followers gathered and cried that humanity would be lost unless they saved appearances by some trickery. Let us drug the watchmen, steal the corpse and announce His resurrection! This is a sure way of making people believe in a miracle. Then it will aid us in spreading this new theory. The trick succeeded. All idiots, women and children go gadding about this miracle and hence no one in the city will believe in this God. Not a man lets himself be converted. The life of Jesus is publicly advertised. This empty fairytale finds people who believe it true. His apostles put words into the mouth of their self-created redeemer which He had never dreamt of. Some exaggerated maxims are made the basis of their morals and since this was announced to all the beggars, love of neighbors and charity were made the first virtues. Diverse bizarre ceremonies were introduced under the name "sacraments," one of the most foolish of which is the changing of a piece of bread into the body of Jesus by a few words from a sinful priest (Philosophy in the Boudoir I, 60-64). It is hence not surprising that one frequently encounters the statements by the Marquis that he considers the defamations of the priests and religion to be a moral obligation. The discovery of new insults and curses takes up a good bit of the time of his characters. Dolmance becomes very angry that there is no God for he often wants to insult this *dégoûtante chimère* and at such times desires his existence (Philosophy in the Boudoir I, 125-126).

From these theoretical maxims Marquis de Sade succeeded in arriving at a practical philosophy of life, his "philosophy of vice."

To realize the triumph of vice in human society there must be a suitable pedagogy at hand. Marquis de Sade rightly recognized that the corruption of the youth meant the general downfall of morality. So from the pattern of Mirabeau's *Education of Laura* he wrote the *Philosophy in the Boudoir* as a manual for the education in vice; he developed in it the theoretical principles and practical applications for the seduction and demoralization of a young girl. The education bans all nonsensical religious theories which tire out the "young organs" of the children and substitutes in its place instruction in the "social principles." They are also to be instructed in the difficult science of nature. If any one tries to smuggle in some childish religious fancies, he is to be treated as a criminal (Philosophy of the Boudoir II, 62 ff.). Marquis de Sade correctly saw that custom and habit were everything in education. Hence vice should be made an integral part of the customs and habits of the young people. "So be evil as often as possible! Then vice will gradually assume tremendous pleasurable proportions which cannot be dispensed with. Vice must become a virtue! And virtue a vice! Then there will be a new universe before your eyes, a consuming, passionate fire will heat your veins; it will become the 'electrical activity' that is the principle of life. Every day you will enfold new ruthless plans and see in all parts and in all ways the victims of your perverse feelings. Thus you will reach the rose-covered path that leads to the final goal, the last excesses of unnaturalness. You must never stop, hesitate and rest upon this path for then the highest pleasure will be forever lost to you. Above all, look out for that hydra, religion, whose dangerous whisperings will try to turn you from the good path." Delbène addressed these words to the fourteen-year-old Juliette (Juliette I, 27-30). The same advice was imparted later to the daughter of Saint Fond, her own daughter and Mademoiselle Fontanges. Its effects have already been given in the statistics of Count Belmor.

So vice is systematically introduced into all the social relations; we mention only the most important.

Love and marriage are chimerical concepts for de Sade. With a jesuist casuistry Duvergier distinguished the two kinds of love, the moral and the physical. A woman can morally regard her beloved or husband and love physically and temporarily whoever sets his foot in her garden. Besides the temperament of women demands many lovers (Juliette I, 286). Delbène, that great pedagogue of vice, delivered a long speech on the uselessness of morals for young girls and women. She asked astonishedly in the beginning: is a woman better or worse if a certain part of her body is more or less *ouverte?* According to her, morals must guarantee individual fortune. Otherwise they are worthless. Hence a maiden need not be forced to protect her virginity, if things go well and she burns to lose it. Indeed the more a girl gives herself the more she is to be loved and honored for making so many men fortunate. Hence one should not despise deflowered girls (Juliette I, 108).

As for marriage the question is not whether adultery is a crime in the eyes of the Laplanders who allow it, or of the French who forbid it, but whether humanity or nature is injured by such actions. Coition is as necessary as drink and food. Modesty is only a *conventionnelle mode* whose first origin was as a *raffinement du libertinage*. Now it is only a virtue of "dolts, bigots and idiots." It injures the health because it restrains important secretions. The "horrible results of sexual abstinence" have been described by many authors and especially by the author of *The English Spy* (London, 1784, p. 409-456). The communal possession of women is the only true law of nature and not monogamy, polyandry or polygamy. Since marriage is a subjective concept, independent of others, adultery by the wife does not infringe upon the honor of the husband. Delbène therefore gave many methods of how wives may best fool their husbands (Juliette I, 109-131).

The position of prostitution in society can easily be imagined from the foregoing tenets. Only a woman who has made companions and men happy with her embraces lives in the memory of mankind. Lucretia was very soon forgotten while Theodora and Messalina were sung of in thousands of poems. Shall women be ascetic and live coldbloodedly and unsung or shall she not rather walk the way of fire and blood and passion and satisfy her every desire?

The great influence of the doctrines of race conservation, leading to the theories of Malthus, may perhaps be under-estimated today but in the eighteenth century it was like the Gospel in the middle ages.

To wars, diseases, famines, murders, "acts of God," etc., were added all possible methods of prevention of birth as an additional aid to nature. The spilling of the seed is no crime but a praiseworthy act; for it combines two useful objects, the creation of pleasure and the prevention of the increase of mankind. Less and better people than an influx of stupid masses! It was a natural result of the aristocratic system that limited the number of children mainly for the reason that they could pass on their great fortunes intact into one hand. Thus besides "moral restraint" Marquis de Sade lauded all the preventive means that satisfy pleasure yet prevent conception.

The most decided Malthusian was Saint Fond. He declared that France needed "blood let out of all her veins if she wanted to live." The artists and philosophers must be ejected, the hospitals and other institutions of mercy must be destroyed, and wars and famines must be brought about. At least two-thirds of the population must vanish (Juliette III, 126, 261). Such an attempt was made by Borgia in Rome. Thirty-seven hospitals were destroyed and 20,000 persons burnt to death (Juliette IV, 258). In *Justine* the bishop developed a system of practical Malthusianism. Firstly, all children were to be murdered. Secondly, there were to be periodic visits of the villages by the soldiers and all superfluous members of the family were to be killed. Thirdly, the freedom won by the Revolution must be again taken from the people, so that hunger, disease, etc., would return. Fourthly, a total suppression of all charitable institutions. Lastly, all celibates, pederasts, tribades, masturbators, murderers, poisoners and suicides were to be held in the greatest esteem and honor (Justine IV, 280-293).

Malthus' *Essay on the Principle of Population* first appeared in 1798 but his ideas on the danger of over-population were preceded, as we have seen, not only by Marquis de Sade but by other French philosophers such as Quesnay and Mirabeau. Indeed Oliver Goldsmith in his *Vicar of Wakefield* (1766) showed how great was the preoccupation of the people of the eighteenth century with this problem.

Marquis de Sade developed in many books his theories of crime which were closely connected with his Malthusian ideas. They were very systematically given in the *Philosophy in the Boudoir*, which he had Dolmance read from a brochure bought in the Palais Royal. In *Justine* Bressac declared that crime was a chimera. For murder only changed the form of matter and did not destroy it. Nothing was lost in nature. Hence there could be no crime (Justine I, 209 ff). Delbène gave a different exposition on the necessity of crime. Nature made men differently and gave them different fates. Hence one was fortunate, another unfortunate. The latter were subdued and tortured by the former. Hence crime was a part of the "plan of nature" and was as necessary to her as war, famine and disease (Juliette I, 176).

In the *Philosophy in the Boudoir* crime was analysed with the *flambeau de la philosophie*. There were four general classes of crimes: defamation, robbery, murder and immoral offences.

Defamation is either against an evil or good man. In the first case it does not matter much if one says more or less bad things about him. It does not harm a virtuous man and the poison of the defamer returns to himself. Defamation serves as a purgative and compensatory method. For it places virtue in its right light. For the victim must be in the position to disprove the defamation and hence his virtuous actions become well-known. But a defamer is not dangerous to society. For he serves to place the vice of evil men as well as the good of honorable men into general knowledge and hence should not be punished (Philosophy in the Boudoir II, 78-81).

Robbery was allowed at all times and was indeed praised as in Sparta. Other races considered it a martial virtue. It is certain that it provides strength, courage, dexterity, etc., all notable virtues for a republic. There have even been societies in which the victim was punished for not watching his property any better! It is unjust to sanction possession by a law for then all doors are open to the criminals who are reduced by this knowledge. It is indeed fairer to punish the victim than the thief (Philosophy in the Boudoir II, 81-84). According to Dorval, that great thief and theoretician of his profession, power is the first root of thievery. The stronger steal from the weaker. Nature desires it this way. Laws against thievery are invalid works of men. Man now steals legally. Justice steals when it is paid for its decisions, a service that should be free. The priest steals when he is paid for being a pander between God and man. Dorval enumerated the thefts of all the professions and then gives a history of robbery in all lands concluding with the statement that at the end of the rule of Louis XIV, the people paid 750 millions a year as taxes and only 250 millions went into the state treasury. Hence 500 millions were stolen (Juliette I, 203-222).

Moral crimes must also be regarded indifferently by a

republic for it does not matter whether the person is modest or not.

Modesty is a product of civilization, principally due to the coquettry of women. Clothing, for example, which serves more to excite the curiosity than to protect from the weather. The care and development of clothing reveals the fact that women feared that men would take no notice of them if they were naked. Prostitution is the natural result of moral laws. It is hence viewed as a disgrace because the prostitutes take gifts for the pleasures they both give and receive. For marriage is also prostitution. For a man can get a wife only in most cases when he has a good position. Just as we give the right to pleasure to men so in a republic there can be no double standards and women must be given the same right. The results of such double freedom, children without fathers, are not injurious for all men have a common mother, the "fatherland"! The right of pleasure must be given to the girl from the tenderest age. Indeed the pleasures of love serve to beautify women.

Adultery is a virtue. There is nothing that is so opposite to nature as the "eternality" of the marriage bond. The adulterer is the champion of nature. Many ethnological examples are given to show the usefulness of adultery.

Incest is also a virtue! It serves freedom and strengthens the family love. Incestuous relations are found in all times and places. Again many examples are produced to show that incest bred strong races and was generally beneficial. This custom must be made a law because it has "fraternity" as a basis. But "sorority," too, must not be forgotten. Women have as much right as men.

Rape is also no crime and is less harmful than robbery. For the latter robs property irreparably and the former uses and returns the property. And besides it had to be done sometime or other, with or without the sanction of the church.

To punish pederasty is a barbarity for no "abnormity of taste" can be a crime. Just as little is tribadism a crime. Both practices are highly regarded by the aged. Marital people indeed highly praised them because they enhanced courage and bravery (Philosophy in the Boudoir II, 84-114).

Finally the fourth class, murder. There are two ways to view it, by natural and political law. From the standpoint of nature murder is no crime. There is no difference to nature between men, plants and animals. Man is born, grows, multiplies, dies and returns to the soil as all the other creatures of nature. It is just as great a crime to kill an animal. It is only our vanity that finds a distinction. Of what value can a creature be if its creation cost nature no trouble at all? The creative material of nature proceeds from the decomposition of other bodies. Destruction is a law of nature; but it is merely a change of form, the transition from one existence to another—the metapsychosis of Pythagoras. Therefore murder is no crime since a change is not destruction. As soon as an animal ceases to live other small animals are formed from it. Therefore it is logical to assert that we help the purposes of nature by assisting in the change of forms. It is due to natural impulses that one man kills another just like famine, disease and primal events. Nature has given us hatred, vengeance and war. Therefore murder is no crime against nature.

It is also a great factor in politics. France became free by murder. What is war? A science of destruction. It is strange that men teach the art of war openly, reward those who kill their enemies yet damn murder as a crime.

From the social standpoint murder is also no crime.

What matters a single member to society? The death of a man has no influence upon the entire population. Even if three-fourths of the people die out, there would be no change in the circumstances of the survivors.

How must murder be considered in a martial and republican state? A nation that has thrown off the tryant's yoke to become a republic can maintain itself only by crime. All intellectual ideas in a republic are subjugated under the "physics of nature" and so the freest people give themselves most gladly to murder. De Sade here gave many examples. For example, in China the undesirable children are thrown into the sea and the famous traveller, Duhalde, estimated that the daily toll of victims was more than 30,000! Is it not wiser for a republic to stem the number of its citizens? In a monarchy population must be encouraged since the tyrants can become rich only by the number of inhabitants. Revolutions are only the results of overpopulation.

These ideas of Marquis de Sade did not spring from the brain of a madman. Very similar ideas were developed by the great terrorists of the first French revolution. The justification for crime and murder was a natural trend of the time. It is notable that in his pre-revolutionary work *Aline and Valcour* little or no importance was given to robbery and murder and that he took them both in his system of sexual theories during and after the Revolution.

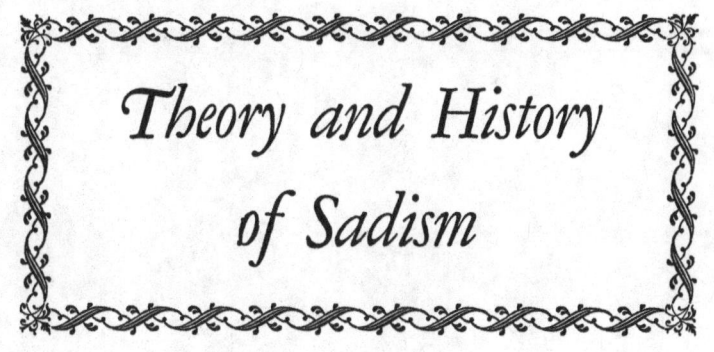

Introduction

According to the Marquis de Sade there is no more immediate relation than that between passion and cruelty. Passion extinguishes sympathy in man and makes the heart cold and hard. (Juliette I, 248). At the same time stronger and stronger charms are necessary to satisfy the growing passion. The nerves need stronger impulses to be awakened and thrilled. It is undoubtedly true that pain excites the nerves more than joy and hence awakens a more lively thrill. The pain of others causes an extraordinary excitation in the libertine. Nature never speaks to us about others but only about ourselves. There is nothing more egotistic than her voice. She praises the search for pleasure and is indifferent if one or the other is agreeable.

This feeling of pleasure from cruelty is inherent in human beings. The child breaks his toy, bites the breast of his wet nurse, strangles the bird, etc. Cruelty is not a result of degeneration since it is found especially among primitive races, but, rather the energy of man which civilization has not destroyed and hence more a virtue than a vice.

The cruelty of women is much more intensive than that of man, a result of their greater energy and greater sensitivity of their organs. Their heated imagination makes them furious and criminal. Would you learn about them? Tell them of a horrible spectacle, a duel, an execution, a fire, a slaughter, murder, disease and death, etc., and see how they flock to the scene. Further proofs for the passionate cruelty of women are given by their preference for poisoning and flagellation.

Our nervous system is so wonderfully formed that convulsions, fits and bloodsheds excite us and consequently are pleasant. This is even felt by persons who fall into swoons at the sight of blood, their own or somebody else's. It is indeed declared that a swoon is the highest power of passion (Philosophy in the Boudoir I, 148-158, Juliette, II, 94-102).

Anthropophagy and Hypochorematophily

Human flesh is the best nourishment for the libertine since it assists in building rich and healthy spermatozoa and quickly replenishes the supply. Who once has eaten this sweet food forever sings its praises. Bread, on the other hand, is the most indigestible and unhealthy food and weakens and unsettles the body. Hence tyrants feed their slaves with water and bread (Juliette II, 323 ff.). Minski especially attributed his strength to his dinners of human flesh (Juliette III, 313).

Closely bound with this anthropophagy is the pleasure received from separate pieces of the body, a kind of anthropophagic fetishism. So the buttocks of the people killed at the orgies were cut off and hung on the walls to serve as passionate excitations (Juliette II, 231). Silvia rips out and eats the genitals of her victim (Juliette VI, 235). Clairwil also uses the cut-off member of the monk, Claude, for her degenerate desires (Juliette III, 101) and explains that that object is so much in her phantasy that she is certain that it will be found in her brain after her death, although in life she only wants it in two different places, back and front (Juliette III, 154). This anthropophagic woman drinks the blood and eats the testicles of the boys she murdered (Juliette III, 72). She also tore their hearts out and used them as phalluses (Juliette III, 252). Minski, the robber at Brisa Testa's, is also a confirmed anthropophagist (Juliette III, 313, etc.).

Hypochorematophily plays a great rôle in de Sade's works. Saint Florent and Rodin find great satisfaction in watching the act of defecation (Justine I, 136 and 304). Mondor, Saint Fond and many others declare it their favorite food. The husband of St. Ange prefers the act *in os* (Philosophy in the Boudoir I, 92). Juliette eulogises: "People are deceived about the excrement of our bowels. It is not unhealthy and is besides very pleasant. One accustoms oneself so easily to its odor! And it's most delicious! The most piquant savor! Of course, in the beginning one must influence his imagination somewhat to this direction. But when one has once reached that degree it becomes a highly joyous and exciting pleasure" (Juliette I, 289). Sexual hypochorematophily has nothing in common with the lunatics who cover themselves with filth. Indeed this strange monomania forms the best proof for our assertion that these conditions may be present in perfectly healthy persons, as is also described by de Sade. Taxil and Tarnowsky give detailed accounts of the medical differences of the reactions of the insane, as well as admitting that they found this practice was not restricted to the madmen.

Other Sexuo-Pathologic Types of de Sade

Krafft Ebing is greatly indebted to de Sade, for the Marquis assembled and described almost all the possible sexuo-pathologic types in his novels. There can be no doubt that the sexual perversions he described were actual accounts of real persons.

All the senses served de Sade to excite the sexual feelings. Let us begin with the ear. There is also a word-sadism! According to Dolmance it is pleasant and exciting to use strong-sounding words of lewd significance in the delirium of passion because it increases the imaginative ability. Endless combinations were sought to discover which gave the greatest pleasure. These people used this vocabulary in polite and genteel society and received great pleasure from shock and shame of the others. Every conversation was spiced with slang and obscenity. Madame St. Ange in the midst of an orgy called out: "Come, let us blaspheme, my friends," and utilized the opportunity to shout at the silent Eugenie: "Swear! you little whore, swear!" (Philosophy in the Boudoir I, 125 and 129).

The eye, of course, has its part in sexual pleasure. Alberti delighted in seeing black women next to white because the contrast heated him (Juliette VI, 238). Great value is placed on the decoration of the rooms so that everything might add to the increase of pleasure (Juliette II, 231). The *voyeurs* are also richly represented. Saint Fond is proud of his "high art of spurring his passions by an industrious abstinency" and therefore sees to it that there is a long interval between coitions. Raimondi is another such *voyeur* who is satisfied with the bare sight (Juliette VI, 150).

The sense of smell is excited by the number of perfumes. In the "*Society of the Friends of Crime*" all participants in the orgies were cleaned and perfumed by young girls and boys (Juliette III, 30). Rabelais described in *Gargantua* the custom of both parties perfuming themselves prior to coition. The odor of women's armpits is especially exhilarating as is that of the faeces (Juliette III, 54). A bishop has his face washed with urine (Juliette III, 51).

Taste also is made good use of. Not only fæces but urine and spermatozoa are swallowed (Juliette I, 172). The *lécheurs* and *gamahucheurs* belong to this category as do the numerous tribadic cunnilinguists (e.g. Juliette III, 55; VI, 152). Dolmance is an individual very active in this direction.

Touch is almost always used as a preliminary to an orgy. By *tâter* and *claquer* of the different parts of the body both parties are brought to the highest degrees of preliminary pleasure.

From the colorful number of the other sexual types, partly already described, we mention only the most notable. Exhibitionism is preached by Dolmance who tells Eugenie to shamelessly uncover all her charms to the world, how to lift her dress up, etc. (Philosophy in the Boudoir I, 147). Saint Fond recommends to men and women clothing that reveal the privates (Juliette II, 197). The satisfaction of cruel desires is achieved by decapitation, quartering, wheel, fire, mad animals, hanging, crucification, etc. Dorval performed a mock execution (Juliette I, 225-230). Another has a mock execution performed on him as a kind of symbolic masochism. Torture is also applied to many victims and flagellation is seemingly the breath of life to de Sade's heroes and heroines. To this category also belongs the monomania of venaesectio and incisio (Justine III, 223).

Zoophilia was highly praised by de Sade as a sexual refinement. "The rooster-cock is delicious but one must wring its neck at the exact moment of the crisis" (Juliette I, 333). The cock is joined in the fourth volume of Juliette with an ape, a goat, and a bulldog in order to satisfy the desires of the connoisseurs (Juliette IV, 262).

Ferdinand of Naples is a necrophile; he satisfies himself on the corpse of a page (Juliette V, 263). Even the statues are used: the statue of Venus in the Louvre (Juliette I, 333).

Finally the realization of bizarre fancies heightens sexual pleasure. Belmor binds his victims fast (Juliette III, 163), the King of Sardinia loves the enema (ibid, 54, 294). Vespoli especially loves lunatics (Juliette V. 345), a Venetian pander, menstruations (ib. VI, 147), a third the depilation of the genitals (Juliette II, 59), a fourth sticks burning candles into the openings of the body (Juliette II, 22), etc., etc., etc.

Curious natural phenomena serve to excite the passion. A eunuch, a dwarf and an hermaphrodite tempted the jaded appetites of the guests (Juliette IV, 262). The sight of great fires heated the senses (ib. IV, 258). The eruption of Aetna (Justine III, 67), of Vesuvius (Juliette VI, 35), the storm on the open sea (Juliette VI, 269) all created sexual pleasures.

Historical events were also favorite excitations. Tiberius, Nero and Theodora were imitated (Juliette V, 362; VI, 319 and 341). Orgies were celebrated in the historically famous cities and in the Temple of Venus at Baiae, etc.

Arrangement of Erotic Individualities

The attempt of Marquis de Sade to derive the individual inclination of the characters in his novels from the physical constitution is very important from a psychiatric and anthropological viewpoint. As an example we give the description of Rodin and his sister Celestine.

"Rodin was a man of 36 years, brunette, bushy eyelashes, pleasant eyes, heroic appearance, and high stature. His whole body breathed health and, at the same time, passion." *Membrum erectum valde durum erat* (Justine I, 252).

"Celestine, the 30-year-old sister of Rodin, tall, thin,

expressive eyes, and a sensuous appearance. She was a brunette, hirsute, had a very long clitoris, virile anus, slight bosom, passionate temperament, and cruel desires." She had *tous les goûts*, especially a preference for women and only gave herself to men as a *pathicus* (Justine I, 253).

Marquis de Sade described Celestine in the above as very hirsute. Tardieu believed that this was a characteristic of extremely erotic women. He also spoke of an *abondance du système pileaux*, later of a brilliant gleam of the eyes and a passionate appearance, thick red lips and a pronounced development of breasts and sexual parts. A man inflicted with satyriasis has a rigid, covetous glare, bloodshot eyes, a passionate mouth, pale face, indecent mannerisms and a challenging posture.

All kinds of persons take part in the orgies in the novels of Marquis de Sade. Yet in all the wild frenzies each participant had a definite rôle assigned. Each had a task and a definite pleasure to consummate. Delbène said: "Let us bring some order in our pleasures. We shall enjoy them better if we arrange them better" (Juliette I, 6).

The tribade, Zanetti, was well experienced in the formation of such obscene groups (Juliette VI, 160). The young student Eugenie was given detailed instructions as to these arrangements by Madame St. Ange and Dolmance in that text book of sexual pleasure, *Philosophy in the Boudoir*. Madame de St. Ange brought Eugenie to an alcove whose walls were covered with mirrors. There she had to repeat a thousand times all the different erotic positions so that she could see with her own eyes the most appealing postures for the different types and so that the other party could be in the position to see any part of the body he desired. So the lovers saw nothing but similar groups and imitators of their own pleasures, only marvellous pictures of passion (Philosophy in the Boudoir I, 40). An especial piece was the *cavalcade* which the lustful monk, Clement, introduced in *Justine*. In this position two girls got down on all fours. Similar obscene positions are to be found on almost every page of *Justine* and *Juliette*.

Lying and Sexual Perversions

At all times lying has been the steadfast associate of prostitution and all manners of sexual debaucheries. We can rightly assert that every *roué* is a liar and that their statements can never be relied upon. "The mania for lying," says Parent Duchatelet, "is universal among prostitutes and hence any one seeking information from them must be very suspicious about their declarations."

Behrend in addition asserted: "Prostitutes lie for the sake of lying. It does not matter whether the matter is important or not or whether the lie will injure anyone. I have even seen them lie in circumstances that were to their own disadvantage."

Almost all the heroes and heroines of de Sade's novels were experienced liars. Proficiency in lying was a condition for the initiation into the "*Society of the Friends of Crime*." Baron Munchausen would have tipped his hat at the lies that were told at the orgies of the club, that is if he were not otherwise distracted (Juliette III, 59).

Lying even afforded a sexual pleasure to these libertines.

True, Dolmance extolled his love for truth but his statement was immediately questioned by that past-mistress of lies, Madame St. Ange. Dolmance then gayly replied: "Yes, just a couple of little lies and untruths. But that has to be in such a society as ours where people hide their vices and only show us their virtues. It would be dangerous to be frank. For that would place one in a disadvantageous position. Hypocrisy and lying are enjoined upon us by society. No one is as corrupt as I. Yet all consider me to be a respectable man" (Philosophy in the Boudoir).

De Sade's View of the Nature of Sexual Perversion

The great majority of the perverts described by de Sade in his novels are products of their environment. Most of the libertines arrived at their diverse perverse sexual pursuits from experience and the desire for "refinements." The entire *Philosophy in the Boudoir* was written with the purpose of instructing Eugenie in all the forms of vice and sexual perversions.

De Sade excellently described how this novice in vice eagerly and ardently heard the theories and placed them into practice. Dolmance said that the power of imagination was the prickles of pleasure, forever finding new kinds of sexual satisfaction (Philosophy in the Boudoir).

THEORY AND HISTORY OF SADISM

The phantasy gradually becomes receptive to ideas that originally arouse the greatest disgust in the mind and imagination. Dolmance drastically described how the young girl first exhibited the greatest distaste for pædicatio, then found more and more pleasure in it until this kind of sexual satisfaction became her especial preference.

The cynical apostle of pederasty, Dolmance, very candidly gave the reason for his preference, which we have seen was purely anatomical. The chemist, Almani, a zoöphilist, became a sexual pervert by the "study of nature" (Justine III, 67).

Only in two places have we found an indication of an hereditary nature of sexual perversion. Clement believed that it was due to the function of the organs. Hence the sexual pervert was "a sick person like an hysterical woman." He should be as little punished as any other sick persons, for he is not the master of himself. He is to be pitied not blamed. When anatomy becomes a perfect science then the connection between the constitution of man and sexual desires will be easily seen. Laws, morals, religions, paradises, hells, gods and gallows, all will collapse when it is found that the perversions are due to differences in blood, nerves and organs, factors over which man has no determining voice (Justine II, 212-213).

Bressac believed that the pathicus was by nature entirely different from other men. His passions were "inherent as a result of an entirely different structure. It would be an arch-stupidity to punish them" (Justine I, 162-164). For a medical as well as legal discussion of the above question we refer to Dr. Albert Moll's excellent work *Perversions of the Sex Instinct*.

Delbène said: "Vice should not be suppressed for it is the only fortune of our life" (Juliette I, 25). It must only be surrounded with such a mystery that will never be unravelled or detected. This mystery will lend an especial charm to vice.

Juliette was amazed at the quiet and peace at the great orgies in the "*Society of the Friends of Crime*," and drew the conclusion that man regarded nothing else in the world with as much care as his passions (Juliette III, 53).

Hence all orgies took place in dark, remote spots, in lonely castles, in caves, cellars, forests, mountains, near and in the sea, in torture-rooms and execution chambers. Hence the anthropophagist Minski became the "Hermit of the Apennines" and lived in a guarded and secluded house on a small island (Juliette III, 313).

Even for Dolmance there were certain things that "absolutely needed the veil" and which he hid from the eyes of the good Madame St. Ange (Philosophy in the Boudoir II, 153).

Definition of Sadism

Let us first give some definitions of other authors. Lacassagne explained sadism by a "mental state" which the sexual instinct excited or satisfied under the influence of an impulse for destruction.

According to Krafft Ebing sadism is that form of perversion of the sexual life by which a person finds a sexual pleasure in causing other people pain and in using their powers upon them. He places in contradistinction to sadism, masochism (after the writer, Sacher-Masoch), the desire to be ruled, beaten and mishandled by another, giving the victim great sexual pleasure thereby. He holds that sadism and masochism are the main forms of psycho-sexual perversions, which may appear in the entire field of vagaries of the sexual instincts in the most different geographical regions.

Schrenck Notzing believes, however, that the differences between the active and passive roles in the novels of Marquis de Sade and Sacher-Masoch is not as sharp as Krafft Ebing declared. He deduces both concepts from a higher concept, *algolagnia* (*álgos*, pain; *lágnos*, sexual excitation) and describes sadism as active algolagnia and masochism as passive algolagnia. According to this author there are other forms of algolagnia; the onanistic (self-mutilation, self-flagellation, etc.), the visual (sexual excitation at the sight of fights, etc.), the zoöphilic and finally the ideal or symbolic algolagnia in which "pain plays the rôle for its own self without secondary significance and imaginative embellishments and without any consideration for active and passive views."

Thoinot believes that "sadism is a perversion of the sexual life which finds sexual pleasure in causing pain to others whether he himself causes the pain or whether he has some one else do it."

Eulenburg preceded the concept of Schrenck Notzing with the words *lognomania* (sadism) and *machlomania* (masochism). Later writers follow in the main the above authorities. Moll in *The Perversions of the Sex Instinct* gives a more complete list.

A definition of sadism that will include all forms of passive and active algolagnia, zoöphilia, necrophilia, symbolic algolagnia, etc., is essential. It should be remembered that since actual and ideal destructive processes in nature appear as causes of sexual excitation and satisfaction, such as eruptions, storms, fires, murders, etc., sadism must be defined in the following way.

Sadism is the purposively sought or accidentally presented connection of sexual excitation and pleasure with the actual or also only symbolic (ideal or illusory) occurrences of strange and terrifying events, destructive processes and actions, which threaten or destroy life, health and property of men or other living beings whereby the person receiving sexual pleasure from such events may be the originator or spectator, voluntary or involuntary.

We believe that this definition covers all cases of sadism, including word-sadism, torture, forms of rape, etc.

Judgment of de Sade According to His Life and Works

The most important question is: was the Marquis de Sade insane?

Only too easily, in face of the present social, political and legal opinion, will the average person assent. Yet from a cultural and medical standpoint we are fully convinced that the greatest number of sexual perverts are perfectly healthy mentally and that their perversions are due to seduction and to sexual super-excitation.

Modern studies have modified Krafft Ebing's views.

Indeed, he, himself, once admitted that "the most horrible sexual madnesses are otherwise accompanied by perfect health." Moll rightly remarked that this was a tacit approval of the theory that sexual perversity was not in itself a proof of insanity.

Eulenberg also states that "the greater percentage of algolagnists are not mad in the narrower sense. They are almost all of excellent physical condition."

Two doctors have recently expressed themselves on the mental condition of de Sade, who, as we have seen, was considered by Royer Collard as quite healthy. Dr. Eulenburg states that "even the leading specialists of our time would not have declared that he was insane or at least have denied him free will." Dr. Marciat believes that Marquis de Sade "was not insane in the exact sense of the word." At the most he could be accused of "moral insanity," but only from the viewpoint of *Justine* and *Juliette*. "But it must also be remembered that Mirabeau, Musset and many others wrote obscene books." Cabanès is positive in his statement that the Marquis was sane.

Rather than moral insanity (*folie morale*) we believe that de Sade was inflicted with a form of perversion that may be inadequately described as "impulsive madness," proceeding from the social organism: an impulsive origin of action without a clear, definite goal.

After these preparatory orientations let us investigate the life and works of Marquis de Sade with the view of obtaining some conclusions on his mental status.

1. De Sade was a Provençal and hence had the "southern hot blood" and the passionateness of his countrymen.
2. In relation to his heredity little is demonstrable. Yet it is probable that de Sade "inherited" from his uncle an inclination for the gallant life and for writing. We know

that at his return from the war at the age of 23 he had written an obscene book.

3. There are no trustworthy observations on the childhood of de Sade.

4. It is notable that de Sade spent the formative years of his life, from 17 to 23, in the war, away from home and family. It is certain that the degeneration of Marquis de Sade had its start during this period of war under the enormous moral corruption of the French army.

5. The unhappy marriage did not play the important rôle in his life that Marciat ascribed to it.

6. It is pretty certain that Marquis de Sade neither destroyed nor killed the victims at his two great scandalous affairs.

7. It is certain that the long prison sentences caused important physical and mental damages.

8. That de Sade was of a strong sexual excitability is testified by the observation of his friend by Brierre de Boismont.

9. Very notable appear some mental anomalies of his prison life: the mistrust, the lying and the raging fits at the visit of his wife.

10. After his release the Marquis appeared more tractable and showed that he had not lost all moral feeling by rescuing his parents-in-law.

11. The mere extent and conception of his chief works, *Justine* and *Juliette* are astonishing.

12. The great amount of cleverly combined details, the development of gradual dramatic action, the excellent memory and the wealth of examples all denote a great mental ability.

13. The diversity of the writings plainly indicates the influence of the time and the milieu.

14. Michelet and Taine rightly called him the "Pro-

fessor of Crime." He was the theoretician of vice, inasmuch as he collected and described with faithful accuracy from his own experience and observations all the contemporary anomalies of the sexual life of his time in his main works. Marquis de Sade wrote in the form of a novel what Krafft Ebing did in his scientific work, *Psychopathia Sexualis* a hundred years later.

15. Thereby his works have a decided cultural and historical value since they acquaint us with all phases, nuances and characteristics of the sexual life in France in the *ancien régime* and in the great Revolution.

16. De Sade's theories of vice were a product of the Revolution and found many analogies therein.

17. In the works that were written before and after *Justine* and *Juliette* and the *Philosophy in the Boudoir* de Sade developed more or less moral views.

18. Even in the above notorious works de Sade had a certain moralistic tendency in his views against the *ancien régime*.

19. De Sade showed in his works that he had read all the contemporary and scientific literature.

20. As a philosopher he was little more than mediocre. His philosophy was an eclectic potpourri. His proofs consisted of senseless tautologies and more senseless premises.

From these facts we base our judgment. Marquis de Sade was not insane. He had, perhaps by heredity, a neuropathic personality, which in the midst of a dangerous milieu easily started him on the path of vice. He saw on all sides his friends become sexual perverts by seduction and custom and his high blood did not fare well at the lengthy prison sentences. There is plainly apparent in his successive works a gradual loss of power of the mind. We have already sufficiently noted the relation of the contents of de Sade's notorious works with the culture of his age.

The great gap between de Sade as a person and de Sade as a writer is thereby partly bridged. We can easily bridge the entire gap if we recall that the power of imagination of perverts reaches almost unimaginable dimensions. "Many patients of this kind, perverts, masturbators, and especially algolagnists were disillusioned as soon as they tried to realize the effects of their imagination. They lived in their dreamy tempestuous world of sexual orgies and were sobered by reality." This is by far the most reasonable explanation for Marquis de Sade. He is personally not to be compared with such a man as Gilles de Rais.

The Spread and Effect of Marquis de Sade's Works

We have already mentioned that the pornographic writings of Marquis de Sade were sold openly under the Directory and were to be had from bookstores and catalogues. A great capitalist financed their publication and sale which extended to many foreign lands. Hence it is not strange that in spite of the confiscation and destruction of *Justine* and *Juliette* by Napoleon I (1801) they spread to enormous extents by frequent reprints. New confiscations in 1815, 1825 and 1843 also served only to heighten the curiosity to see and possess these notorious works.

Indeed the publisher, himself, asked that the book be suppressed for then he would have been certain that it would find many purchasers.

As early as 1797 Villers wrote about the spread of *Justine*: "Everybody wants to know just what kind of a book it is. *Justine* is eagerly sought for, treasured and loaned, an edition is suppressed and two spring up to take its place."

For over a century authors, bibliophiles and scientists snapped up every copy that appeared on the market. Janin declared that "every respectable library has its quota of the works of Marquis de Sade. Often enough they stare out from a stack full of innocent books. All the auctioneers have told me that there is the most spirited bidding when a book of his is placed under the hammer." The first and second editions of his works, including the monumental combined edition of *Justine* and *Juliette* has fetched at all times extremely high prices. Nevertheless all his works are difficult to procure even in French for all the editions were usually de luxe and limited and were confined to the sanctum of bibliophiles from which they appeared only at the death of the owner. In Germany *Justine* and *Juliette* were issued privately by the Bibliophile Society in an edition of 350 copies. *Justine* has alone been translated into English and I understand that it is extremely rare.

Two important French writers, Rétif de la Bretonne and Charles Villers, almost at the same time, start the long list of "de Sade literature." First: *Anti-Justine or the Delights of Love, written at the Palais Royal in 1798 by M. Linguet in two volumes.* Sixty illustrations were announced on the title-page but they never appeared. Of the eight parts that Rétif promised in the preface only the first was published. Of the first edition only two copies were preserved in the National Library after the great confiscation and destruction of all the obscene books found in bordellos and bookstores.

According to Monselet, *Anti-Justine* contained obscene descriptions from Rétif's own life and was supposed to form a supplement to his *Monsieur Nicolas*. The work was divided into forty-eight chapters on various obscene subjects. Rétif, however, managed to give a kind of moral twist to them and declared that it was a "kind of antidote" to the poison of the infamous *Justine*, which "would render the name Linguet immortal."

He set out with a warning to women against cruelty. But *Anti-Justine* was for this reason just as obscene as *Justine* since the men had for them a substitute that could be used without the cruelty of de Sade's works. Rétif continually repeated that these "antidotes were extremely urgent," thus testifying to the enormous spread of de Sade's works. Rétif ended the book with cynical remarks on the illustrations that were supposed to accompany the book, referring undoubtedly to the exceptionally obscene pictures of *Justine* and *Juliette*.

Villers, a French emigrant, settled in Germany after the Revolution. In 1797 there appeared a *Letter on the Novel Entitled "Justine or the Misfortunes of Virtue."* This has been definitely proven to have been written by Villers. "I have started and thrown away this horrible work over a dozen times, but its great fame caused me to read it to the very end. *Justine* could have been conceived only in the most barbarous and bloody convulsions; it is the true fruit of the Revolution. There are works that appear to have been inspired by the Graces; *Justine* must have been inspired by the Furies. It is written with blood and stinks of blood. It is to books what Robespierre is to men." Villers then set forth the philosophic theories of de Sade and succinctly and distastefully summarized the contents of *Justine*. He closed his essay with the words: "What can one think of an age that can find an author to write, publishers to print and a public to read such a work as *Justine*?"

Sadism in Literature

Marquis de Sade found many literary imitators. We shall name only the most important authors and works in which are plainly seen a direct influence of the theories of Marquis de Sade.

A mild imitation of de Sade was Toulotte's *The Dominican or the Crimes of Intolerance and the Effects of Religious Celibacy* (1802). It had the same taste for the union of cruelty and pleasure and contained many episodes from the life of the *célèbre marquis* but was in the main uninteresting and poorly executed. It was condemned on July 12, 1827, and confiscated on April 5, 1828.

In 1835 some bookseller conceived the brilliant idea of placing the title *Justine or the Misfortunes of Virtue* on the contents of a very poor novel. A selection from the preface of the real *Justine* was used. The story, in which thieves and rascals of the worst kind attempted to construct some weak principles of immorality, was ascribed to a hack-writer, Rabau, and was published in Bordeaux. The book was publicly sold and the resulting scandal was great. The publisher was finally fined and imprisoned.

A writer directly influenced by the works of de Sade was Jacques Baron Révérony de Saint Cyr, the first true "sadistic" author. He wrote many plays, novels and scientific works on this subject. He died of insanity. Some of his works were: *Pauliska or Modern Perversity, Recent Memoirs of a Polonaise* (1798), *Sabina d'Herfeld or the Dangers of Imagination* (1797-1798), *The Torrent of Passion or the Dangers of Gallantry* (1812). The descriptions and doctrines are all direct imitations of de Sade.

"A respectable man always has a volume of Marquis de Sade in his pocket," wrote Borel in his novel, *The Lycanthrope*. Proudhon declared that George Sand was a "worthy daughter of Marquis de Sade" and taught similar doctrines, especially in her *Lelia*. Proudhon, himself, taught the same views on robbery as did de Sade.

The French revolutionist Fourier developed a sadistic theory of love. In his *Harmony* every woman had to have: two children from an *époux*, one child from a *géniteur*, a favorite and assorted lovers. This harmonic world was protected from over-population by four organic means: gastrosophic regime, feminine vigor, integral exercise and *coutumes phanérogames*.

Modern French literature is plentifully supplied with authors of a sadistic bent. We mention below only the most striking.

The sensualism of Baudelaire that, according to Bourget, "reached complete sadism" is so well known that any description is unnecessary. The *Diaboliques* of Barbey d'Aurevilly describe the self- and reciprocal atrocities of men and women. Satan is invoked, praised and served by the sadistic assemblage. Paulhan in his *New Mysticism* and Joseph Péladan in his *Vice Supreme* express similar ideas as de Sade on the joys of stealing and other persons' sufferings.

The much beloved hypochorematophily of de Sade found a devotee in Maurice Barrès. He has his "little princess" relate: "When I was twelve years old I loved to take off my shoes and stockings and wade with my bare feet in the warm dung. I used to spend hours doing this. My whole body thrilled at the contact."

J. K. Huysmans again depicted the problem of education of the *Philosophy in the Boudoir* in his *Against the Grain*. Des Esseintes met in the Rue de Rivoli a sixteen-year-old, poorly dressed boy who asked him for a light for his cheap cigarette. Des Esseintes gave him a perfumed, Turkish cigarette, brought him to a bordello where the prostitutes dazzled him. The madame asked des Esseintes why he brought the boy. He answered: "I'm simply making a murderer out of him. I am going to bring him here for the next fourteen days to accustom him to pleasures which he has not the means to satisfy. Later he will steal so that he can afford to visit you. I hope that he will also murder. Then my purpose will be achieved." He then sent the boy out with the words: "Go now, do unto others what you do not want others to do unto you. You will go far with this fundamental principle."

In the already quoted *Là-Bas* of Huysman, Durral relates the history of the bluebeard, Gilles de Rais, the arch-criminal of the fifteenth century and a true sadist.

Emile Cheve and Paul Bourget have also given many personal sadistic descriptions. Alfred de Musset in his *Gamiani or Two Nights of Excesses* is believed to have taken revenge on his former mistress, George Sand, by describing her in his heroine, Gamiani, a tribade of the most savage kind. An intercourse between a woman and an ass, from the prototype of the *Golden Ass of Apuleius*, is also described.

German literature also has its sadistic authors. Heinrich von Kleist described in his Penthesilea how a love-mad woman had her beloved torn to pieces by blood-hounds and then joined the dogs in ripping out his entrails.

A German novel in which the Marquis de Sade is often mentioned and in which sadism plays an important rôle is the notorious *Memoirs of a Singer* (Boston, 1862). It is supposed to be an autobiography of the famous singer, Wilhelmine Schroeder Devrient (1804-1860). The novel consists of letters to a doctor describing the progress of the singer in the art of love. *Justine* has especially influenced the second part of this book and we therefore quote the important details.

In Budapest Devrient became acquainted with a certain Anna, a demi-mondaine and connoisseur of the notorious corruptions of the Hungarian capital. She asked Anna of her opinion of *Justine* which she had bought in Frankfurt am Main, but which repelled more than attracted her. Anna then advised her to attend the whipping of a thief. This afforded the singer great pleasure and the victim, the thief Rosa, became a participant in the tribadic orgies. The idea of artificially deflowering Rosa gave her infinite joy and on the same evening the act was consummated by a "double" artificial phallus while Anna sucked the "virgin blood" after the operation. Next all the notorious bordellos of Budapest were visited. Respectable Budapest society celebrated a great orgy in one of the bordellos: the only coverings of the ladies and gentlemen were masks. The details of this orgy were largely taken from *Justine*. There a certain Ferry re-deflowered the poor Rosa. Devrient and Rosa then travelled to Italy where they became acquainted with a fifty-nine-year old English libertine, Sir Ethelbert Merwyn, who taught them all the sexual vices of Italy. He then brought them to Rome where after an execution of a man and woman in a church, an unbelievable orgy of monks, nuns, boys, and animals of all kinds took place.

Some Sadistic Moral Crimes

The hundreds of criminal sadisms that have attracted the attention of the authorities and that have appeared in print seem to justify the statement that in almost all the cases their prototypes could be found in either *Justine* or *Juliette*. For example, the well-known cases of "Jack the Ripper" of London, Ben Ali of New York, and Piper and Pomeroy of Boston, all find their counterparts in de Sade's works. We quote some interesting examples of these crimes from the works of Garnier, Moll, Krafft Ebing, etc.

A degenerate Russian prince has his mistress turn her back upon him and defecate on his breast. Only in this way could he become excited (cf. Juliette III, 54).

The *Journal L' Evenement* of March 4, 1877, told of a gardener who fell in love with the statue of Venus de Milo and was caught by the police in the picture salon attempting intercourse with it (cf. Juliette I, 334).

A married man complained to Krafft Ebing that every time he approached his young and nervous wife he would have to inflict some wound upon himself. She would then fiercely suck the blood from the wound and become greatly excited. A commander of the post had his mistress draw blood from her genitals so that he could excite himself by sucking in the blood (cf. Juliette III, 233, ff.).

The details of this truly sadistic affair are to be found in the Paris newspaper *Gil Blas*. The complaint was against Michel Bloch, a diamond broker and many times a millionaire, a man of about sixty years, happily married, father of two young girls. A co-defendant was a procuress, Madame Marchand, who introduced Bloch to his victims. The first meeting of Bloch and the complainant, Claudine Buron, took place in the following manner: The girl was brought into a room of Marchand and had to undress completely in company with two other girls, who had already made the acquaintance of Bloch. Completely naked and with handkerchiefs in their hands all three entered a blue room in which the defendant awaited them. The girls had to silently file past him with a smile on their lips (this was expressly demanded). He was then handed needles, handkerchiefs and a whip. The novice, Claudine Buron, had to kneel down before him. He stuck about one hundred needles in her breasts, back and almost all parts of her body. He then folded a handkerchief in three corners, fastened it securely with needles on her breasts, and suddenly ripped off the handkerchief with brutal force. Not until then did he fall upon the young girl, beat her, tear her hair from all parts of her body and finally satisfy himself sexually upon her before the eyes of her companions. These other girls had meanwhile wiped the sweat from his

THEORY AND HISTORY OF SADISM

brow and had assumed "plastic positions." All three were then released by Bloch and given a gift of 40 francs.

When the incident became public and loud cries of indignation arose, Bloch assumed an attitude of wonder that such a great fuss was made about a little fun. He was fined and imprisoned for six months. The madame was given a year in jail. The girl received 1000 francs damages (cf. similar scenes in Juliette II, 284; III, 55).

In 1840 the American Embassy at Madrid caused great excitement by a scandalous affair closely resembling the one perpetrated in Marseilles by Marquis de Sade in 1772. The ambassador had often before shown eccentricities of the kind of Marquis de Sade. One day he invited 20 "manolas" to a supper and distributed to these girls strong irritants which excited them to the wildest scenes under the American Eagle.

This short list could be multiplied almost ad infinitum. Scarcely a day goes by that similar "imitations" of the heroes and heroines of Marquis de Sade do not appear in the daily newspapers. We would like though, in addition, to refer to the extremely interesting masochistic case, unique in its complexities, that is given by Dr. Albert Moll in his *Perversions of the Sex Instinct*.

Conclusion

In conclusion we wish to reiterate that the works of Marquis de Sade have a significance in the history of human culture that is far from the fields of pornography and the extraordinary anti-moral theories. For Marquis de Sade was the first person who considered all the phenomena of nature and of the social organism from the viewpoint of the human sexual life.

Even if we forget the dreadful panoramas of perverse sexual feelings that sprang from a profound knowledge of sexuo-pathologic phenomena, the works of Marquis de Sade deserve the most serious attention for scientific investigators in the cultural, political, juridical and medical fields.

Bibliography

PUBLISHED WORKS OF MARQUIS DE SADE

Justine, ou les Malheurs de la Vertu; en Hollande, chez les Libraires associés. [Paris.] 1791. 2 vols. 8 vo.

Justine, ou les Malheurs de la Vertu; en Hollande, chez les Libraires associés. [Paris.] 1791. 2 vols. 12mo.

Justine, ou les Malheurs de la Vertu; à Londres. [Paris, chez Cazin.] 1792. 2 vols. 16mo.

Justine, ou les Malheurs de la Vertu; 3me édition corrigée et augmentée; à Philadelphie. [Paris.] 1794. 2 vols. 18mo.

Justine, ou les Malheurs de la Vertu; à Londres. [Paris.] 1797. 4 vols. 18mo.

Justine, ou les Malheurs de la Vertu; en Hollande. 1800. 4 vols. 18mo. [Reprint of the Cazin Edition of 1792.]

Juliette, ou la suite de Justine. 1796. 4 vols. 8vo. [n. p.]

La Nouvelle Justine, ou les Malheurs de la Vertu, suivie de l'histoire de Juliette, sa sœur. Ouvrage orné d'un frontispiece et de cent sujets gravés avec soin; en Hollande. [Paris.] 1797. 10 vols. 18mo.

[This is the definitive edition of both works. *Justine* occupies 4 volumes and *Juliette* 6. The original issue contains a frontispiece and 100 illustrations, of which 40 belong to *Justine* and 60 to *Juliette.*]

Aline et Valcour, ou le Roman philosophique; écrit à la Bastille un an avant la Révolution de France, orné de quatorze gravures, par le citoyen S——. A Paris, chez Girouard, Libraire, rue du Bout-de-Monde, no. 47. 1793. 8 parts, in 4 vols. 18mo.

[This same edition was reissued twice, in 1795, with different title-pages.]

La Philosophie dans le Boudoir; ouvrage posthume de l'auteur de *Justine*. A Londres [Paris], aux dépens de la compagnie. 1795. 2 vols. 16mo.

Oxtiern, ou les Malheurs du Libertinage; drame en 3 actes et en prose, par D.A.R.S. A Versailles: Blaizot. An VIII. [1800.] 8vo.

[This is the only play by de Sade that was published. It was originally produced at the Théâtre Molière in October, 1791.]

Les Crimes de l'Amour, ou le Délire des passions. Nouvelles historiques et tragiques, précédées d'une Idée sur les Romans, par D. A. F. Sade, auteur d'*Aline et Valcour*. A Paris: chez Massé. An VIII [1800.] In two forms, 4 vols. 12mo, or 2 vols. 8vo.

Voloë et ses deux Acolytes, ou Quelques décades de la vie de trois jolies femmes. Histoire véritable du siècle dernier, par un contemporain; à Turin. [Paris.] An VIII. [1800.] 12mo.

Les 120 Journées de Sodome, ou l'Ecole du Libertinage, par le Marquis de Sade. Publié pour la première fois d'après le manuscrit original, avec des annotations scientifiques par le Dr. Eugène Dühren. Paris: Club des Bibliophiles. 1904. Imperial 8vo.

[The first and only edition of this work, which was written in 1785.]

Docri, ou la Bizarrerie du sort; conte inédit, par le Marquis de Sade, publié sur le manuscrit, avec une notice sur l'auteur. Paris: Charavay frères. 1881. 12mo.

[With an etched frontispiece by G. Charpentier. Edition limited to 269 copies. The *Notice sur l'auteur*, of 23 pages, is signed *A. F.* and is by Anatole France.]

Valmor et Lydia, ou Voyage autour du Monde de deux amants qui se cherchent. Paris: Pigoreau. An VII. [1799.] 3 vols.

[This is an abridged version, with the names slightly altered, of part of *Aline et Valcour*, and is a pirated edition.]

Alzonde et Koradin. Paris: Cerioux et Moutardier. 1799. 2 vols. 12mo.

[The same remarks apply to this as to No. 16.]

Discours prononcé à la Fête décernée par la Section des Piques aux mânes de Marat et de le Pelletier, par Sade, citoyen de cette Section et membre de la Société populaire de la Section des Piques, rue Saint-Fiacre, no. 2. [Paris, 1793.] 8vo.

[A pamphlet of 8 pages.]

Pétition de la Section des Piques aux Représentants du peuple Français. Paris. [1793.] 8vo.

L'Auteur des Crimes de l'Amour à Villeterque, folliculaire. Paris: Massé. An IX. [1801.] 12mo.

Couplets chantés à Son Eminence le Cardinal Maury, le 6 Octobre, 1812, à la maison de santé près de Charenton.

[Published in the Revue Rétrospective, Paris, 1833, vol. i., p. 262.]

WORKS IN THE STYLE OF DE SADE

L'Anti-Justine ou les Délices de l'Amour. Par M. Linguet. Epigraphe: Casta placent superis.—Manibus puris sumite (cunnos). Avec soixante figures. Première partie. Fleuron: Tête de faune couronnée de feuilles et de raisins. Au Palais-Royal; chez feue la veuve Girouard, très-connue. 1798. Deux parties in-12. The preface: "Blasé sur les femmes. Depuis longtemps, la *Justine* de Dsds me tomba sous la main; elle me mit en feu . . . Personne n'a été plus indigné que moi des ouvrages de l'infâme de Sade, que je lis dans une prison. Ce scélérat ne présente les delices de l'amour, qu'accompagnés de tourments de la mort même." The purpose of the author (Rétif de la Bretonne): "Mon but est de faire un livre plus savoureux que les siens, et que les épouses pourront faire lire à leurs maris; un livre où le libertinage n'ait rien de cruel pour le sexe des Grâces; où l'amour, ramené à la Nature, exempt de scrupules et de préjugés, ne présente que des images riantes et voluptueuses."

Pauliska, ou la Perversité moderne, mémoires récentes d'une Polonaise. Paris, Lemierre et chez Courcier, an VI (1798), 2 vols. 12°. Jacques Baron Révérony de Saint-Cyr. (1767-1829) is the author.

Sabina d'Herfeld ou les Dangers de l'imagination. Paris, 1757-1758. 2 vols. 12°. Author: Révérony de Saint-Cyr.

Le Torrent des passions, ou les Dangers de la galanterie. Paris, 1818. 2 vols. Révérony de Saint-Cyr.

Le Dominicain, ou les crimes de l'intolérance et les effets du célibat religieux par T . . . e (E. L. J. Toulotte), Paris, Pigoreau, 1903, 4 vols. 12mo.

Justine ou les Malheurs de la Vertu; avec préface par Marquis de Sade. Paris, Oliver, Impr. Maltesse, 1835. A castrated imitation of de Sade's work of the same name.

Aus den Memoiren einer Sängerin; Boston. Reginald Chesterfield (Verlagsbureau Altona). 2 vols., 1862 and 1875. 8vo.

Virilités; Emile Chevet, Paris, A. Lemerre, 1882, 18°.

WORKS ON DE SADE

Apollinaire. *L'Œuvre du Marquis de Sade*. Pages choisies, comprenant des morceaux inédits et des lettres publiées pour la première fois, tirés des Archives de la Comédie Française. Introduction, essai bibliographique et notes par Guillaume Apollinaire. Ouvrage orné de huit illustrations hors texte. Paris: Bibliothèque des Curieux. 1912. 8vo.

Bloch (Iwan), see under Dühren (Dr. E.). Nos. 62 and 64.

Bonneau. *La Curiosité Littéraire et Bibliographique*. Articles littéraires; reproduction, extraits et analyses d'ouvrages curieux; notices de livres rares; anecdotes, etc. Paris: Liseux. 1880-83. 4 vols. 8vo.

[Vol. i., pp. 105-158. *La Première Edition de Justine, ou les Malheurs de la Vertu*. Vol. iii., pp. 131-176, *Analyse de Juliette, ou les Prospérités du Vice, par le Marquis de Sade*. Both by Alcide Bonneau. The latter also contains *Le Fauve*, a poem from *Virilités*, par M. Emile Chevet which concerns the Marquis and his work.]

Brunet. *Le Marquis de Sade, l'Homme et ses écrits*. Etude bio-bibliographique [par P. G. Brunet]. Sadopolis: chez Justin Valcourt, à l'enseigne de la "vertu malheureuse," l'an 0000. [Bruxelles: J. Gay. 1866.] 12mo.

Cabanès. *La Prétendue Folie de Marquis de Sade*. Pages 259-320 dans le *Cabinet Secret de l'Histoire*, par A. Cabanès. 4e série. Paris. 1900. 8vo.

Coulmier. Lettre du 23 Mai 1810, écrite à Madame Cochelet, du directeur Coulmier, sur les spectacles arrangés par Sade à Charenton. [First appeared in the *Revue Anecdotique*, vol. x. (new series, vol. i.) 1869, pp. 101-106.]

Dawes. *The Marquis de Sade: His Life and Works*. London, 1927. 8vo.

[This book, accredited to an Englishman, C. R. Dawes, is nothing but a paraphrase of this foregoing work of Iwan Bloch, *Marquis de Sade: The Man and His Age!* Whole chapters are taken word for word from Bloch's book! Not only does this English "edition" fail to give any credit to Bloch but it also mentions his name only once! Such conduct is sufficient to damn both publisher and alleged "author," C. R. Dawes. They have been guilty of an even greater crime in being prurient enough—such people would be—to omit all the references, quotations and discussions of Bloch on de Sade's sexual life and all the sexual references from his works. Such a contemptible castration and condensation has, of course, vitiated and nullified all possible benefit from Bloch's work from a medical and cultural standpoint. Any reader having a copy of Dawes' "work" can immediately see that the book is nothing but an expurgated paraphrase of this translation of Bloch's Marquis de Sade. The reader may rest assured that the present translation has omitted no line from the German edition that might possibly detract from its medical, forensic or cultural value. There are no prurient "expurgations" in this present translation. I have given so much space to this pirated castration because there has never been such a bold and hypocritical theft of another man's work in the history of literature. Both author and publisher deserve the greatest condemnation for their cowardice and thievery.—*The Translator*.]

Détention du Marquis de Sade. Article in the *Revue Rétrospective*, 1883, vol. i., p. 256 et seq.

Dühren. *Neue Forschungen über den Marquis de Sade und seine Zeit*, von Dr. Eugen Dühren. [Iwan Bloch.] Berlin, 1904. 8vo.

Eulenburg. *Der Marquis de Sade*, von A. Eulenburg. Published in *L'Avenir*. 7th year, No. 26, 25th March, 1899.

Ginisty. *Lettres inédites de la Marquise de Sade*, par Paul Ginisty. Published in *La Grande Revue*, 3rd year, No. 1, 1st January, 1899.

Ginisty. *La Marquise de Sade*, par Paul Ginisty. Paris, 1901. 8vo.

Jacob. *La Vérité sur les deux procès criminels du Marquis de Sade*, par le Bibliophile Jacob. [Paul Lacroix.] First published in the *Revue de Paris*, 1837, pp. 135-144.

Jacobus X. *Le Marquis de Sade et son Œuvre, devant la Science médicale et la Littérature moderne*, par le Dr. Jacobus X—. Paris: Carrington, 1901. 8vo.

Janin. *Le Marquis de Sade*, par Jules Janin. First published in the *Revue de Paris*, 1834, pp. 321-360.

Janin. *Marquis de Sade (Le)*, par Jules Janin. La vérité sur les deux procès criminels du Marquis de Sade, par le Bibliophile Jacob, le tout précédé de la Bibliographie des Œuvres du Marquis de Sade. Paris, chez les Marchands de nouveautés. 1834. 12mo.

Marciat. *Le Marquis de Sade et le Sadisme*, par le Dr. Marciat, in *Vacher l'éventreur et les crimes sadiques*, par A. Lacassagne, Lyon et Paris. 1899. 8vo.

Marquis de Sade (Le), ses aventures, ses œuvres, passions mystérieuses, folies érotiques. Avec 116 illustrations. Paris: Fayard. [No date.] 8vo.

Sade. *Les Crimes de l'Amour*, précédé d'un Avant-propos, suivi des Idées sur les Romans, de l'auteur des Crimes de l'Amour à Villeterque, d'une Notice bio-bibliographique de Marquis de Sade, l'homme et ses écrits, et du discours prononcé par le Marquis de Sade à la Section des Piques. Bruxelles: Gay et Doucé. 1881. 8vo.

Summers. *The Marquis de Sade: a study in Algolagnia*, by Montague Summers, M.A., F.R.S.L. London, 1920. 8vo.

Uzanne. *Idée sur les Romans*, par D. A. F. de Sade, publiée avec préface, notes et documents inédits, par Octave Uzanne. Paris: Rouveyre, 1878. 8vo.

Villers. Lettre sur le roman intitulé *Justine, ou les Malheurs de la Vertu*, par Charles Villiers. Nouvelle édition par A. P. Malassis. Paris, 1877. 12mo.

[The original appeared in 1797, in *Le Spectateur du Nord*, vol. iv.]

WORKS RELATING TO DE SADE AND HIS AGE

Baudot. *Notes Historiques*, de M. A. Baudot. Publiées par Madame Edgar Quinet. Paris.

Bégis. *Notes de Police*, par Alfred Bégis. Published in *La Nouvelle Revue*, November to December, 1880.

Biographie universelle et portative des contemporains depuis 1788 jusqu'à nos jours. Paris, 1836. Vol. v.

Biographie Générale. Paris. Vol. xlii.

Bossard. *Gilles de Rais, Maréchal de France, dit Barbe-Bleue (1404-1440)*, par l'Abbé Eugène Bossard, d'après les documents inédits réunis par M. René de Maulde. Deuxième edition. Paris: Champion, 1886. Royal 8vo.

Brillat-Savarin. *Physiologie du Goût*, par Brillat-Savarin. Paris, 1825. 8vo.

Casanova. Mémoires de Jacques Casanova de Seingalt. Paris, 12 vols. (n. d.).

Deffand. *Lettres de la Marquise du Deffand à Horace Walpole (1766-1780)*. Première édition complète, augmentée d'environ 500 lettres inédites. Publiées d'après les Originaux, avec une Introduction, des Notes et une Table des Noms, par Mrs. Paget Toynbee, éditeur des *Lettres d'Horace Walpole*. Londres: Methuen et Cie. 1912. 3 vols. 8vo.

Dulaure. *Histoire physique, civile et morale de Paris*, par J. A. Dulaure. Paris, 1821. 8vo.

Ellis. *Studies in the Psychology of Sex*. Vol. iii. Analysis of the Sexual Impulse; Love and Pain; The Sexual Impulse in Women, by Havelock Ellis. Second edition, revised and enlarged. Philadelphia, 1913. 8vo.

Espion Anglais (L'). London, 1784. 8vo.

Fraxi. *Index Librorum Prohibitorum*: being Notes Bio- Biblio- Iconographical and Critical, on Curious and Uncommon Books, by Pisanus Fraxi. London: privately printed. 1877. Royal 4to.

Fraxi. *Centuria Librorum Absconditorum*: being Notes Bio- Biblio- Icono-graphical and Critical, on Curious and Uncommon Books, by Pisanus Fraxi. London: privately printed. 1879. Royal 4to.

[With a frontispiece and 10 plates. Edition limited to 250 copies. Contains references to de Sade (pp. 253, 268, and 457).]

Fraxi. *Cantena Librorum Tacendorum*: being Notes Bio- Biblio- Iconographical and Critical, on Curious and Uncommon Books, by Pisanus Fraxi. London: privately printed. 1885. Royal 4to.

[With a frontispiece and 3 plates. Edition limited to 250 copies. Contains several short references to de Sade.]

Gay. *Bibliographie des Ouvrages relatifs à l'Amour, aux Femmes, au Mariage, et des livres facétieux, pantagruéliques, scatalogiques, satyriques, etc.*, par M. le C. d'I—[Jules Gay]. 4me édition, entièrement refondue, augmentée et mise à jour par J. Lemonnier. Paris, 1894-1900. 4 vols. Royal 8vo.

Goncourt. *La Femme au dix-huitième Siècle*, par Edmond et Jules de Goncourt. Paris, 1863. 8vo.

Krafft-Ebing. *Psychopathia Sexualis*, with especial reference to antipathic sexual instinct: a medico-forensic study, by Dr. R. v. Krafft-Ebing. London, 1901. 8vo.

Legouvé. *Histoire morale des Femmes*, par E. Legouvé. Paris. 1848. 8vo.

Maréchal. *Dictionnaire des Athées*, par Sylvain Maréchal. 2me édition, par J. Lalande. Bruxelles, 1833. 8vo.

Mayne. *The Intersexes: a history of similisexualism as a problem in social life*, by Xavier Mayne. Privately printed, 1908. Royal 8vo.

Mémoires Secrètes pour servir à l'histoire de la République des Lettres en France, ou Journal d'un Observateur (1762-1784). Paris. 12mo.

[By Bachaumont and others, in many volumes. Vol. vi., pp. 162-163, under date 27th July, 1772, gives a much exaggerated account of the scandal of Marseille.]

Michaud. *Biographie Universelle, ancienne et moderne*. Paris. 1863. 8vo.

Michelet. *Histoire de la Révolution Française*, par Jules Michelet. Paris, 1869. 9 vols. 8vo.

Mirabeau. *Vie Privée, Libertine et Scandaleuse de feu Honoré-Gabriel-Riquetti*, ci-devant Comte de Mirabeau, Député du Tiers-Etat des

Sénéchauffées d'Aix et de Marseille, membre du départment de Paris, commandant de bataillon de la milice bourgeoise du district de Grange-Batellière, président du club Jacobite, etc., etc., etc. A Paris, rue de l'Echelle, en Suisse, à Londres, en Prusse, et en Hollande, chez tous ses créanciers. 1791. 8vo.

[With portrait, engraved title-page, and 5 plates, and a dedicatory letter addressed *A Monsieur Satan* and concluding *de votre Altesse Diabolique, le très humble, très obéissant et très dévoué serviteur, Mirabeau*. It is, of course, not by Mirabeau, and was published shortly after his death. A scurrilous production, typical of its period.]

Nodier. *Souvenirs, épisodes et portraits pour servir à l'histoire de la Révolution et de l'Empire*, par Charles Nodier. Paris, 1831. 2 vols. 8vo.

Palache. *Four Novelists of the Old Régime: Crébillon, Laclos, Diderot, Rétif de la Bretonne*, by John Garber Palache, London, 1926. 8vo.

Parc aux Cerfs (Le), ou l'origine de l'affreux déficit, par un zélé Patriote. A Paris: sur les débris de la Bastille. 1790. 8vo.

Pigoreau. *Petite Bibliographie biographico-romancière*, etc., par Pigoreau. Paris, 1821. 8vo.

Pitou. *Analyse de mes malheurs et de mes persécutions depuis vingt-six ans*, par Louis Ange Pitou. Paris, 1816. 8vo.

Rétif. *L'Anti-Justine, ou les délices de l'amour*, par Rétif de la Bretonne. Nouvelle édition sans suppressions conforme à celle originale de 1798. Amsterdam. [Paris.] 1864. 2 parts in 1 vol. sq. 12mo.

Speculator Morum. *Bibliotheca Arcana seu Catalogues Librorum Penetralium*, being brief notices of books that have been secretly printed, prohibited by law, seized, anathematized, burnt, or Bowdlerized, by Speculator Morum. London, 1885. 4to.

Taxil. *La Corruption fin de siècle*, par Leo Taxil. Nouvelle édition. Paris, 1894. 8vo.

Fin

www.ingramcontent.com/pod-product-compliance
Lightning Source LLC
LaVergne TN
LVHW031629070426
835507LV00024B/3391

www.ingramcontent.com/pod-product-compliance
Lightning Source LLC
LaVergne TN
LVHW031629070426
835507LV00024B/3391